Nelson Cuthbert

Cuthbert's exercises in arithmetic

For use in the senior classes of public schools

Nelson Cuthbert

Cuthbert's exercises in arithmetic
For use in the senior classes of public schools

ISBN/EAN: 9783337274726

Printed in Europe, USA, Canada, Australia, Japan

Cover: Foto ©Paul-Georg Meister /pixelio.de

More available books at **www.hansebooks.com**

CUTHBERT'S
Exercises in Arithmetic

FOR USE IN THE

SENIOR CLASSES OF PUBLIC SCHOOLS.

PART II.

A COLLECTION OF PROBLEMS

SUITABLE FOR

CANDIDATES FOR THE ENTRANCE AND PUBLIC SCHOOL LEAVING EXAMINATIONS

WITH ANSWERS.

SECOND EDITION.

BY

W. N. CUTHBERT,

Toronto.

TORONTO:
THE COPP, CLARK COMPANY, LIMITED.
1896.

PREFACE TO FIRST EDITION.

The Second Part of my Exercises in Arithmetic consists of a collection of Problems which are *original in construction*, and which were made for use in the different classes of the Public Schools in which I have taught.

As already stated, the Problems will be found *suitable for candidates* preparing for the Entrance Examination to High Schools and Collegiate Institutes, and for candidates preparing for the Public School Leaving Examination.

W. NELSON CUTHBERT.

Verschoyle, *May 1st, 1894.*

PREFACE TO SECOND EDITION.

The author has much pleasure in thanking those who have called his attention to the errors which had crept into the First Edition. These have been corrected; and in presenting the Second Edition he does so, hoping that it will meet with the same marked favor from the profession as did the First.

At the suggestion of many P. S. Inspectors and Teachers, the Answers have been incorporated, and fourteen new Exercises (182 Problems) have been added in Fifth Class work, covering the P. S. L. Examination Papers up to date.

W. NELSON CUTHBERT.

Toronto, *May 1st, 1896.*

The boy stood on the back yard fence,
  Whence all but him had fled;
The flames that lit his father's barn
  Shone just above the shed;
One bunch of crackers in his hand,
  Two others in his hat,
With piteous accents loud, he cried,
  "I never thought of that!"
(A bunch of crackers to the tail
  Of one small dog he'd tied;
The dog had sought the well-filled barn
  And 'mid its ruins died!)

The sparks flew wide, and red and hot:
  They lit upon that brat;
They fired the crackers in his hand,
  And eke those in his hat.
Then came a burst of rattling sound—
  The boy! Where had he gone?
Ask of the winds that far around
  Strewed bits of meat and bone,
And scraps of clothes, and knives, and tops
  And nails, and hooks, and yarn—
The relics of that dreadful boy
  That burned his father's barn!

ARITHMETIC.

PART II.

FIRST CLASS.

On the Circle.

A circle is composed of an indefinite number of sectors, the sum of which is equal to the area of the circle.

By dividing and sub-dividing these sectors the radii come very close together, and the area of a small sector differs very little from the area of a triangle formed by the radii and the line joining these at the base; and when the radii are indefinitely close together the base of the sector is an indefinitely small arc (which may practically be regarded as a straight line), and the sum of all these arcs is equal to the circumference of the circle.

For the sake of illustration, then, we may regard the circumference of a circle to be composed of an indefinite number of straight lines; and by drawing an indefinite number of straight lines (radii) from the center of the circle to its circumference, we can get an indefinite number of triangles (sectors).

Now the area of each of these triangles is equal to half the base multiplied by the altitude (the radius, or half the diameter, of the circle); therefore, *half the circumference of the circle* (half the bases of these triangles) *multiplied by half the diameter of the circle* (the altitude of these triangles) *is equal to the area of the circle.*

8   EXERCISES IN ARITHMETIC.

This may be better explained by reference to the following figures:

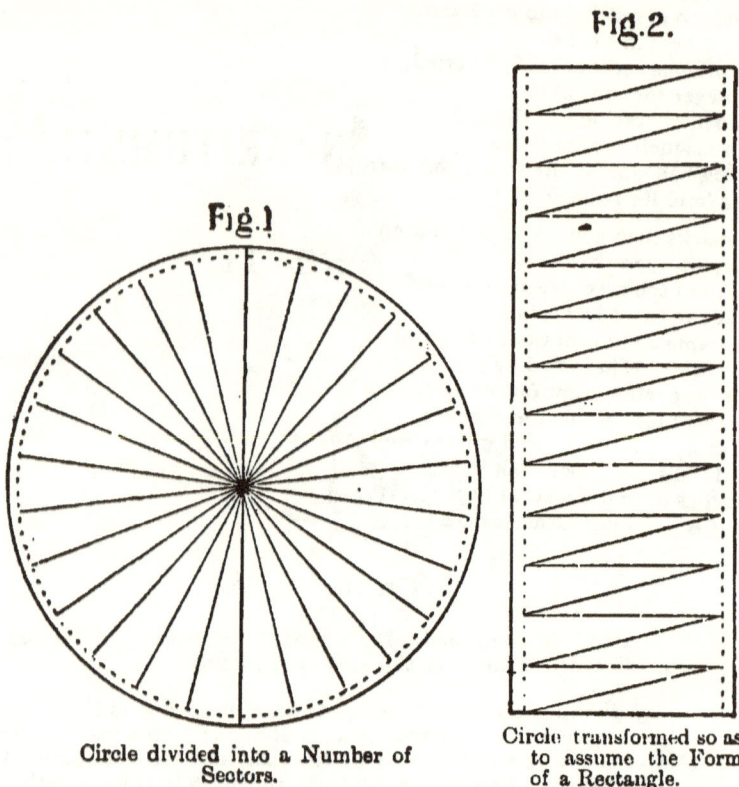

Circle divided into a Number of Sectors.

Circle transformed so as to assume the Form of a Rectangle.

Figure 1 represents a circle divided into a definite number of sectors by lines drawn across the circle through its centre and terminating near the circumference, one line however going the whole way across the circle and dividing it into two semi-circles. An indefinite number of sectors is impossible; but the more sectors, the *more nearly perfect* the demonstration and the better the shape of the rectangular figure represented in Fig. 2.

Figure 2 represents the circle transformed into a rectangle with the serrated edges brought into close contact so as to form a figure of rectangular shape, each half of the circumference of the circle having assumed a practically straight line, thus forming the sides of the rectangular figure, and each half of the diameter of the circle forming the ends of the rectangular figure, which for the purpose of illustration and explanation may be regarded as a rectangle.

Now, the area of a rectangle is equal to the measure of the length multiplied by the measure of the width ; and the measure of the length of this rectangle is half the circumference of the circle ; also the measure of width is half the diameter (radius) of the circle ; therefore *half the circumference of a circle multiplied by half the diameter is equal to the area of the circle.*

Pupils must admit that the circumference of a circle is equal to $3\frac{1}{7}$ times the diameter. This, however, may be demonstrated, in a way, by using a circular ink-bottle and a piece of cord. The circumference may be shown *to measure* the diameter *more than three times.* It measures it $3\frac{1}{7}$ times, nearly, which is practically correct.

Now, if $3\frac{1}{7}$ times any given number equals a certain number, then $3\frac{1}{7}$ times the half of that given number equals the half of the certain number, as for example :

$3\frac{1}{7} \times 14 = 44.$

$\therefore 3\frac{1}{7} \times \frac{14}{2} = \frac{44}{2}.$

And $3\frac{1}{7} \times$ diameter of a circle $=$ circumference.

$\therefore 3\frac{1}{7} \times \frac{1}{2}$ diameter of a circle $= \frac{1}{2}$ circumference.

But $\frac{1}{2}$ *circumference* $\times \frac{1}{2}$ *diameter of a circle* $=$ *area,* therefore, by substituting, we have :

$(3\frac{1}{7} \times \frac{1}{2}$ diameter$) \times \frac{1}{2}$ diameter $=$ *area.*

But half the diameter ($\frac{1}{2}$ diameter) $=$ the radius (r.).

Substitute again, and :

$3\frac{1}{7} \times r. \times r. =$ area.

That is $3\frac{1}{7}$ r.^{2} $=$ area.

Now, representing $3\frac{1}{7}$ by π. we have, π r.^{2} $=$ area of a circle.

See Exercise *LXIV.* for examples on the circle. Other examples are interspersed through the Fourth and Fifth class work.

WEIGHTS OF VARIOUS ARTICLES ESTABLISHED BY CUSTOM.

A barrel of flour $=$ 196 lbs. (net).
" " " beef $=$ 200 lbs. (net).
" " " pork $=$ 200 lbs. (net).
" " " white-fish $=$ 200 lbs. (net).
" " " trout $=$ 200 lbs. (net).
" ' " salt $=$ 280 lbs. (net).
" " " lime $=$ 220 lbs. (net).

Hay well settled 4½ lbs. to the cubic foot.
Corn on cob, in bin 22 lbs. to the cubic foot.
Corn shelled 45 lbs. to the cubic foot.
Wheat 48 lbs. to the cubic foot.
Oats 25½ lbs. to the cubic foot.
Potatoes 38½ lbs. to the cubic foot.
Sand (dry) 95 lbs. to the cubic foot.
Clay (compact) 135 lbs. to the cubic foot.
Marble 169 lbs. to the cubic foot.

Anthracite (stone or hard) coal = 33 cub. feet per ton.
Bituminous (lignite or soft) coal = 42 cub. feet per ton.

A Surveyor's chain is 66 feet long.
"   "   "   22 yards long.
"   "   "   4 rods long.
"   "   " 100 links long.

Exercise I.

1. Divide $990 among A B and C, giving B twice as much as C, and A $30 more than ⅔ of the remainder.

2. A can walk 4 miles, 80 rods, an hour, and B can walk 110 yds. in a minute. How long will it take A to overtake B if the latter has 2 minutes the start?

3. A can do a piece of work in 6 days, B in 9 days and C in ten days. A and B work together at it for 2 days, then B and C work together at it for ½ a day. How long will it take a boy, who does ⅓ as much in a day as C, to finish it?

4. A has half as much money as B, and B has one-fourth as much again as C. What per cent. of A's money is ⅓ of C's?

5. Two men carry a weight of 3 cwt. 41 lbs. between them, and their loads are to one another as 6 : 5. By how much does one load exceed the other?

6. A man sold a horse which cost him $154, losing by the sale 10 per cent. of the proceeds. Find the price at which he sold the horse.

7. Find the cost of paving a square court-yard 24 yds. to a side, at 3 cents a sq. foot.

FOURTH CLASS.

8. The Province of Manitoba contains 116000 sq. miles. What is the Province worth at $2.50 an acre?

9. If 7 pears buy 5 peaches, and 8 peaches buy 15 apples, and there are 90 apples in a peck, how many doz. pears will 100 quarts of apples buy?   *70 dozen*

10. A man mixed 14 bushels of clover seed with 26 bushels of timothy seed, and sold 30 bushels of the mixture. What was the value of the clover seed sold at $6 a bushel?   *$63*

11. A farmer sowed 21 bushels, 55¼ lbs. of wheat on 7 acres, 40 sq. rods of land. How many ounces was that to the sq. foot?   *7/5 (3*

12. Simplify $\frac{8}{135} + \frac{1}{230} + \frac{7}{325}$.   *19/30*

13. The larger wheel of a bicycle is 4⅓ yds. in circumference, and the smaller wheel is 2½ feet in circumference. How often will the same points in the wheels come in contact with the ground, simultaneously, in going 5 miles, 950 yards?

Exercise II.

1. Find the cost of a tract of land 75 chains long by 15 chains wide at $60 an acre.   *$6750*

2. Multiply 64 acres, 121 rods, 30 yds., 2 ft., 96 inches by 8; divide the result by 9; and reduce the quotient, thus obtained, to square inches.

3. A man walked 25 miles on Monday, 1600 rods on Tuesday, 36960 ft. on Wednesday 7040 yds. on Thursday, 560 chains on Friday, and 640 perches on Saturday. (a) How many miles did he walk during the week? (b) How many inches?

4. In 41080 inches of wire, how many rods, yards, feet and inches are there?

5. A and B owned a flock of 642 sheep. A's share of the flock was 5 times B's; but when they divided the sheep, A got 500 sheep and $210 in money for his share. At this rate what was the value of the whole flock?   *$3852*

6. A man owns a horse 16½ hands high; how much less in height is he than his owner who is 5 ft. 8 inches high?   *2"*

7. Bought 84000 grains of tea. Paid 5 cents an ounce for ¼ of it, and 85 cents a lb. for the remainder. What did the tea cost me?   *$10*

8. Show, by a diagram that 10 chains square is ten acres.

9. Bought 672000 grains of tea at 87½ cents a lb. and sold it for $105; find my gain per cent.

10. What will 40 chains, 40 rods of fencing cost at 40 cents a rod?

11. If a five-cent register stamp be 2¼ inches long and ¾ of an inch broad, what would it cost to paper a wall 20 ft. long by 9 ft. high with 5-cent register stamps?

12. A seed merchant mixes 15:6 lbs. Hungarian seed worth $2.50 a bushel with 12 bushels of millet worth $3.20 a bushel. Find the value of 11 bushels of the mixture.

13. (a) What is the value of 1 mile 18) rods of rope at 5 cents for 10 yards? (b) How often is the G.C.M. of 155 and $151\tfrac{9}{10}$ contained in their sum?

Exercise III.

1. A railway train going 15 miles an hour takes 3 minutes to cross a bridge 660 yds. long. Find the length of the train.

2. The simple interest on $800 for a certain time at 5½ per cent. is $264. Find the time.

3. A boy sold a coat which cost him $24 losing 20 per cent. of the proceeds. Find the price at which he sold it.

4. The total cost of 66 lbs., 10⅔ ozs. butter at 21½ cents an oz., and a certain number of bushels of wheat at 87½ cents a bushel, was $58.60. Find the number of bushels of wheat.

5. A manufacturer sold his goods to a wholesale merchant, gaining 20 per cent. The wholesale merchant sold to the retailer at an advance of 8⅓ per cent. What would the manufacturer have gained on the sale of 6660 dollars' worth of goods, had he sold direct to the retailer at wholesale prices?

6. Simplify (a) $(3\tfrac{1}{2}+2\tfrac{1}{4})\times 3\tfrac{1}{3}-(1\tfrac{1}{2}-1\tfrac{1}{4})$; (b) $(3\tfrac{1}{2}+2\tfrac{1}{4})\times(3\tfrac{1}{3}-1\tfrac{1}{2})-1\tfrac{1}{4}$.

7. If ⅚ of a car-load of cheese cost $540, what would be the value of ten such car-loads?

8. If 9620 lbs. of wheat at 75 cents a bushel, 480 lbs. apples (undried) at 90 cents a bag, and 4 tons of bran cost $183.85, what was bran a cwt.?

9. If 9 oxen or 12 sheep can feed on a certain field for 6 days, how many days could 20 sheep and as many oxen feed on a field 3¼ times as large?

FOURTH CLASS. 13

10. By selling an article for 4 shillings, 9d., I lose 5 per cent. At what price, in Canadian currency, must I sell it in order to gain 140 per cent.?

11. From 45 miles, 80 rods, 4 yds., 2 ft., 5 inches subtract 13 miles, 180 rods, 5 yds., 2 ft., 8 inches.

12. At what time are the hands of a watch equidistant from the figure VI?

13. (a) A cheese-monger sold 2184 cheeses at $30 each. On one-half of them he gained 30 per cent., and on the other half he lost 30 per cent. How much did he gain or lose on the whole lot? (b) The difference in weight of two chests of tea is 12 lbs. 8 ozs., and the value of both at 54 cents a lb. is $47.25. How many lbs. are there in each chest? (c) Find the value of 46 bushels, 15 lbs., 17 bushels, 16 lbs., 47 bushel, 26 lbs., 10 ozs., 75 bushels, 30 lbs., 6 ozs., 57 bushels, 18 lbs., 20 ozs., 19 bushels, 10 lbs., 12 ozs., and 14 lbs. 8 ozs. of wheat at 72 cents a bushel.

Exercise IV.

1. If a man walk 41 miles, 725 yds. during a week as follows,—6 miles on Monday, 650 rods on Tuesday, 18270 yds. on Wednesday, 26400 feet on Thursday, 800 chains on Friday, 443520 inches on Saturday, and the remainder of the distance the next day, find the length of the Sabbath day's journey.

2. A rectangular farm cost $10980 at $45 an acre. It was 122 chains long. How wide was it in rods?

3. If 5 doz. bananas or 3 doz. pine-apples are worth $1.20, what would 15 doz. of each kind cost?

4. A bought 5 stacks of hay of 16400 lbs. each at $15 a ton. He sold ⅔ of it at $17 a ton, and the rest at $16 a ton. How much did he gain or lose?

5. Seven men engage to dig a ditch in 42 days, but owing to sickness one man is unable to work. How long will it take the rest of the men to dig the ditch?

6. A mixture of 50 gallons of liquid is 70 per cent. alcohol. How much alcohol must be added to make it 80 per cent. alcohol?

7. If $1\frac{3}{5}$ of a lottery ticket is worth 13 florins, and a florin is worth 2 sh. Sterling, what is the value, in Canadian money, of ⅔ of a lottery ticket?

8. Find the H.C.F. of 1 rod, ¼ of a yard, and 2 feet; and the L.C.M. of 4716, 3930, and 9170.

EXERCISES IN ARITHMETIC.

9. If, by selling an article for $51 a merchant lose 15 per cent., what per cent. would he gain, should he receive $75 for the article?

10. A miner after losing ⅛ of 13⅓ per cent. of his money has ⅓ of 90 per cent. of it left, and the difference between the amount lost and the amount left is $81.60. What was he worth at first?

11. A, B and C, have together $700. A has 3 times as much as B, and C has $20 more than 7½ times as much as A and B together. How much money has C?

12. A glazier cuts 48 panes of glass, each 12 inches long, out of a plate of glass 12′ 0″ × 3′ 4″. How many feet in length will the edges of all these panes of glass measure?

13. A fruiter divided a basket of 46 doz. and 8 peaches, equally, among 8 of his customers. One of these customers then divided his share among his three boys in the following manner: To Tom he gave 2 for Will's 3, and to Will 4 for Sam's 5. What per cent. of the original basket of peaches have Tom and Will, together, then?

Exercise V.

1. How many lbs. of coffee worth 35 cents a lb. must a grocer mix with 6 lbs. of chicory at 40 cents a lb. to make a mixture worth 38 cents a lb.?

2. How many yds. of paper 2 feet wide will be required for a hall-way 72 feet long and 14 feet high?

3. A man earning $1.80 a day works from 1 o'clock p.m. till 4.30 o'clock p.m. What does he earn, 8 hours being a day's work?

4. After taking 10 gallons from a barrel of vinegar, and then ⅔ of the remainder, it was found to still contain 25 gallons. How many gallons were there in the cask at first?

5. A man buys a farm for $6250, pays taxes $32, insurance on building $36.75. What does he make per cent. on his investment, if he rent the farm for $350 per annum?

6. What is the duty, at 15 per cent., on 320 boxes raisins, each containing 50 lbs. at 8 cents a lb.?

7. Find (a) the volume of a cube whose edge is 13 feet, 8 inches, (b) the surface of the cube.

8. A wholesale and retail man deducts 33⅓ per cent. from his retail price in serving a wholesale customer. What per cent. will the retailer now make by selling to compete with the whol sale man at retail prices?

FOURTH CLASS.

9. Divide $1450 among A, B and C, so that $3\frac{1}{2}$ times A's, twice B's, or 4 times C's shall all be equal.

10. If the carriage of 16 tons, 200 lbs. of goods for 70 miles cost $18, what weight, at the same rate, should be carried 210 miles for $135?

11. If 9 horses require as many oats as 15 ponies, and 20 ponies are fed 36 days on 240 bushels of oats, how long would 630 dollars' worth of oats feed 27 horses, when oats are $37\frac{1}{2}$ cents a bushel?

12. A pile of wood is 60 feet long, 25 feet wide, and 6 feet high. How many cords of fifteen-inch wood are there in the pile?

13. (a) A sold a horse to B, losing $8\frac{1}{3}$ per cent.; B sold it to C for $240, gaining thereby $9\frac{1}{11}$ per cent. What did the horse cost A? (b) Find the amount of $720 for 3 years, 2 months at 8% per annum. (c) Had 5 times 76 bushels, 1 peck, 1 gallon, 3 quarts, 1 pint of wheat; sold 303 bushels, 10 lbs., 5 ozs. of it; find the value of the remainder of my wheat at $1.20 a bushel.

Exercise VI.

1. At what time after 5 o'clock are the hands of a clock equidistant from the figure V?

2. At what time after 11 o'clock are the hands 3 min. more than half an hour apart?

3. At what time after 9 o'clock are the hands of a watch opposite to each other?

4. At what times after 7 o'clock are the hands of a watch (a) first at right angles? (b) coincident? (c) at right angles the second time?

5. What time after 11 o'clock are the hands of a watch equidistant from the figure XI?

6. At what time past 11 o'clock are the hands of a watch 11 min. apart the second time?

7. A watch which loses 5 seconds in every 2 minutes is set right at 8 o'clock a.m. What will be the true time when its hands are together between 4 and 5 p.m.?

8. At what time after 10 o'clock will the hands of a watch be together?

9. By the clock it is VII. How far will the hands be apart when the minute hand has gained 11 minutes on the hour hand?

10. At what time after III o'clock are the hands of a watch 40 minutes apart?

11. At what time after 4 o'clock will the hands of a watch be equidistant from the figure IV?

12. It is 3 o'clock. By the time the minute hand has gained 11 minutes on the hour hand, how many minutes will there be between the hands?

13. By the clock it is 12 o'clock. In what time will the hands be (a) 5 min., 41 seconds apart? (b) at right angles to each other for the first time? (c) 22 min. apart? (d) opposite each other? (e) at right angles the second time? (f) 5 min. apart second time? (g) equidistant from the figure XII?

Exercise VII.

1. A, B and C engaged an opera house for a certain concert. B contributed $170, C $250, and A secured the services of a comedy company to give the concert. The total receipts from the concert were $1340, of which A's share was $500. Find each artist's fee, given that the company consisted of 21 artists including the leader, whose fee was $50.

2. A laborer agreed to dig a certain ditch at 12 cents a rod. The first week he dug 25 rods more than the half of it, and the next week he finished the remaining 215 rods of the ditch. (a) What were his daily wages on an average? (b) What was the difference between his daily wages each week?

3. If a farmer can keep 20 cows, that each makes 73 dollars' worth of butter a year, on 45 acres, 60 sq. rods of pasture-land for which he pays an annual rent of $3.20 per acre, what is his yearly gain from the cows, supposing him to put aside $374.80 for losses and expenses during the year?

4. Reduce $2\frac{2}{3}$ lbs. Avoirdupois to the fraction of $\dfrac{2}{\frac{2}{3} \text{ of } \frac{3}{4}}$ lbs. Troy.

5. By how much is $\frac{5}{7}$ greater than $\cdot 714285$?

6. Oats are worth $\frac{3}{8}$ of 7 sh., 6d. (Sterling) a bushel, and hay is worth $15 a ton. How many bushels of oats ought to be given for 730 lbs. of hay?

7. What is $\frac{2}{3}$ of 5 acres, 80 sq. rods, 4 sq. yds.?

8. How many cows must a person buy at $34 each, so that, after allowing $73\frac{1}{2}$ cents for the food of each for a week, he may then, by selling each of the lot at 36.91\frac{2}{3}$, gain 172.48\frac{1}{2}$?

9. A stack of hay will keep 36 cows or 27 horses for a week; how many days will it keep 10 cows and six horses? 14 / 14

10. Find the sum of the 5 numbers which follow $\overline{\text{X}}$CDCCCLXXX, and express your answer in Roman numerals?

11. A battalion, coming home from battle, has only $\frac{3}{4}$ of its original number of men. It has lost $\frac{1}{10}$ in killed, $\frac{1}{8}$ in prisoners, and 25 in deserters. Find the original number of men in the battle? 1000

12. A man having $\frac{4}{5}$ of $100, gave away $\frac{2}{5}$ of his money and then lost $8 at billiards. What has he still left? 40

13. (*a*) What is the value of 7 times $\frac{5}{7}$ of 4 acres, 40 sq. rods, 16 sq. yds. of land at $38.72 an acre? (*b*) Bought 16 crates of eggs of 40 doz. each at 15 cents a doz.; two out of every score were bad; sold the remainder at 25 cents a doz.; what did I gain, after paying a comission merchant $7.70 for selling the eggs? $40.30

Exercise VIII.

1. What is the value of $2\frac{2}{3}$ of £$3\frac{3}{4}$ divided by $3\frac{3}{8}$?

2. At what time after 9 o'clock will the hands of a clock be one minute apart? 9.45

3. Out of a heap of Canadian cent pieces, weighing 57 lbs. 8 ozs., 4450 cent pieces are taken and the heap then weighs 13 lbs. How many cent pieces were in the heap at first?

16 4. Find L.C.M. of: (*a*) 7 feet, 6 inches, and 4 feet, 6 inches; and (*b*) $\frac{1}{8}$, $\frac{7}{8}$, $\frac{18}{45}$, and $\frac{4}{7}$. 22'-6" 112

16 5. If $\frac{5}{6}$ of 2 lbs. of sugar cost as much as 2 lbs., 8 ozs. of rice, and if $3\frac{3}{4}$ lbs. of rice cost 15 cents, what is the value of a barrel of sugar weighing 300 lbs.? 27

16 6. If 6 elephants eat 50000 lbs. of hay in 20 days, how many tons would last 56 elephants 33 days? 385 tons

16 7. A field 60 chains long and 80 rods wide will produce 21600 bushels of potatoes. What is the rate per acre? 180 Bush

8. A goldsmith earned £3 Sterling in 5 days of 2 hours each; what were his daily wages in dollars and cents?

16 9. What will it cost to pave a court-yard 50 yds. long and 60 feet wide with square paving-stones 9 inches to a side, at 5 cents each stone? $800.00

10. If the true discount on $1978, for a certain time at 5 per cent. be $258, on what sum should the true discount, for the same time, at 8 per cent. be $444 ?

11. A fruit-dealer bought 24 baskets of grapes at $3 a basket. If each basket held 40 lbs. and he sold the lot at 15 cents a lb., find his gain or loss per cent.

12. A man rolling a wheel-barrow takes 96 steps, each 2 feet, 9 inches long, in a minute. How often will the wheel of the barrow, which is 14 inches in diameter, revolve in an hour ?

13. (a) Find the cost of carpeting a room, 24 feet, 10 inches long, by 16 feet, 8 inches wide, with carpeting 27 inches wide, running lengthwise of the room, and allowing 8 inches per strip for waste, the carpet costing $1.25 per yd. (b) A dealer bought brooms at $24 a gross, and sold them out at 25 cents each ; find his gain per doz. (c) The sum of three numbers is 3258, and $\frac{3}{4}$ of the first is $\frac{5}{6}$ of the second ; also $\frac{4}{5}$ of the second is $\frac{7}{8}$ of the third ; find the numbers.

Exercise IX.

1. A man draws wood to supply a contract of 700 cords of twenty-inch wood. His sleigh-box is 14 ft. long, and he puts on 2 tiers, each 2 ft. 6 in. high, the length of his sleigh-box, at each load. How many loads will he require to draw to fill the contract ?

2. How many bushels of pease at 80 cents a bushel must be mixed with 60 bushels of oats at 30 cents a bushel, to make a mixture on which may be gained $6\frac{1}{4}$ per cent., by selling the mixture at 55 cents a bushel ?

3. Find the value of ten rectangular plots of ground, each 55 by 40 yards, at $110 an acre.

4. The selling price of a pair of boots is $1\frac{1}{2}$ times the cost price and the gain at which they were sold is $2. Find the cost price of the boots.

5. A sold a farm to B, gaining $5\frac{3}{5}$ per cent. of the cost. B then sold it to C for $3610, losing thereby 5 per cent Find A's cost price.

6. Divide $640 among A, B and C, so that B may have 6 times as much A, and that C may have $1\frac{1}{2}$ times as much as B.

7. If $\frac{1}{3}$ of $\frac{8}{11}$ of a farm be worth $5800, find the value of 80 per cent. of it.

8. If a lb. of tea is worth 3 lbs. of coffee, and 12 lbs. of coffee are worth 15 lbs. of rice, what is the value of a chest of tea weighing 70 lbs., when rice is worth 28 cents a lb.?

FOURTH CLASS.   19

9. Find the cost of papering the walls of a room, 20 ft. long by 16 ft. wide, with paper 21 inches wide, worth 12½ cents a single roll, allowing 12 ft. for doors and windows.

10. A man after spending $2 more than $\frac{7}{10}$ of his money found that he had still left 40 per cent. of what he had spent. How much did he spend?

11. A produce dealer paid $80 for butter, $C0 for beef and $120 for cheese. He then sold the whole for $325, gaining 20 per cent. on the butter and 11⅔ per cent. on the beef. What per cent. did he gain on the cheese?

12. Tom and Will receive $34\frac{2}{7}$ per cent. of a basket of 78 dozen and 4 oranges, divided among three boys Tom, Will and Sam. If Tom got 4 for Sam's 5, and Sam got 3 for Will's 4, what fractional part of the basket of oranges was divided among the three boys?

13. Sold a horse for $180 which was $35 more than he cost me. Allowing $15 for his keep while I owned him, what per cent. did I make by the transaction?

Exercise X.

Find the prime factors of :

1. 340, 2800 and 2940.
2. 4860, 5964 and 4500.
3. 8400, 3824 and 1380.
4. 4400, 864 and 5400.
5. 280, 640 and 7722.
6. 960, 1800 and 2500.
7. 45045, 8778 and 15400.
8. 1280, 7200 and 8100.
9. 3300, 6500 and 3900.
10. 1800, 5200 and 7500.
11. 1150, 5640 and 1820.
12. 2100, 8700 and 3500.

Exercise XI.

Find the L.C.M. of:
1. 3, 9, 18, 24, 46, 21.
2. All the *prime* numbers between 7 and 23 inclusive.
3. All the *even* numbers between 8 and 30 inclusive.
4. 12, 14, 21, 32, 48 and 56.
5. 2, 4, 9, 18, 10, 30, 180.
6. 4, 9, 7, 8, 6, 12, 14, 28, and 56.
7. 6, 2, 18, 10, 17, 51, 9.
8. 3, 16, 28, 14, 36, 20, 1260, 1680, 1008 and 720.
9. 4, 7, 14, 36, 21 and 100.
10. All the *odd* numbers between 7 and 25 inclusive.
11. All the *composite* between 8 and 28 inclusive.
12. All the *even* numbers between 32 and 42 inclusive.
13. 740, 1554, 1054, 4278 and 1035.

Exercise XII.

1. Find the L.C.M. of all the *prime* numbers between 2 and 17 inclusive.
2. Find the L.C.M. of all the *even* numbers between 7 and 21.
3. Find the L.C.M. of 36, 42, 48, 70, 75, 60, 120, 7, 4, 35, 25, 10 and 5.
4. Find the L.C.M. of 8, 3, 16, 48, 20, 56, and 75.
5. Find the L.C.M. of 2, 9, 18, 45, 63, 70 and 72.
6. Find the L.C.M. of all the odd numbers between 8 and 28.
7. Find the L.C.M. of all the composite numbers between 15 and 25 inclusive.
8. Find the L.C.M. of 8, 19, 27, 56, 54, 57 and 7182.
9. Find the L.C.M. of 11, 2, 22, 75, 150, 60 and 20.
10. Find the L.C.M. of 3, 28, 56, 15, 45, 60, 27, 36, 48, 90, 125 and 420.
11. Find the L.C.M. of 6, 9, 18, 24, 36, 108, 96 and 432.
12. Find the L.C.M. of 34, 170, 95 152, 52, 117 and 60.
13. (a) Find the L.C.M. of 41, 39, 123, 40, 75, 110. (b) Find the L.C.M. of $5\frac{1}{3}$, $41\frac{9}{11}$, $4\frac{2}{3}$ and $11\frac{1}{2}$.

Exercise XIII.

Find the H.C.F. of :

1. 19557 and 156933.
2. 10244 and 103228.
3. 1344 and 1536.
4. 3384, 8272, 7567 and 2209.
5. 1561, 1477 and 1681.
6. 8277, 10947 and 11303.
7. 5187, 5850 and 1339.
8. 6231, 5967 and 4692.
9. 8185736 and 20578792.
10. 1560, 1599 and 2223.
11. 8544, 22161 and 203187.
12. 1247, 1505, 1720 and 3827.
13. 37665, 76167 and 61101.

Exercise XIV.

Find the G.C.M of :

1. 225, 1575, 9000 and 9225.
2. 16287 and 67818.
3. 6902 and 8265.
4. 428108 and 586749.
5. 640, 724, 968 and 3828.
6. 1470, 4907 and 567.
7. 4100, 8282, 12341 and 3239.
8. 1860, 3906 and 5208.
9. 444, 1480, 1665, and 1369.
10. 984, 1476, 2952, and 241572.
11. 14385, 20391, and 49287.
12. 10767, 9409, and 203021.
13. 7029, 6039 and 9999.

Exercise XV.

1. Find the L.C.M. of 6, 8, 24, 42, 88, 96, 170 and 5610.

2. Divide the L.C.M. of 7, 21, 49, 105, 154, and 84 by the H.C.F. of 37191 and 69531.

3. Divide the L.C.M. of 8, 20, 16, 48, 40 and 168 by the H.C.F. of 8904 and 16632.

4. Divide the L.C.M. of 9, 16, 21, 42, 85 and 147 by the H.C.F. of 19257 and 21609.

5. Divide the L.C.M. of 9, 10, 11, 12, 13, 14, 16 by the H.C.F. of 9009 and 67067.

6. Divide the L.C.M. of 26, 28, 30, 32, 34, 36, 39, by the H.C.F. of 51051 and 468741.

7. Find the product of the H.C.F. and L.C.M. of 128, 384, 768, and 2304.

8. What is the *least* number which will leave a remainder when divided by any number between 11 and 19 inclusive?

9. Divide the L.C.M. of $\frac{2}{3}$, $\frac{3}{5}$, $\frac{4}{7}$ and $\frac{1}{8}$ by the G.C.M. of $\frac{4}{5}$, $\frac{5}{8}$, $\frac{7}{15}$ and $1\frac{1}{24}$.

10. Find the L.C.M. of $\frac{3}{10}$, $\frac{7}{15}$, $\frac{11}{30}$, and $\frac{4}{15}$.

11. Find the L.C.M. of $(3\frac{11}{13} \div 6\frac{4}{15})$ and $(\frac{9}{13} \times 1\frac{5}{8})$.

12. Find the L.C.M. of $(8\frac{7}{13} \times 1\frac{2}{37})$ and $12\frac{3}{4} - 11\frac{7}{8} + 4\frac{1}{6} - 1\frac{3}{24}$.

13. (a) Find the G.C.M. of $\left\{ \dfrac{\frac{2}{3}-\frac{1}{2}}{\frac{1}{3}-\frac{1}{6}} + \frac{3}{8} \text{ of } \frac{1}{5} \times \frac{3}{4} \right\}$ and $\dfrac{\frac{3}{8} \times \frac{1}{6} \times \frac{3}{4}}{1\frac{5}{3} \text{ of } \frac{13}{25} \text{ of } \frac{3}{5}}$.

(b) Find the G.C.M. and L.C.M. of $\dfrac{\frac{5}{6} \div 5}{\frac{3}{8} \div 4} + \frac{1}{2}$ of 22 and $(\frac{3}{5} \div \frac{4}{5})$ of $\frac{3}{8} + \frac{2}{3} \div \frac{3}{4} + \frac{5}{8}$. (c) Sold 8484 lbs. wheat at 96 cents a bushel, and with the proceeds bought $226\frac{9}{25}$ yds. carpet. What was the carpet worth per yd.?

Exercise XVI.

1. Find the value of $1\frac{2}{5} + 2\frac{3}{4} + 3\frac{1}{8} + 4\frac{5}{8}$.

2. Find the sum of $3\frac{5}{11}$, $\frac{9}{15}$, $4\frac{13}{38}$, $\frac{17}{66}$.

3. What is $\frac{39}{138} + \frac{14}{230} + \frac{27}{322}$?

4. Add $5\frac{3}{10}$, $3\frac{7}{24}$, $5\frac{3}{8}$ and $\frac{11}{16}$.

5. Find the sum of $5\frac{3}{20}$, $2\frac{9}{17}$, $\frac{13}{18}$ and $\frac{11}{14}$.

6. Find the value of $1\frac{7}{18} + 5\frac{2}{3} + 3\frac{10}{27} + 4\frac{7}{54}$.

FOURTH CLASS.

7. What is (a) $6\frac{3}{4} - 2\frac{3}{5}$? (b) $11\frac{9}{51} - 8\frac{9}{17}$? (c) $12\frac{1}{13} - 9\frac{4}{11}$?

8. Subtract $18\frac{13}{18}$ from $25\frac{3}{20}$, and $18\frac{39}{31}$ from $24\frac{2}{13}$.

9. Subtract $12\frac{13}{18}$ from $20\frac{5}{14}$, and $5\frac{9}{7}$ from $10\frac{1}{4}$.

10. Simplify: (a) $9\frac{11}{12} - 4\frac{5}{8}$; (b) $13\frac{4}{195} - 8\frac{37}{234}$.

11. Subtract (a) $8\frac{7}{8}$ from $9\frac{3}{16}$; (b) $7\frac{3}{34}$ from $10\frac{2}{17}$.

12. Subtract $\frac{6\frac{1}{4}}{1}$ from $\dfrac{40\frac{3}{7}}{10\frac{13}{18}}$.

13. (a) Subtract $\dfrac{13\frac{3}{7}}{13\frac{3}{4}}$ from $3\frac{3}{7}$ of $19\frac{1}{5}$. (b) Add $\frac{3}{4}$ of a sq. rod, $\frac{5}{8}$ of a sq. yd., $\frac{9}{5}$ of a sq. foot $\frac{27}{35}$ of a sq. inch.

Exercise XVII.

1. Multiply (a) $8\frac{4}{7}$ by $1\frac{4}{11}$; (b) $14\frac{1}{8}$ by $7\frac{1}{17}$.

2. What is $3\frac{5}{8} \times 1\frac{7}{8} \times \frac{3}{10} \times 1\frac{13}{14}$?

3. Simplify $7\frac{1}{8} \times \frac{5}{27} \times \frac{2}{13} \times \frac{3}{8} \times 6 \times 5\frac{3}{8} \times 3\frac{3}{11}$.

4. Multiply $2\frac{1}{5}$, $1\frac{5}{22}$, $1\frac{7}{8}$, $\frac{3}{20}$, $\frac{5}{8}$ together.

5. Simplify $1\frac{3}{8} \times 2\frac{7}{16} \times 3\frac{9}{25} \times 4\frac{21}{26} \times 1\frac{9}{11}$.

6. What is $8\frac{5}{17} \times 3\frac{5}{24} \times 2\frac{3}{7} \times 3\frac{3}{8} \times \frac{17}{144} \times 16$?

7. Divide (a) $19\frac{5}{18}$ by $1\frac{1}{104}$; and (b) 131 by $4\frac{1}{5}$.

8. What is (a) $52 \div 3\frac{1}{4}$? and (b) $8\frac{5}{8} \div 7\frac{1}{6}$?

9. Simplify $\left\{\dfrac{10\frac{13}{18}}{6\frac{8}{25}} \div 5\frac{13}{18}\right\}$; and $\left\{\dfrac{52}{3\frac{1}{4}} \div 9\frac{3}{8} \text{ of } 4\frac{1}{16}\right\}$.

10. What is (a) $22\frac{19}{25} \div 2\frac{143}{88}$? and (b) $13\frac{2}{235} \div 8\frac{1}{15}$?

11. Divide $21\frac{1}{4}$ by $4\frac{1}{5}$; $11\frac{1}{11}$ by $\frac{8\frac{1}{8}}{9}$ of $\frac{1}{12}$; $7\frac{5}{16}$ by $4\frac{74}{101}$.

12. What is $\dfrac{5\frac{5}{24}}{4\frac{1}{8}} - (\frac{9}{10} \text{ of } 3\frac{3}{4})$?

13. Divide (a) $\dfrac{7 \ (1\frac{1}{2} \text{ of } \frac{9}{14})}{\frac{1}{8}\left\{\dfrac{3}{3\frac{1}{2}} \text{ of } 7\right\}}$ by $\frac{9}{14}$; (b) $\left\{\dfrac{25\frac{3}{3}}{4\frac{1}{12}} - (1\frac{3}{8} \text{ of } 5\frac{1}{1})\right\}$ by 4.

Exercise XVIII.

1. Add $\frac{7}{8}$, $3\frac{1}{4}$, $2\frac{2}{3}$, $\frac{5}{6}$ and $\frac{3}{8}$.

2. Simplify $\frac{1}{6}$ of $\frac{2}{3} + \frac{1}{3}$ of $\frac{2}{7} + 1\frac{1}{2}$ of $\frac{5}{6} + \frac{1}{252}$ of 11.

3. Simplify $\left\{ 2\frac{1}{3} - \left(\frac{25}{27} + \frac{11}{27}\right) \right\} + \left(\frac{1}{2} + \frac{1}{3} + \frac{1}{4} + \frac{1}{5}\right) + \frac{15\frac{3}{8}}{2\frac{1}{4}}$.

4. Simplify $\left\{ \left(\frac{3}{8} + 1\frac{1}{16} - \frac{1}{2}\right) \times \left(4\frac{2}{5} - 3\frac{2}{15} + \frac{7}{10}\right) \right\} + \frac{5}{32}$.

5. Simplify $\dfrac{7\frac{1}{6} \text{ of } 5\frac{3}{8} + 2}{3\frac{1}{7} \text{ of } 2\frac{4}{11} - 1} - \dfrac{104}{405}$.

6. Simplify $\frac{2}{3}$ of $\frac{5}{8} + 1\frac{1}{14}$ of $\frac{63}{75} + \frac{7}{10} - \frac{1}{60}$.

7. Simplify $\dfrac{\frac{2}{3} \text{ of } 1\frac{1}{7} \times 2\frac{2}{3} \text{ of } 4\frac{3}{8} \text{ of } 1\frac{1}{5}}{31\frac{9}{7} - 21\frac{9}{21} - \frac{17}{21}} \times 1\frac{1}{8}$.

8. Simplify $\left\{ \dfrac{1}{1 + \frac{7}{6\frac{2}{3}}} + \dfrac{7}{13\frac{2}{3}} \right\}$.

9. Simplify $\dfrac{3\frac{1}{2} + 2\frac{1}{12} + 3\frac{3}{16} - 7\frac{19}{24} + \frac{1}{48}}{\dfrac{1\frac{2}{3} + \frac{3}{5}}{\frac{2}{3} \text{ of } 2\frac{1}{8}} \quad \dfrac{10 - 7\frac{1}{2}}{3\frac{1}{3} - 1\frac{1}{6}}} \times 1\frac{1}{15}$.

10. Simplify $\dfrac{3}{8 - \dfrac{7}{2 - \frac{3}{4}}} + \dfrac{5}{6 - \dfrac{5}{2 - \frac{5}{6}}} + 1 + \dfrac{3}{1 + \dfrac{3}{1 + \frac{1}{2}}}$.

11. Simplify $\dfrac{\frac{1}{2} + \frac{1}{3} \text{ of } \frac{1}{4} + \frac{5}{6}}{\frac{1}{13} \text{ of } (1 + 5\frac{1}{2}) + \frac{5}{6} \text{ of } \frac{1}{23} \text{ of } (7 - 2\frac{2}{5}) - \frac{1}{4}} \div 17$.

12. Simplify $\dfrac{\dfrac{\frac{1}{8} + \frac{5}{6}}{24\frac{1}{2}} + \frac{1}{2} \text{ of } \frac{3}{4} \div \frac{5}{3} - \frac{9}{20}}{30}$.

13. Simplify $\left\{ \dfrac{\frac{1}{2} - \frac{1}{3}}{\frac{1}{3} - \frac{1}{4}} \text{ of } \dfrac{\frac{1}{4} - \frac{1}{5}}{\frac{1}{5} - \frac{1}{6}} \text{ of } \dfrac{\frac{1}{6} - \frac{1}{7}}{\frac{1}{7} - \frac{1}{8}} \right\} \times \dfrac{5\dfrac{1\frac{17}{20}}{4}}{40}$.

FOURTH CLASS.

Exercise XIX.

1. What fraction divided by $\frac{2}{3}$ of 12 will give $\frac{4}{5}$ for quotient?

2. How many vests, each containing $\frac{3}{4}$ of a yard, can be made out of 24 yards of cloth?

3. How many poor people can be supplied with $\frac{4}{5}$ of a lb. of meat each, out of a basket containing 25 lbs., $9\frac{3}{5}$ ozs.?

4. A lady bought three pieces of cloth; the first contained $39\frac{1}{2}$ yds.; the second $28\frac{1}{4}$ yds.; the third $25\frac{3}{8}$ yds. How may yards, in all, did she buy?

5. If $\frac{5}{8}$ of a mill is worth $5225, what is $\frac{3}{4}$ of the remainder worth?

6. Express the following in fractions with the least common denominator, and find the difference between the greatest and the least: $\frac{3}{7}$, $\frac{9}{10}$, $\frac{11}{21}$ and $\frac{23}{35}$.

7. If $27\frac{2}{3}$ miles are travelled in $2\frac{5}{8}$ hours, how long will be required for $11\frac{21}{23}$ miles?

8. A man has $\frac{4}{15}$ of an acre in one plot; $\frac{5}{8}$ of an acre in another; $1\frac{7}{10}$ acres in another; and $4\frac{3}{8}$ acres in a fourth. How many acres has he altogether?

9. A dairyman sells $6\frac{3}{5}$ lbs. of cheese from a piece weighing 20 lbs., 4 ozs. How much of the piece has he left?

10. A man who owns $\frac{7}{64}$ of a ship, sells $\frac{1}{2}$ of his share; what fraction of the whole ship does he still possess?

11. The sum of three numbers is $\frac{99}{32}$; the least is $\frac{1}{2}$ and the greatest $1\frac{1}{4}$; what is the *product* of the three numbers?

12. A house and lot together cost $2400; the lot cost $\frac{1}{7}$ of what the house cost; find the cost of each.

13. (a) The remainder 9 is $\frac{1}{5}$ of the divisor and $\frac{3}{8}$ of the quotient; what is the dividend? (b) A cistern loses, by leakage, 4 gallons 3 quarts, 1 pint, in 7 hours, 48 minutes; what is its hourly rate of loss?

Exercise XX.

1. What is the value of $2\frac{2}{3}$ of $3\frac{1}{4}$ divided by $3\frac{1}{4}$?

2. Add together $\frac{3}{4}$, $\frac{13}{16}$, $\frac{13}{32}$, and $\frac{7}{160}$; and divide the sum by the difference between $\frac{1}{2}$ and $\frac{7}{40}$.

EXERCISES IN ARITHMETIC.

3. Arrange the following fractions in order of magnitude $\frac{2}{3}$, $\frac{4}{5}$, and $\frac{3+4}{4+5}$.

4. (a) Find the L.C.M. of 1547, 1729 and 4199; (b) Add $\frac{7}{1541}$, $\frac{8}{2717}$ and $\frac{10}{4199}$.

5. The numerator of a fraction is 3, and the fraction becomes $\frac{3}{14}$ when divided by 2. What is the fraction?

6. The numerator of a fraction is 16, and the fraction becomes 144 when multiplied by 46. What is the fraction?

7. Simplify $\dfrac{\frac{6}{8} \text{ of } 7\frac{3}{11}}{1\frac{1}{8} - \frac{1}{4}} + \dfrac{40}{20} - \dfrac{8\frac{1}{2}}{8\frac{7}{8}} \div 11\frac{3}{32}$.

8. Simplify $\dfrac{5\frac{2}{3} + \ldots \quad (4\frac{2}{3} - 4\frac{7}{12}) \text{ of } \frac{2\frac{1}{4}}{}}{5\frac{2}{3} - 5\frac{1}{5} \quad 4\frac{2}{3} + 4\frac{7}{12} \text{ of } \frac{2\frac{1}{4}}{}}$.

9. The less of two numbers is $\dfrac{54\frac{2}{3}}{\frac{1}{3} \text{ of } 8\frac{1}{3}}$; and their difference is $\dfrac{1\frac{4}{5}}{\frac{9}{10}}$; what is the greater number?

10. Simplify (a) $\frac{1}{7}$ of $\frac{3}{8} \div 1\frac{2}{7} + \frac{4}{15} \times \frac{5}{8} - \frac{9}{7} \div 1\frac{4}{5}$ of 3; (b) $\left\{ \dfrac{\frac{1}{4} + \frac{1}{3}}{1\frac{1}{4}} - \dfrac{1}{2} + \dfrac{\frac{1}{2\frac{1}{3}}}{} - \dfrac{\frac{1}{3}}{2\frac{1}{12}} + 7 \right\}$ of $\dfrac{\frac{1}{7} + \frac{1}{9}}{\frac{1}{9} + 1\frac{1}{7}}$ of \$210.

11. Divide $\frac{5}{126}$ by the difference between the greatest and least of the following fractions: $\frac{14}{15}$, $\frac{17}{18}$ and $\frac{21}{23}$.

12. What number added to $\frac{5}{8} + \frac{4}{5}$ will give that number which, when subtracted from $3\frac{7}{12}$, leaves $1\frac{1}{3}$?

13. (a) Simplify $\dfrac{\frac{1}{3}(\frac{1}{2} + \frac{1}{7}) - \frac{1}{7}}{1 + \dfrac{1}{2 - \frac{1}{4}}}$ (b) Multiply the sum of $\frac{1}{2}$, $\frac{1}{3}$, and $\frac{3}{4}$ by the difference between $\frac{4}{5}$ and $\frac{2}{3}$. (c) Illustrate $\frac{1}{2}$ of $\frac{3}{4}$, $\frac{1}{4}$ of $\frac{4}{5}$, $\frac{7}{8}$ of $\frac{1}{2}$, $\frac{1}{4}$ of $\frac{1}{3}$. (d) If a plot of ground $\frac{3}{8}$ of a mile square be divided into 750 lots of equal size, what part of an acre will each lot contain?

(e) Simplify $\frac{3}{4} (\frac{2}{3} \cdot \frac{1}{4})$ of $\frac{5}{8} \cdot \frac{9}{7} \div \dfrac{1}{3\frac{1}{2}}$.

FOURTH CLASS.

Exercise XXI.

1. Reduce the difference between 14 tons, 16 cwt., 11 lbs. and 13 tons, 18 cwt., 20 lbs., to ounces.

2. A boy, having a basket of oranges, gave away a certain number of them, and then he bought at a fruiter's 5 times as many as he gave away, after which he had $26\frac{2}{3}$ dozen or twice as many as he had at first. How many more did he buy than he gave away?

3. A has a field $60\frac{1}{2}$ rods square, around which, on the inside, he makes a roadway 10 rods wide. How many acres and square rods does the roadway contain?

4. When apples are 32 cents a bushel, a barrel costs $1.27; at this rate, what will a barrel cost when apples are 40 cents a bushel, the cost of packing being 15 cents a barrel?

5. A does $\frac{1}{8}$ of a piece of work in $1\frac{1}{2}$ days, when he is joined by B, and together they finish the work in 5 days from the time when A began the work. How many days would the work have occupied each alone?

6. There are 917 square yards in a path which surrounds a plot containing 1 acre, 80 sq. rods and whose length is 80 rods; find the width of the path.

7. How far may a man row down a river at the rate of 12 miles an hour, so that he may walk back at the rate of $2\frac{1}{2}$ miles an hour and be occupied 7 hours, 15 minutes in travelling?

8. From 2 acres, 140 sq. rods, take 1 acre, 150 sq. rods, and reduce the difference to inches.

9. A man, having 75 acres, 130 sq. rods of land, sold 13 acres, 150 sq. rods, 30 sq. yards. What is the remainder worth at 8 cents for every 5 square yards?

10. From a square stick of timber, 15 inches to the side, and containing 3 cubic yards, 8 cubic ft., a piece 4 ft. long is cut. How many cubic inches are still left?

11. A man buys 50 bushels, 1 peck and one pint of wheat for $64.34, and sells 10 bushels, 2 gals. and 1 quart of it for $16.45; what per cent. is he clearing?

12. Mr. C has 40 bushels, 5 lbs of barley on his wagon, and Mr. D has 30 bushels, 25 lbs. of wheat on his wagon; what fraction of C's load is D's?

13. How many small boxes, each $3'' \times 2'' \times \frac{3}{4}''$, can a traveller pack into a box $3' \times 2' 6'' \times 2' 2''$?

Exercise XXII.

1. If $\frac{5}{9}$ of a house is worth $250, what is the value of two such houses? $900

2. If $\frac{8}{11}$ of a boat is worth $1200, what is the value of $\frac{7}{10}$ of it?

3. If $\frac{3}{7}$ of $3\frac{1}{2}$ of a farm cost $4900, what is the farm worth? $3430

4. If $\frac{4}{15}$ of a bushel of potatoes cost $2, what is $2\frac{2}{3}$ pecks worth at the same rate?

5. What is $\frac{4}{7}$ of an acre of land worth, if $\frac{3}{8}$ of an acre is worth $18?

6. If $\frac{3}{4}$ of a coal mine is worth $9000, what is the value of $\frac{1}{12}$ of it?

7. If $\frac{1}{7}$ of $\frac{7}{9}$ of an estate is worth $900, what is the value of the estate?

8. What is $\frac{1}{2}$ of $\frac{4}{5} \div \frac{9}{10}$ of an orchard worth, when $\frac{4}{9}$ of it is worth $500?

9. A man sold three quarters of beef for $36, and one quarter of mutton for $3. At that rate, what was the value of the whole of his beef and mutton?

10. When $\frac{1}{4}$ of a gross of lead pencils cost $4, what will half a gross cost? What is that apiece?

11. If $\frac{3}{4}$ of $\frac{4}{5}$ of a wagon-load of turf will cover 60 square feet of ground, what will 50 such wagon-loads cover?

12. How many carrots will grow on nine acres, if 180 bushels grow on $\frac{8}{10}$ of an acre?

13. (a) If $\frac{4}{5}$ of a stack of hay is worth $28, what is the value of $\frac{8}{15}$ of $2\frac{2}{3}$ of it? (b) Find a multiplier which will give the amount of any sum of money at simple interest for 5 years at 4 per cent. Use the multiplier to find the amount of $560 for the said time at the said rate.

Exercise XXIII.

1. A and B do a work in 8 days, B and C in 10 days, A and C in 15 days; all three work together at it for 4 days and then A leaves; the other two go on for 2 days longer and, then, B leaves. In how many days will C finish the work alone? $10\frac{2}{5}$ dys

2. At what price per yard must a merchant mark silk which cost him $3.20 a yard, so that he may throw off 20 per cent. and still be making a profit of 25 per cent. on cost? $5.00

FOURTH CLASS. 29

3. Find the simple interest on $415.50 for 4 years at 7 per cent. per annum. *$116.34*

4. Express ($\cdot 27$ of 13s. 4d.)+($\cdot 194$ of £2 10s.) as the decimal of £18 2s. 6d. *$\cdot 637$*

5. What is the value of ($\frac{3}{4}$ of $\cdot 16 \div \cdot 375$)² of $90 ? *$10*

6. On what sum is $157.50 the true discount for 2 years, 6 months, at 7 per cent. per annum ?

7. A dealer can sell 700 bushels of barley for $490 cash, or for $560 due in 1 year 6 months hence. Which offer had he better accept, money being worth 8 per cent. per annum ? *The latter*

8. Simplify $\left\{ \left(\frac{41}{20} + \frac{7\frac{1}{2}}{91} \text{ of } 4\frac{1}{3} \right) + \left(\frac{7}{8} \text{ of } 7\frac{6}{21} - \frac{1}{8} \right) \right\}$
$\div \left\{ \frac{3\frac{1}{2}}{9} \text{ of } 1\frac{1}{14} - \frac{2239}{5400} \right\} \times \frac{7}{45}.$ *607*

9. What time after 12 o'clock will the hands of a watch be *first* at an angle of 120 degrees ? *21·91*

10. An agent sold 215 ~~bushels~~ *bbls* of apples at $2.30 a barrel on a commission of 4 per cent. ; find the amount of his commission *$19.78*

11. A and B own $\frac{2}{3}$ of a pit of apples, and C the rest. A's share is 3 times B's and the difference between B's and C's shares is 58 bushels, 1 peck, 2 quarts, 1$\frac{1}{3}$ pints. How many bushels of apples does the pit contain ? *350 bushels*

12. A man exchanges 20 pecks of clover seed at $5 a bushel for hay at 80 cents a cwt. How many tons and lbs. does he get ? *1 ton 11*

13. (a) Find the value of 4 barrels of eggs, of 96 doz. each, at 35 cents a score. (b) A can mow $\frac{1}{3}$ of a field in 3 days, and B can mow $\frac{1}{5}$ of the same field in 3 days. In what time could both, working together, mow $\frac{8}{15}$ of the field ? *3 dys.*

Exercise XXIV.

1. A line X is one-third as long again as a line Y, and Y is three-fourths as long again as a line Z. What fraction of X is $\frac{1}{2}$ of Z ?

2. Divide $225 between A and B, giving A $1\frac{1}{7}$ times as much as B. *$120 $105*

3. A man sold a lot, losing thereby 25 per cent. of the cost of the lot, and with the proceeds he bought a bankrupt stock of groceries which he immediately sold for $3500, thereby gaining 16$\frac{2}{3}$ per cent ; find the cost price of the lot and his total gain or loss per cent. by his transactions.

EXERCISES IN ARITHMETIC.

4. If pure silver be worth $15 a lb., find the value of 192 ounces of English *standard* silver.

5. A's age is 66⅔ per cent. of B's, and 7 years ago the half of the sum of their ages was 13 years; find their ages.

6. Divide $615 among A, B, C, D and E, giving A $30 less than C, C $10 more than B, B $100 less than E, E $40 more than A and B together, and D half as much as all the others together.

7. The wheels of a road-cart are each 14 feet, 8 inches in circumference, and together make 14400 revolutions in going 2 hours'. How fast does it go per hour?

8. A cistern contains 8000 gallons of water, but when 300 cubic feet are withdrawn, the cistern is found to still contain 61250 lbs. of water. How many gallons of water are there in a cubic foot?

9. The sum of $135 was paid as a week's wages to an equal number of men, women and boys; the men received $1.25, the women 75 cents, and the boys 50 cents a day. How many men were there?

10. How many chains is it from Winnipeg to Calgary, a distance (by railway) of 955 miles?

11. At 30 cents a load, it cost $66 to gravel a walk, 80 rods long, by 9 feet wide, with gravel 6 inches deep. How many cubic feet make a load?

12. For every 2 ounces of green tea in a mixture there are 5 ounces of black tea. How many lbs. of each are there in 14 lbs. of the mixture?

13. How much heavier would 12 barrels of pork be than 1 cubic yard, 2 cubic feet of water?

Exercise XXV.

1. Simplify $\dfrac{\tfrac{1}{11} \text{ of } 9\tfrac{3}{13} \text{ of } 3\tfrac{1}{4} \text{ of } 9\tfrac{7}{10}}{\tfrac{4}{17} \text{ of } 3\tfrac{9}{13} \text{ of } 12\tfrac{1}{4} \text{ of } 2\tfrac{10}{33} \text{ of } \tfrac{7}{20}}$ of $100.

2. If 9 hats cost as much as 25 silk ties worth 99 cents each, how many hats could be bought with $330?

3. A whaler, in pursuit of a whale, lost ⅓ of his whale-line; he then added 500 feet to the remainder, when he found it to be ¼ longer than it was at first; find the cost of the original whale-line at 25 cents a yard.

FOURTH CLASS.

4. A man sold a horse for $100, thereby losing $16\frac{2}{3}$ per cent. of his purchase. What per cent. of his sale would he have gained, had he sold the horse for $200?

5. Divide $47.50 among A, B and C so that, B shall have $\frac{2}{3}$ of A's share and C $\frac{2}{3}$ of B's share.

6. A person agrees to complete a piece of work in 30 days. (a) What part of it ought to be done in 24 days? (b) How much less than $\frac{7}{8}$ of it will be done?

7. A bill of 55 lbs. of mutton and 45 lbs. of veal amounted to $13.35. The veal cost 3 cents a lb. more than the mutton. What is the value, at this rate, of one cwt. of mutton?

8. A person who paid away $\frac{5}{17}$ of the contents of his purse, and was robbed of $\frac{1}{12}$ of the remainder, found that he had still left $4.50. How much had he at first?

9. Two horses are worth as much as 5 oxen, and 3 oxen as much as 16 sheep. What will be the value of a horse, if the price of a score of sheep is $300?

10. A buys 75 tons, 2 cwt. of hay at $14 a ton; B buys 64 cords of wood at $9.75 a cord, and C buys 8 pigs each weighing 115 lbs. at $3.25 a cwt. How much does A pay more than B and C together?

11. In marking questions *one* is the maximum, and *six* the minimum. What per cent. does a candidate make who receives 4 marks?

12. If $8 be allowed as the interest on $160 for a certain time, what will be the interest on the same sum for twice that time at half the rate?

13. A man owning a section and a half of land in Manitoba sold two rectangular lots out of it, the first, 50 by 40 rods at $150 an acre, and the second 90 by 70 rods at $80 an acre. What was his average selling price per acre?

Exercise XXVI.

1. A and B start from Montreal for Ottawa at the same time that C starts from Ottawa for Montreal, a distance of 100 miles. A and B travel, respectively, 10 and 8 miles an hour, and C 11 miles an hour. (a) In how many hours will C be midway between A and B? (b) How far will C be distant from A?

2. A rectangle contains 9600 square yards of area, and its sides are to one another as 3 : 2. Find the number of yards in a side and an end of the rectangle.

3. Suppose that ·8 is represented by unity, what number will represent ·04$\frac{3}{8}$?

4. Bought a hind and a fore quarter of beef weighing 252 pounds, paying 7$\frac{1}{4}$ cents a lb. for the hind quarter and 5$\frac{1}{3}$ cents a lb. for the fore quarter, and found that I had paid 24$\frac{1}{2}$ cents more for it than I would, had I bought both at the average price per lb. Find number of lbs. in the hind quarter.

5. Bought 13 horses at 14$\frac{2}{7}$ per cent. below their real value. I then sold them at 20 per cent. less than they cost me, which was $286 below their real value. Find the cost price of a horse.

6. The difference between 2 per cent. of a number multiplied by 5 and 3 per cent. of it multiplied by 7 is 22. What is the number?

7. A farm is 391 rods long and 345 rods wide, and it is divided up into square fields of the largest possible size. How many acres and sq. rods are there in 32 of these fields?

8. Bought 70 gals. wine at $3.20 a gallon. How much water must I add so that I may gain $9.75, by selling the mixture at $2.75 a gallon?

9. A safe and its contents are, together, worth $189, and the safe is worth $\frac{2}{7}$ of its contents. Find the value of each.

10. How far from the end must I cut a board, 14 inches wide, to have a piece containing 14 sq. feet?

11. Divide $600 among A, B and C in the ratio of 3 : 4 : 5.

12. A man has a certain sum of money of which he spends $\frac{1}{4}$, then $\frac{1}{3}$ of the remainder, and lastly $\frac{1}{5}$ of what still remains, when he finds he has $300. How much money had he at first?

13. A man buys horses at an average price of $90 each, feeds them at a cost of 90 cents each, and then sells them at $125 each, gaining on the lot $1193.50. How many horses did he handle?

Exercise XXVII.

1. What time between 8 and 9 o'clock are the hands of a clock 7 minutes apart?

2. A and B run a mile race. A gains one rod on B in every 176 yards. How far will B be from the winning-post when A arrives there?

FOURTH CLASS.

3. A speculator buys a tract of land at $15 an acre, and by selling it off in lots makes 80 per cent. on all he sells; so that, after reserving a "quarter section" for a farm, he finds that he has realized, on what he has sold, $11040 more than the whole tract cost him. How many acres were there in the tract bought?

4. A cwt. of beef in England is worth $36.50 Canadian currency. At how many pence per lb. must it be sold to gain 40 per cent.?

5. A miller received $265.12½ for flour at 87½c. a bag. How many barrels and pounds of flour did he sell, and what did a bag hold, given that flour is worth $3.50 a cwt.?

6. At 11 cents a rod, what will 4 miles 110 rods of fencing cost?

7. Bought 20 lbs. black tea and 15 lbs. green tea for $26.60. The black tea cost 28 cents a lb. more than the green tea. Find the cost price of a ten-pound "caddie" of green tea.

8. From 21 acres take 19 acres, 3 roods, 30⅞ sq. yards.

9. A man spent ¼ of a certain sum of money, then $4 more than ⅛ of the remainder, then ⅞ of what still remained all but $6, when he had yet left $16. What was the original sum?

10. What time after 9 o'clock are the hands of a watch equidistant from the figure IX?

11. Sixteen men can do a piece of work in 10 days. How long will it take them when assisted by 4 men?

12. A fruit dealer bought 6 barrels of apples at $2.45 a barrel. The six barrels contained 83 doz. each, and he sold them out at 5 for 3 cents. Find his gain per cent.

13. (a) If a quart contain 78 cubic inches, how many bushels of grain will a uniform circular elevator, 42 feet in diameter and 91 feet high, hold? (b) How often does the L.C.M. of 19½, 4½ and 40½ contain their H.C.F.? (c) A has twice as much money as B. A receives $70, and B receives 30% less money than A, but finds that his money is increased by 116¾% of what it was at first. How much money had A and B (together) at first?

Exercise XXVIII.

1. Find the total cost of putting a board fence, 4 boards high, round a lot, 84 rods, 4 yds., 2 feet long, by 59 rods, 2 yds., 6 inches wide, with inch-lumber 7 inches wide at $12 a thousand, the posts being 7 feet apart, and costing 7 cents each, and the labor of making the fence being at the rate of $33 a mile.

2. Find the cost price of cheese, per cwt., if the sale of 50 cwt. for $250, gives a profit of ⅑ of the original cost.

3. Find the value of the syrup contained in a vessel, which is exactly filled by emptying into it the contents of 24 dozen uniform circular tin pails, each 14 inches in diameter and 12 inches deep, when a gallon of syrup weighs 13½ lbs., worth 8¾ cents a lb.

4. If a carat be $3\frac{1}{10}$ grains, how many carats would a diamond be, which weighs $\frac{2331}{28800}$ of a lb. ?

5. A, B and C are partners in a business. A has in it $7000, B $4000, and C $5000. They gain in 5 years, $16000. A then retires from the business ; what should he take with him ?

6. Sixty cents will buy 4 cocoanuts, 12 oranges, or 20 bananas ; how many dozen bananas are worth as much as 2 dozen oranges and 4 cocoanuts ?

7. A newsboy bought a certain number of papers at 3 cents each. He sold them, gaining $3, which was $9\frac{1}{11}$ per cent. of his sales. Find the number of papers bought.

8. Find the number of acres, sq. rods, etc., in a tract of land consisting of 50 square fields, each 14 chains 40 links to a side.

9. Bought 36 dozen oranges and lemons for $16.80, the lemons at 3 cents each, and the oranges at 5 cents each. How many dozen more lemons were there than oranges ?

10. By what fraction must $\dfrac{1\frac{1}{4}}{1\frac{1}{12}}$ of $\frac{2}{3} + \dfrac{2\frac{1}{2} - 1\frac{1}{8}}{\frac{3}{4} + 1\frac{1}{8}} - \dfrac{8\frac{1}{5}}{7\frac{2}{3}}$ be divided in order to give a quotient of $\frac{2}{3}$?

11. A boy's home is situated one-third of the way from N to M, two villages on the bank of a river. The boy can row from home to M and back in 2 hours, 8 minutes, and he can row from home to N in 40 minutes. He leaves home at 8 a.m., and rows to N, then, from N to M, where he stays 48 minutes, after which he rows home. What time does he reach home ?

12. Divide the number 1089 in the proportions of ⅛, ⅑ and 1/10.

13. In Winnipeg, a man paid $55 a foot frontage for a store site. What was land, an acre, in Winnipeg ?

Exercise XXIX.

1. A man invested $1540 in sheep ; he then sold a certain number for $297 at $4.95 a head, losing thereby 11¼ per cent. of his sales. How many sheep did he buy ?

FOURTH CLASS.   35

2. A person borrows a certain sum of money for 4 years, 6 months, at 5½ per cent. and returns, at the end of that time, $1122.75. What was the sum borrowed? $900

3. A gentleman from London (Eng.) paid £240 Sterling for a "quarter section" of land in Alberta, N.W.T. What was land per acre there?

4. If the import duties on hogs into Canada be 80 cents a cwt. more than 25 per cent. of the cost per cwt. in Illinois, and the packer pays $4860 duty on a car-load of 1500 hogs averaging 180 lbs. each, what is pork per cwt. in Illinois?

5. If a twenty-five cent piece weigh 3 dwts., 18 grs., how many five-cent pieces would weigh 3¾ lbs. Avoidupois? How much is the pure silver in them worth at $18.28¼ a lb.?

6. Two horses are loaded, one with a cubical tank, 3 feet to a side, filled with sand which is 1⅔ times as heavy as water, and the other with 9 barrels flour. If the tank weigh 70 lbs. and each barrel 12 lbs.; which horse is drawing the greater load, other things being equal?

7. Find the cost of wire, at 8 cents per 5 yds., to enclose a field 36 by 45 rods, the field being rectangular in form, and the fence 5 wires high. $71.28

8. How many feet of lumber, inch-measure, will be required to plank a play-ground, 166 feet long by 66 feet wide, with plank 2½ inches thick?   2739o

9. The mean height of 5 trees is 91 feet. What must be the height of a sixth tree, which brings the average up to 94 feet?   109

10. Simplify (a) 5⅔ of $\tfrac{1}{15} \div (6\tfrac{1}{2} - \tfrac{2}{75}) + \dfrac{35\tfrac{1}{2}}{81}$; (b) $[\{2\tfrac{1}{4} \div 2\tfrac{4}{4}\} \div \{2\tfrac{1}{3} \div (6\tfrac{1}{3} \div 1\tfrac{29}{72})\}] \div 1\tfrac{13}{14}$.   (a) ½   (b) 2¾   2 3/4

11. A man owns a farm, divided into 121 plots of rectangular shape, each 90 by 80 yds., which he has planted with potatoes. Find the value of the crop, supposing 350 bushels to grow on an acre, and potatoes to be worth 60 cents a bushel.   3780 0

12. A drover paid $18595.50, in Toronto, for 200 head of prime cattle, averaging 1771 lbs. each. He shipped them to Liverpool at a cost of $16.06 a head, and sold them in the English market at 9 pence a lb. Find his gain.   42 854

13. The larger wheel, of a bicycle, which is 15 feet in circumference, makes 63963 revolutions less than the smaller wheel in going 20 miles, 60 rods, 15 feet. Find the circumference of the smaller wheel.

7 above, double the perimeter

Exercise XXX.

1. How often does the L. C. M. of 3, 6, 17, 18, 42 and 64 contain the G. C. M of 18996 and 29932 ?

2. (a) Resolve 180, 630 and 7350 into their prime factors. (b) Use these factors to prove the truth of each of the following statements :—

   I. "The G. C. M. of two or more numbers is composed of *all the factors which are common* to these numbers."

   II. "The L. C. M. of two or more numbers is composed of *the smallest selection of factors* that includes the factors of each given number."

3. (a) Resolve 1365 and 4550 into their prime factors. (b) From the factors thus obtained select those factors which form (I.) the G. C. M. ; and (II.) those which form the L. C. M. (c) Show (I.) that the G. C. M. and L. C. M. are composed of all the factors of these *two* numbers ; and (II.) that the G.C.M. is composed of all the factors rejected by the L. C. M., and *vice versâ* ; (III.) that the G. C. M. × L. C. M. = the product of the numbers. (Why?); (IV.) that the G. C. M. × L. C. M. ÷ one of the numbers = the other number, and *vice versâ* ; and (V.) that the L. C. M. of the two numbers = their product ÷ their G. C. M., and *vice versâ*.

4. Find the L. C. M. of $\frac{1}{10}$, $\frac{4}{5}$, $\frac{9}{35}$ and $\frac{5}{12}$.

5. "The principle of finding the G. C. M. of two numbers depends upon the following axioms :" (1) "'A measure of any number is also a measure of any *multiple* of that number." (2) "A measure of each of two numbers is also a measure of their *sum or difference*." With the numbers 264 and 312 prove these axioms to be true.

6. The H. C. F. of two numbers is 74, and their L. C. M. is 15,540 ; one of the numbers is 1554 ; find the other.

7. The H. C. F. of two numbers is 240, and their L. C. M. is 2880. Find the numbers.

8. Find the L. C. M. of $\frac{4}{5}$, $\frac{5}{7}$ and $\frac{8}{105}$, and divide it by the last fraction.

9. Find the H. C. F. and L. C. M. of $(8\frac{1}{2}\frac{0}{1} \div \frac{1}{5}\frac{0}{6})$ and $(1\frac{1}{2} \times 1\frac{1}{4} \times 2\frac{1}{2} \times 3\frac{1}{3})$.

10. (a) Find the H. C. F. and L. C. M. of $(\frac{1}{4}$ of $\frac{1}{3} \div \frac{1}{24} \times \frac{3}{8})$ and $(\frac{1}{4} \times \frac{1}{3}$ of $\frac{1}{24} \div \frac{3}{8})$. (b) How often is the H. C. F. contained in each ?

11. Find the L. C. M. of 4662, 7175, 7770, 6993, and 6970.

12. Find the L. C. M. and H. C. F. of $\frac{2}{3}$ of $\frac{5}{7}$, 9, $\frac{2\frac{1}{3}}{7}$ and $\frac{1\frac{2}{3}}{2\frac{1}{2}}$.

FOURTH CLASS.   37

13. Find the greatest number which will divide 2733 and 5191, leaving as remainders, respectively, 13 and 23.

Exercise XXXI.

1. If 240 bushels of oats are worth 15 sheep, 16 sheep worth 2 oxen, 7 yoke of oxen worth 256 hogs, 48 hogs worth 14 tons bran; how many bushels of oats must be given for 13 tons of bran?

2. Simplify: $\left\{ \dfrac{5\frac{2}{3} \text{ of } 7\frac{2}{9}}{8\frac{7}{24} - 3\frac{5}{12}} \right\} \div \left\{ \dfrac{1\frac{3}{5}}{3 + \dfrac{1}{3\frac{1}{3}}} + \dfrac{1\frac{2}{3} \text{ of } 4\frac{2}{7}}{1\frac{2}{8} \text{ of } 3\frac{6}{7}} \right\}$.

3. A fruiter buys apples at 2 for 3 cents, and as many pears at 2 for 5 cents. How many can he then sell for $1, an equal number of each, in order neither to gain nor lose?

4. A boy can get 10 candy-sticks at a confectioner's each 8 inches long, for 20 cents; or he can get a dozen sticks of the same kind, each 7 inches long, for 18 cents. (*a*) In which kind had he better invest? (*b*) If, on a certain occasion, he gained 10 cents by the better investment, how many sticks did he buy?

5. Of two numbers 3 times one is equal to twice the other, and the sum of three times the one and twice the other is 2460, what are the numbers?

6. How often will a harrow, 12 feet by 15 feet, move the length of itself in harrowing a field of 20 acres?

7. A cubical block of iron, 4 inches to a side, weighs 40 lbs.; find the weight of a circular disk of iron whose diameter is $3\frac{1}{2}$ inches and whose thickness is $3\frac{1}{2}$ inches.

8. How much sugar at 4, 6, 8 and 15 cents a lb. will be required to form a mixture of 13 barrels of 270 lbs. each, worth 10 cts. a lb.?

9. How much per cent. will a grocer gain who sells a mixture of 15 lbs. tea at 55 cents a lb., 9 lbs. of which cost 60 cents a lb., and the balance 40 cents a lb.?

10. Find the cost of painting a hall-way, 60 feet long, 10 feet wide, and 12 feet high, at 54 cents per sq. yard, allowing for two doors, each 6 feet by 3 feet, and one window 10 feet by 4 feet.

11. The cost, gain, and selling price of an article, together amount to $56; and the gain, at which it was sold, is 40 per cent.; find the cost price.

12. A man sows 16 lbs. millet seed on every 242 sq. yards of his ground. Find the cost of seeding 20 acres with millet seed at $1.80 a bushel.

13. (*a*) How many bushels shelled corn are there in a bin 8 feet square at the base, and 10 feet high ? (*b*) Divide the L.C.M. of 6·25, 25 and 10·6 by their H.C.F. (*c*) If 9 boarders (in a certain boarding-house) consume ⅔ of a barrel of flour per week, and the host, at the end of 8 weeks, admits 3 new boarders, what will be the amount of the flour bill at the end of a period of 13 weeks, flour being worth $4.41 per barrel ?

Exercise XXXII.

1. A stationer bought 138 reams of paper at $2 a ream, of which he kept 18 reams for his own use. At what price per quire must he sell the remainder that he may have his own for nothing ?

2. Soap is bought and made up into uniform cakes, the selling price per cake being the same as the buying price per 4 ozs. What must be the weight of each cake so as to insure a gain of 6¼ per cent. ?

3. Divide $199.36 between A and B in the ratio of ·2̇ : ·3̇4̇.

4. A grocer buys some tea at 6sh. a lb. and some at 4sh. a lb. In what proportion must he mix them, so that, by selling the mixture at 5sh. 3d. a lb., he may gain at the rate of 20 per cent. ?

5. If ⅔ of a mine be worth $198,000, find the value of 8·3̇ of the mine.

6. How many square feet are there in the surface of a cube, one of whose edges measures 8ft., 4 inches ?

7. A sold a house for a certain sum, losing thereby 8¼ per cent.; B sold it to C for $240, gaining 9 1/11 per cent. What did the house cost A ?

8. A farmer weighed 5 loads of hay on the market and received a ticket, marked 10950 lbs. If his wagons weighed 1250 lbs each, and he got $18 a ton for his hay, how much of his hay money would he have left, after buying 66lbs. of sugar at 11lbs. for a dollar, 50 lbs. 2¾ ozs. tea at 52¾ cents a lb., and 80 yards of cotton at 12½ cents a yard ?

9. A can do a piece of work in 16 days, B can do ¾ of it in 9 days, and C can do ⅓ of it in 1¼ days. How long will it take C, alone, to finish the work after A and B have worked together at it for 3¾ days ?

FOURTH CLASS. 39

10. A man paid $20160 for a farm at $24 an acre. What will it cost to put a fence around it, at 80 cents a rod, and two cross fences, one lengthwise and the other crossing it at right-angles, given that it is 200 rods wide and the cross fences cost 55 cents a rod less than the outside fence?

11. A tradesman earns $40\frac{5}{8}$ cents an hour. How many £, Sterling, does he earn in a month, at this rate, working 8 hours a day? (a month = 4 weeks).

12. A salt merchant sells 500 bbls. salt at $1.40 a barrel, on a commission of $1\frac{3}{4}$ per cent. How much does he remit?

13. (a) Find the average cost price of 80 lbs. tea at 60 cents a lb., 40 lbs. at 50 cents a lb., and 30 lbs. at $53\frac{1}{2}$ cents a lb. (b) Find the L.C.M. of $2\frac{1}{4}$, $3\frac{3}{4}$ and $11\frac{1}{4}$; how often does it contain all these numbers?

Exercise XXXIII.

1. A can do a piece of work in 4 days, B in 9 days, and C in 10 days. If $8.30 is paid for the work, how much of this does each one receive?

2. A drover marketed $\frac{1}{4}$ of his herd at M. at $80 a head, $\frac{1}{3}$ of the remainder at N. at $100 a head, and the remainder at R. at $90 a head. If he had marketed twice as many at N. and half as many at M., he would have gained $800. How many cattle did he market at R.?

3. A and B have each a flock of sheep. A lost $\frac{1}{8}$ of his flock worth $5 each, and B sold $\frac{1}{10}$ of his flock valued at the same rate as A valued his, one man losing what the other man realized. If A had sold his sheep instead of losing them, they would both have realized, for the sheep sold, $300 cash. Find the value of both flocks at this rate.

4. Bought a *quarter-section* of land in Manitoba; but land having risen, I sold $\frac{3}{8}$ of my land for what the whole of it cost me. What per cent. did land rise in value?

5. Simplify $\frac{3}{8}$ of $\frac{1}{8} + \frac{1}{2} - \frac{1}{4} \div \frac{1}{8}$ of $1\frac{1}{4} + \frac{4}{5}$ of $\frac{23}{40} \div \frac{9}{10} \times \frac{3}{8}$.

6. A farmer laid out $2940 in purchasing an equal number of sheep, hogs and cows. Each sheep cost $8, each hog $\frac{3}{4}$ as much as a sheep, and each cow as much as 2 sheep and 2 hogs together. Find the number bought altogether.

7. Along a certain street, one mile long, there is a house every 40 yards, and a tree every 16 yards. How many houses will have a tree in front?

40   EXERCISES IN ARITHMETIC.

8. The product of two numbers is 5103, and their G.C.M. is 9. Find their L.C.M.

9. Divide 493 into two parts such that ½ of the greater is equal to ⅜ of the less.

10. A grocer sold two kinds of tea, the dearer kind at 90 cents a lb. and the cheaper kind at 50 cents a lb. He received $204 for 280 lbs., sold. How many lbs. of each kind did he sell?

11. A man and a boy, working together, earn as much in 21 days as the boy alone can earn in 69 days. If the man's daily wages are $1.60, what are the boy's daily wages?

12. Seven-eighths of the selling price of certain goods is ten per cent. less than the goods cost. Find the gain per cent. at which the goods are sold.

13. (a) A man wishing to sell his farm asked 14¾ per cent. more than it cost him, but finally sold it for 6¼ per cent. less than his asking price, gaining thereby $500. How much did the farm cost? What was his asking price, and for what did he sell it? (b) Bought 5600 lbs. of coal in Scranton at $6 a "*long*" ton, and sold it in Woodstock, Ont., at 85 cents a cwt. per "*short*" ton. What did I gain?

Exercise XXXIV.

1. A can do a work in 12 days, B in 15 days, and C in 20 days, working alone. If A and C work together at it for 7 days, what should be paid B, who finishes it, given that A, B and C can earn $6 a day when working together?

2. A man borrowed $560 at the Ontario Bank on February 1st, 1888, at 8 per cent. per annum. He paid back, at a certain date, $595.84. Find the date on which he returned the money, allowing 365 days to a year.

3. A fifty-gallon cask is ⅔ full of wine, which is 83⅓ per cent. pure. Twenty per cent. of the contents is then withdrawn, and the cask is filled with water. What percentage of the contents is pure wine now?

4. A has 11 times and B 13 times as much money as C, and 25 per cent. of the difference between A's money and B's money is $4. How much money have they all?

5. A hatter sold two hats, getting 20 per cent. less for the second than for the first. He lost 12½ per cent. on the first, but gained 40 per cent. on the second, which made his total gain, on both hats, 30 cents. Find the cost price of each hat.

FOURTH CLASS. 41

6. What is the difference in cost, at 50 cents a square yard, of paving a square plot of ground 35 yards to a side, and one in the form of a circle, 35 yards in diameter?

7. A and B sold potatoes, each making the same rate per cent. profit. A's cost 40 cents a bushel and he sold at 45 cents. B's cost 24 cents a bushel, and a merchant bought 54 dollars' worth of potatoes from him. How many bushels did he get for that money?

8. The interest is $\frac{1}{4}$ of the principal, and half the difference between the interest and the principal is $300. If the time is 6 years, 3 months, what is the rate per cent.?

9. If coffee is mixed with 40 per cent. of its own weight of cocoa, and 10 per cent. of its weight of chicory, what per cent. of the whole mixture is the coffee?

10. What is the value, at $70 an acre, of a semi-circular tract of land whose radius is 100 rods?

11. Simplify: (a) $(3\frac{1}{2}+4\frac{1}{8}) \div \frac{5}{18}$ of $\frac{80}{125} \div \frac{2}{3} + \frac{3}{4} \div \frac{9}{10} \times \frac{7}{12}$ of $\frac{84}{56}$; (b) $8\frac{1}{2}+4\frac{1}{8} \div \frac{5}{18}$ of $\frac{80}{125} \div \frac{2}{3}+\frac{3}{4} \div \frac{9}{10} \times \frac{7}{12}$ of $\frac{84}{56}$.

12. A boy's age now is one-third of his father's age, but six years ago he was one-ninth of his father's present age. How old is the boy?

13. (a) A stick, placed vertically down in water, appears, owing to refraction, only $\frac{7}{8}$ of its real length; find the depth of a pond in which a stick, placed vertically down, appears to be 14 feet long, and which exactly measures its depth. (b) A man being asked how old he was, answered: "If I were as old again as I am, and half as old again, and 9 years older, I would then be 99 years old." How old was he?

Exercise XXXV.

1. Paid $235.20 for the use of $840 at 8 per cent. For what length of time did I use it?

2. If, to 6 cwt., 72 lbs. of sugar, 448 ounces of sand be added, what percentage of the whole mixture is sand?

3. A man speculates with $\frac{1}{5}$ of his income, gives away $\frac{1}{18}$ of the remainder in charity, and banks the remaining $1200, after spending $150 for clothes. Find the amount of his income.

4. If 28 barrels of sugar and 420 boxes of cheese fill a car, and 16 barrels of sugar and 32 boxes of cheese fill $\frac{1}{5}$ of a car, how many barrels of sugar and boxes of cheese can I ship in two such cars, filling a car with each?

5. The sum of three numbers is 260; and eight times the first, twice the second, and once the third are all equal. Find the numbers.

6. A rectangular court containing 2 acres is closely paved with flag-stones, 9 inches in thickness. How many cords of stone are there in the pavement?

7. Multiply 47 acres, 134 sq. rods, 13 sq. yds., 2 sq. ft., by 108, using the factors 9 and 12.

8. A man, owning $\frac{2}{3}$ of a section of land in Shoal Lake District, sold $\frac{3}{4}$ of his share at $15 an acre. How much did he realize on his sale?

9. What is 95 times $\$\left\{\dfrac{1}{2-\frac{3}{4-\frac{5}{6}}}-\dfrac{1}{2+\frac{3}{4+\frac{5}{6}}}\right\}$? $54

10. A pile of 30-inch wood is 80 ft. long, 20 ft. wide, and 14 ft. high. What is it worth at $1.80 a cord? (Side measurement.) $504

11. The sum of two numbers is $76\frac{2}{3}$, and their difference is 46. The larger number is how many times the smaller?   4 times

12. By selling a mixture of 300 lbs. of black and green tea at 42 cents a lb., a merchant lost $14\frac{2}{7}$ per cent. of the cost price of the mixture. If the black tea cost 55 cents a lb. and the green tea 40 cents a lb., in what ratio were they mixed?

13. (a) Find a fourth proportional in the ratio as 7:147::16:
(b) Bought 640 bags of flour at $1.50 a bag; kept out 40 bags for my own use, and sold ½ of the remainder at $1.25 a bag. For how much, per bag, must I sell the rest in order to gain $120 on the whole lot? $2.35

Exercise XXXVI.

1. Find the amount of $450 lent out for 7 years at 5 per cent. $607.80

2. A man put $1600 into a grocery business, and at the end of 5 years withdrew $2000. What rate per cent. did he realize on his investment?   5%

3. In what time will $800 amount to $1600 at 8 per cent.?   12½

4. A person can buy a farm for $20000 payable in 4 years with interest at 5 per cent., or he can buy it for $16000 cash. Which is the better bargain for the buyer provided he can get money at 4 per cent.?   latter by $5440

FOURTH CLASS. 43

5. A mixture of brandy and water is as 4 : 1. How much of the mixture must be drawn off and water put in its place that the mixture may contain brandy and water as 3 : 2 ?

6. A feed merchant chops a mixture of 20 bushels of pease at 70 cents, 32 bushels of oats at 35 cents, and 8 bushels of barley at 60 cents a bushel; the mixture increases, in the chopping, 15 per cent., and he then sells it, by measure, at 50 cents a bushel. What does he gain ?

7. One-fifth of the time a man works at a job he gets $2.75 a day, ½ of the time $3.25 a day, and for the remaining three days, which the job lasts, he gets $4 a day. What does he receive for the job ?

8. If a skein of linen makes 15 knots of 110 threads each, and each thread is 2 feet 9 inches long, how many miles and yards of thread will 13 lbs. of linen make, given that a skein weighs 14 grains ?

9. How many tons of bran at $16 a ton should I receive for 4560 feet of lumber at $18 a thousand feet, 6480 lbs. of wheat at $1.05 a bushel, 1720 lbs. hay at $15 a ton, and a pile of wood 160 feet long and 5 feet high at $2.50 a cord, the length of the wood being 22 inches ?

10. Divide 882 acres, 101 sq. rods, 19 sq. yds., 4 sq. feet, 72 sq. inches by 63, using the factors 7 and 9.

11. If 10 turkeys and 4 ducks are worth $11.20, and 4 turkeys and 10 ducks are worth $8.26, what is the value of 36 ducks ?

12. If a laborer earns $1.50 a day when wheat is $1.10 a bushel, what should he receive when wheat is $1.10 a cental ?

13. If a train travel 203 miles in 6 hours, including on an average 2 minutes per hour for stoppages, how far will it travel in 99 hours when 5 minutes per hour, on an average, are lost by delays ?

Exercise XXXVII.

1. At what rate per cent., simple interest, will $1170 bear $31.20 interest in 8 months' time ?

2. A man exchanged 11 tons of hay, which cost him $88, for 15 sheep at $6 each and 2 pigs at $10 each. What per cent. did he gain by the exchange ?

3. A garrison of 7200 men had provisions for 9 months. How many men must vacate the garrison at the end of six months that the provisions may last till the end of the year ?

4. If 4⅝ ounces of tea cost 60 cents, what will 29 lbs. cost ?

5. A cart wheel is 84 inches in diameter; how often will it turn in going 11 miles?

6. If 60 lbs. of coffee, sold for $27, gains 12½ per cent. of the cost price, find the cost price per lb.

7. If 15 men or 33 women can reap a field of wheat in 30 days, in how many days could 45 men and one woman reap ten such fields?

8. Sold barley at 80 cents a bushel, gaining 14⅔ per cent. Find the cost, at this rate, of 2500 bushels of barley.

9. How many lbs. of tea at 46, 50, 75 and 80 cents per lb. respectively, will make a mixture worth 60 cents a lb.?

10. Sold a lot for $960, losing ⅛ of the proceeds. Find my gain per cent., had I sold the lot for $1500.

11. If 10½ lbs. of milk make a lb. of cheese, which sells at 12½ cents a lb., find the value of the cheese made from 560 tons of milk.

12. A salt merchant bought 56 tons of salt at $8 a ton; put it into barrels, at a cost of 15 cents a barrel, and then sold it all at $1.50 a barrel; find his gain.

13. (a) Find the cost of carpeting a room 30 feet 10 inches, by 24 feet 8 inches, with carpeting 30 inches wide, at $1.80 a yard, the carpet to run lengthwise of the room and 4 inches to be allowed, per strip, for waste. (b) An agent charged $15 for selling a sewing-machine worth $75; what per cent. on the cost price did he collect?

Exercise XXXVIII.

1. What principal will produce $376 interest in four years at 5 per cent.?

2. What will it cost to put a board fence, 5 boards high, round a lot 60 rods long by 220 yards wide, the lumber used being inch boards, 16½ feet long and 1 ft. wide, worth $18 a thousand feet; the posts 16½ feet apart, from centre to centre, and costing $50 a thousand; and the cost of labor, in building the fence, 10 cents a rod?

3. A can do a piece of work in 16 days, B can do ¾ of it in 9 days, and C can do ⅓ of it in 1¼ days. How long will it take C to finish the work, after A and B have worked together at it for half a day?

FOURTH CLASS.

4. If a train lost 5 minutes per hour in performing a journey of 154 miles in 4 hours, how many minutes an hour would it lose when it performed a journey of 9576 miles in 10 days, its rate of travelling being uniform?

5. How much water must be added to a mixture of 240 gallons of brandy and water $\frac{7}{8}$ pure, so that the brandy may be 70 per cent. of the whole mixture?

6. How many seconds will there be in the year 1900?

7. A merchant fails in business, owing $36000. His assets are $27000. What will a creditor lose to whom he is indebted $720?

8. Six persons on a journey of three months spend $365; how long, at this rate, may 9 persons journey on four times half that sum?

9. A pile of 22-inch wood cost $727.65 at $1.96 a cord. It was 180 ft. long, 20 ft 2 inches wide, and 6 ft. high. (a) How was it measured? (b) Which way was it piled?

10. At $120 an acre, a plot of ground is worth $4500. It is 75 rods wide; what will it cost to enclose it with a fence at 87½ cents a rod?

11. How much tea at 50 and 70 cents per lb., respectively, will make a mixture of 13 lbs. worth $7.50?

12. Pure wine is worth 4.66\frac{2}{3}$ a gallon. How much water is there in a mixture of 100 gallons worth 382.66\frac{2}{3}$?

13. (a) A had $17 less than B, and $21 less than C. He then gave B $5 and C $11. How much money had C more than B then? (b) If 40 oranges be sold for $1.20, and the gain thereby be 20 per cent., find the cost price per dozen.

Exercise XXXIX.

1. A boy walks from A to B, a distance of 15 miles. For the first quarter of his journey he goes at an average rate of 120 yards a minute, and for the rest of the way at 90 yards a minute. How long will it take him to perform the journey?

2. Bought oranges at 3 for 5 cents, and sold them at 50 cents a dozen; what per cent. did I gain?

3. If $\frac{2}{3}$ of a herring cost $\frac{3}{8}$ of a dime, how many herrings will $1.80 buy?

EXERCISES IN ARITHMETIC.

4. A table, 4ft. 8in. long, by 2ft. 11in wide, is covered with Canadian cent pieces placed in rows contiguous to one another, and none touching more than four others. If each cent piece is an inch in diameter, find the surface of the table that remains uncovered by coins.

5. Sold $\frac{1}{12}$ of my goods at a loss of $33\frac{1}{3}$ per cent. By what increase, per cent., must I raise the selling price of the remainder to gain 5 per cent. on the entire cost of my goods?

6. A speculator bought 3200 dollars' worth of land at $2.50 an acre. He sold 200 acres of the land at $3 an acre, and 540 acres at $5.00 an acre. At what price per acre must he sell the remainder so that his total receipts may be equal to 5·21625 times the cost of his land?

7. Simplify: $\frac{1}{15} \times [\{ (4\frac{1}{3} - 2\frac{1}{4}) \times (7\frac{1}{3} + 2\frac{1}{15}) - (8\frac{1}{3} - 3\frac{1}{4}) + (2\frac{1}{15} - \frac{1}{15}) \} \div (\frac{1}{4} + \frac{17}{20}) \} + \frac{127}{240}]$.

8. Find the *least* number that may be exactly divided by 9, 11, 51 and 36. Find the *sum* of the *several quotients*.

9. Had a certain sum of money; spent $\frac{1}{4}$ of it, then $\frac{1}{3}$ more than $\frac{1}{2}$ of the remainder, and had still left $2; find the original sum.

10. An egg dealer buys eggs at 40 cents a score, and sells them at 30 cents a dozen. On a certain day, he received $21 for eggs; how much of this was profit?

11. A man lost $\frac{1}{3}$ of his money and $5 more, then $\frac{1}{11}$ of the remainder all but $5, and still had money enough left to buy 66lbs. 10$\frac{3}{4}$ozs. of butter at $37\frac{1}{2}$ cents a lb. How much money had he at first?

12. A farmer bought 30 sheep at $8 a head due in six months. He sold $\frac{1}{2}$ of them, immediately, for $123 cash, and the rest at $9 a head due in four months. What did he gain, 6 per cent. per annum being allowed off a debt for immediate payment in cash?

13. (a) A paid $840 dollars for hay, and sold part of it for $405 at $15 a ton, gaining, on what he sold, $81. How many tons did he buy? (b) If 8 bushels of wheat sow 4 acres 80 sq. rods of land, what will the wheat cost, for a "quarter-section" of land, when wheat is $1.35 a bushel?

Exercise XL.

1. Bought 20 tons 3 cwt. oat hulls at 3.87\frac{1}{2}$ a ton, and sold the whole of it out at 20 cents a cwt. Find my gain.

2. Divide 270 cocoa-nuts among three boys, giving the first half as many as the second, and the third 20 more than $\frac{2}{3}$ of the remainder.

3. How often does the L. C. M. of 3, 6, 18, 17, 42 and 64 contain the H. C. F. of 18996 and 29932?

4. Twelve dollars are paid down for a suit of clothes, and this is $\frac{4}{5}$ of the price of it. How many bags of apples, at 30 cents a bag, will pay the balance due on it?

5. A bought potatoes at 75 cents a bushel, and B bought apples at 72 cents a bag. How many bushels of apples should B give A for 1200 bushels of potatoes?

6. A certain number divided by 2, 3 or 9, leaves respectively remainders of 1, 1 and 4, and the sum of the three quotients is 793. Find the number.

7. A certain kind of grain is \$1.25 a cwt., or \$.70 a bushel. How many lbs. in a bushel of that grain?

8. Divide \$28.80 among A, B, C and D, so that A's share shall be \$4.70 more than B's, and that C's share shall be \$10.40 less than A's and B's together, and that D shall have \$3.60 less than the combined shares of A, B and C.

9. The sum of \$12.50 is made up of five-cent and ten-cent pieces, there being 10 more five-cent than ten-cent pieces. How many are there of each?

10. Find the cost of 298400 shingles at \$4.80 a thousand.

11. Find the cost of 1022 lbs. of oatmeal at fifty cents a stone.

12. What is $40\left\{\frac{\cdot 6}{\cdot 25}+\frac{\cdot 24}{\cdot 96}+\cdot 325-\cdot 150\right\}$?

13. (*a*) I buy an article for \$280 a ton. At what price per lb. must I sell it in order to gain $14\frac{2}{7}$ per cent.? (*b*) Divide \$650 among A, B and C, so that A may receive $\frac{7}{13}$ of the whole, and that B may receive $\frac{1}{5}$ as much as C.

Exercise XLI.

1. A man after selling ·375 of his farm, had still left ·8 of the remainder, having lost, in speculation, $12\frac{1}{2}$ acres worth \$70 an acre. How much was his farm worth?

2. Simplify:

(*a*) $\frac{1}{4}\div\frac{5}{6}$ of $\frac{9}{10}\times\frac{3}{5}$.
(*b*) $\frac{1}{4}\times\frac{5}{6}\div\frac{9}{10}$ of $\frac{3}{5}$.
(*c*) $\frac{1}{4}$ of $\frac{5}{6}\times\frac{9}{10}\div\frac{3}{5}$.

3. Find the amount of $840. for 8 years at 3½ per cent. interest, per annum.

4. A bicyclist rode from Regina to Carron, a distance of 54 miles, at the rate of 8 miles an hour. Half an hour after a cow-boy left Regina on horseback and reached Carron 15 minutes before the bicyclist. Find the cow-boy's rate per hour.

5. What will be the cost of covering with lead, a flat roof, 40 feet long, 24 feet wide, the lead being $\frac{1}{16}$ of an inch thick, weighing 702 lbs. to the cubic foot and costing 5 cents a lb. ?

6. The distance between two towns is 44 miles, and on a certain map their places are marked 5½ inches apart. On what scale is the map drawn ?

7. Bought 8 dozen bundles of gloves of a dozen pair each, and sold them all for $1382.40, gaining 33⅓ per cent. What did they cost me a pair ?

8. The interest on a certain sum for 3 years, 6 months at 8 per cent. per annum is $75.60. What fraction of the principal is the yearly interest ?

9. At what rate per cent. will $1170 produce $31.20 as interest in 8 months ?

10. A cart holds 1½ cord-feet of stone. How many such cart-loads of stone will it take to build a wall under a barn 80 feet long, by 48 feet wide (outside measurement), the wall being 18 inches thick and 8 feet high, allowance being make for 4 doors each 7′ × 6′ and ten windows each 4′ × 3′ ?

11. A ton of bricks measures 20.83 cubic feet, and a brick is 8 inches long, 4½ inches wide, and 2½ inches thick. How many bricks weigh 13 tons ?

12. In a composition of pure air, oxygen is to nitrogen as 1 : 4. How much per cent. of pure air is the nitrogen it contains ?

13. A sets out on foot at 4 miles an hour, at 7 a.m. ; B sets out 25 per cent. faster, per hour, than A at 10 a.m. ; and C, on horseback, at 12½ miles per hour at 2 p.m. At what o'clock will C be midway between A and B ?

Exercise XLII.

1. Two bicyclists, A and B, going 18 and 12 miles an hour, respectively, start together from the same point at the same time to go in the same direction round a circular course 101 rods, 13½ feet in diameter. (a) In what time will A overtake B ? (b) How far will A have ridden ?

FOURTH CLASS.

2. If 12 men do $\frac{5}{9}$ of a piece of work in 20 days of 8 hours each, in what time would 20 men do 25 times as much work, working 10 hours a day ?

3. Property is assessed at two-thirds of its real value, and a man who owns a farm, the corner of which is within the limits of a town, pays $1\frac{1}{2}$ mills on the dollar for township rates, $1\frac{1}{4}$ county rates, $\frac{3}{4}$ water rates, $2\frac{3}{4}$ school rates, $1\frac{1}{4}$ gas rates, and $1\frac{1}{8}$ railway rates. What does he pay on his property, the real value of which is $54000 ?

4. A can mow 9 acres in 12 days, B can mow 15 acres in 24 days. In how many days could they both, working together, mow 16 acres, 80 rods ?

5. If 15 ozs. of wheat sow 1 sq. rod of land, what will it cost a Manitoba farmer to sow a *section* of land when wheat is 90 cents a bushel ?

6. How many tons, lbs. and ozs. of ice are there on a circular pond, frozen 7 inches thick, if the diameter of the pond be 84 rods, and the ice weigh $\frac{9}{10}$ as much as water ? ($\pi = 3\frac{1}{7}$).

7. A can win from B 10 games of marbles in 30 games played, and B can win from C 5 games in 40 played. How many games could A win from C in 30 games played ?

8. Bought 3360 lbs. of apples (undried) at 20 cents a bushel, and sold them at five-ninths of a cent a lb. What per cent. did I gain ?

9. Sold a house for $2400, gaining $12\frac{1}{2}$ per cent. of the proceeds. How much would I have received for it, had I lost $7\frac{1}{4}$ per cent. of the cost ?

10. What would be the cost of carpeting a room, 53′ 4″ by 42′ 8″, with carpeting 32 inches wide, running lengthwise of the room, if the carpet cost $·75 a yard, and 8 inches be allowed off each strip in matching ?

11. If 6 oxen eat as much as 9 cows, and 150 bushels of barley feed 15 oxen for 48 days, how long can 108 cows be kept for $182.40, when barley is 76 cents a bushel ?

12. A speculator bought a block of land, 140 chains long and 55 chains wide, at $·50 a perch. He then sold 20 per cent. of it at $45 an acre, and the remainder at $90 an acre. What per cent. did he gain or lose ?

13. If $14.40 is the interest on $120 at 6% for a certain time, at what rate per cent. is $34, the interest on $340 for the same time ?

Exercise XLIII.

1. A man bought what he supposed was twenty-four dollars and eighty cents' worth of tea at 40 cents a lb., but the grocer had used a weight of $15\frac{1}{2}$ ounces for a lb. in weighing the tea. (a) What did the merchant gain in money? (b) What per cent. did the customer lose?

2. How many gallons will a tank, 8 feet square at the base and 5 feet deep, hold?

3. How many tons of coal, at $5 a ton, must I mix with 12 tons at $8 a ton, so that, by selling the mixture at $7 a ton, I may gain 25 per cent.?

4. A farmer has a bin, 51 feet long, 4 feet high, and 3 feet wide, filled with oats. What are they worth at 34 cents a bushel? (1 cub. feet = $25\frac{1}{2}$ lbs.)

5. Sixteen lbs. of coffee at 40 cents a lb. were mixed with 4 lbs. at 55 cents a lb., and the mixture sold at $45\frac{3}{20}$ cents a lb. Find the gain per cent. at which the mixture was sold.

6. A corn crib, 6 feet wide at the top and 3 feet wide at the bottom, 10 feet long and 8 feet high, is filled with corn on the cob. What is it worth at 25 cents a bushel? (1 cub. foot = 22 lbs.)

7. Divide $340 among A, B and C in such a manner that $4\frac{1}{2}$ times A's share = $1\frac{1}{2}$ times B's share = C's share.

8. How much coffee at 40 cents a lb. must I mix with 5 lbs. chicory at 25 cents a lb. to make a mixture worth 30 cents a lb.?

9. A wholesale and retail merchant deducts 20 per cent. from his retail price in selling a retailer an invoice of goods. If the retailer gain 40 per cent. in retailing his goods, what per cent. advance on the wholesale merchant's retail price does he sell his goods?

10. A reduction of 20% on the cost price of eggs enables a buyer to purchase 30 doz. more eggs for $18 than he could, before the reduction. Find the price of eggs per doz., both before and after the reduction.

11. A Kauri-pine tree yields 3520 feet of lumber and 200 lbs. of Kauri-gum. If lumber is worth $24 a thousand, and gum 5 cents an oz., find the total value of the tree.

12. Simplify: $\left\{ \dfrac{2\frac{4}{17}}{1\frac{2}{3}} \text{ of } \frac{1}{4} \text{ of } 240 \right\} \div \left\{ \dfrac{\frac{5}{6}}{2\frac{1}{2}} + \dfrac{35}{3\frac{3}{14}} + \frac{7}{8} \right\}.$

FOURTH CLASS. 51

13. I spent ½ of my money and three dollars more, when I had still left ⅝ of my money all but a dollar. How much money had I at first?

Exercise XLIV.

1. A man earned £3 Sterling in 5 days of ten hours each. At this rate, what would half a day's wages be in dollars and cents?

2. Simplify:

$$\left\{ (1\tfrac{1}{6} + \tfrac{4}{5} \text{ of } \tfrac{1}{2}) \times 1\tfrac{3}{4} \times (\tfrac{4}{11} - \tfrac{1}{8}) \right\} + \tfrac{1}{25} + \left\{ \frac{1}{6\tfrac{2}{3}} \div 11\tfrac{1}{4} \right\}. \quad \tfrac{34}{75}$$

3. In what time will $450 amount to $607.50 at 5 per cent. simple interest? *7 yrs*

4. A, B and C together have $279. B has ⅝ as much money as C, and for every $4.50 that A has, B and C together have $11. How much money has each?

5. How many boys, each doing ¾ of a man's work, must be employed with 39 men to do in 12 days what 36 men could do in 20 days?

6. To a certain number 5 is added, and 80 per cent. of the result is then subtracted; to the remainder 15 is added and 5 per cent. of the result is subtracted, leaving 95. What is the number?

7. Eighteen choppers agree to have a contract of wood cut in 40 days. When ¾ of the contract is finished, 6 of the men leave; how much more than an average day's work will be required, on the part of each of the remaining men, to finish the contract on time?

8. If a barrel of white-fish costs $16, how much will 3 dozen of the fish, each weighing 2 lbs., 2 ozs., cost?

9. What sum will amount to $2256 in 4 years at 5 per cent.? *$1880*

10. What will it cost, at 13 cents a sq. yard, to paint the walls, ceiling and floor of a room 42 feet, 6 in. long, 30 feet, 8 in. wide, and 15 feet high, an allowance of 1075 sq. feet, 96 sq. inches, being made for doors, windows and baseboards? *$53.82*

11. A man borrowed $560 at the Bank of Ontario, on Feb. 1st, 1888, at 8 per cent. per annum. He returned the Bank, at the end of a certain time, $595.84. Find the time when he returned it. (365 days = 1 year.) *Nov 19/88*

12. A tank can be half filled by two taps, A and B, in 1 hour, 12 minutes, and it can be filled by B alone in 6 hours, or emptied by a tap C in 2 hours. The tank is empty and A is opened for 40 minutes. A is then closed and B is opened for 3 hours, when the taps are all opened. In what time will the tank be emptied, after all the taps are opened?

13. A debt of $260 is paid in francs, valued at $16\frac{1}{4}$ cents each, at a time when $6\frac{1}{4}$ francs are worth $1.00. What does the creditor gain or lose?

Exercise XLV.

1. C, who earns 50 cents an hour for eight hours a day, can earn as much in 8 days and 2 hours, as A and B together can earn in 6 days of 10 hours each, and A earns 20 per cent. more wages than B. What sum would all three, together, earn in 13 weeks, working 9 hours a day?

2. The Savings' Bank pays 4 per cent. per annum, and D deposits $32 at the beginning of the year; $48 more at the end of three months; $25 more at the end of six months; and $50 at the end of 9 months. At the end of the year he withdraws it all and invests the money in an enterprise, paying 35 per cent. yearly. How much will he have at the end of 6 years from the time when he put the first money in the Savings' Bank?

3. A man bought 80 sacks of bran of 80 lbs. each at $10 a ton, and paid for it with apples at $1.60 a barrel. How many barrels did it take?

4. If 13 geese or 7 turkeys cost $9.10, what will be the value of 42 geese and 13 turkeys?

5. A man walks 860 yards in 8 minutes. How long will he be in going 1806 miles?

6. A fisherman buys codfish at 8 cents a lb. and sells it out at $12 a cwt.; find his gain per cent.

7. A brewer has a vat 30 ft., 9 in. long, 16 ft., 8 in. wide, and 6 ft., 4 in. deep, filled with beer, which he wishes to put into quarter-barrel casks. How many casks does he require, given that a cubic foot contains 25 quarts?

8. The circumference of the hind and fore wheels of a carriage are, respectively, $16\frac{1}{2}$ and $13\frac{3}{4}$ ft. How far has the carriage gone when the hind wheel has made 1536 revolutions *less* than the fore wheel?

FOURTH CLASS. 53

9. A person travelled 1440 miles by water, rail and stage. The distance by stage was ⅛ that by rail, and the distance by rail was 1⅔ that by water. The cost of travelling by water, rail and stage was as 2 : 3 : 5. Find the cost of the journey, given that an *equal* number of miles, by each mode of travelling, averaged 3⅜ cents a mile.

10. A rectangular court is 240 ft. long by 45 ft. wide (outside measurement) and a path of the uniform width of 3 yds. runs round it on the inside. Find the cost of paving the path with flag-stones at 80 cents a sq. yard, and the remainder of the court with turf at $1 50 a hundred sq. feet.

11. If four men can do as much in a day as 7 women, and 2 women as much as four boys, and 7 boys working together for 8 days earn $44, what will be the earnings of 8 men and 6 women working together for 70 days?

12. A freight train is 16 miles ahead of an express which travels at the uniform rate of a mile in 1 min. and 15 seconds. It is run into in 40 min. How many miles an hour was the freight running?

13. What is the value, at $1.60 a cord, of all the 18-inch wood that can be closely piled 6ft. high on ⅛ of an acre of ground?

Exercise XLVI.

1. If 20 of A count for 12 of B, and 45 of B count for 29 of C, and 20 of C for 9 of D, and 6 of D for 100 of E, how many of E count for 150 of A?

2. If 40 apples = 2 dozen oranges, and half a dozen oranges = 9 pears, and 28 pears = 2 lbs. coffee, how many apples are 72 lbs. of coffee worth?

3. If 50 lbs. of dates are worth 80 lbs. candy, and 6 lbs. candy are worth 5 lbs. figs, what is the value of a lb. of dates when figs are 30 cents a lb.?

4. If £6 = 40 thalers, and 25 thalers = 93 francs, and 27 francs = 5 scudi, and 31 scudi = 67½ gulden, how many gulden = £210 10sh.?

5. If 4 horses cost as much as 6 cows, and 9 cows cost as much as 30 sheep, and 45 sheep cost $810, find the value of a car-load of 17 horses.

6. If 4 lbs. of tea be worth 40 lbs. sugar, and 16 lbs. sugar be worth 3 lbs. coffee, and 60 lbs. of coffee be worth 240 lbs. biscuit, how many lbs. of biscuit would 20 lbs. tea buy?

7. If 10 horses can move as much as 6 mules, and 4 mules as much as 1 elephant, and 4 elephants as much as 130 men, how many horses would move as much as 156 men?

8. If 36 bushels oats = 15 bushels wheat, and 5 bushels wheat = 9 bushels pease, and 12 bushels pease = 30 bushels rye, how many bushels of oats should be exchanged for 210 bushels rye?

9. *Five* per cent. of a certain sum and *three* per cent. of another sum amount to $14.65; but when the per cents. are interchanged the amount is $17.75. Find the sums.

10. The map of a certain country is drawn on a scale of $\frac{1}{2}$ of an inch to the mile. What area on the map will represent a lake whose area is 16000 acres?

11. Find the total cost of 17 tons of oats at 50 cents a bushel; 860 cwt. of wheat at $1.11 a bushel; 40 chains, 3 rods of ditching at $2.40 a chain; and 65 tons of iron at 5 cents a lb.

12. A vintner mixed two kinds of wine, worth respectively $3.60 and $4.20 a gallon, in such proportion that by selling the mixture at $5.50 a gallon he made a profit of $42\frac{6}{7}$ per cent. Find the proportion in which the wines were mixed.

13. (*a*) A man sold 13 fowls for $10.40. There were as many geese as chickens, and twice as many turkeys as ducks. Find the number of each sold, given that a turkey sold for $1.10, a goose for 80 cents, a duck for 50 cents, and a chicken for 35 cents. (*b*) From £16 10sh. 8d., take $\{ (\frac{1}{4} \text{ of } \frac{7}{8} \text{ of } \frac{9}{10}) \div \frac{7}{15} \}$ of 62.59\frac{2}{27}$.

Exercise XLVII.

1. What is the G.C.M. of $\frac{5}{8}$, $\frac{2}{3}$, $\frac{2}{5}$, and $\frac{4}{5}$?

2. Is a fraction a number, and why?

3. When *must* the following note be paid at the Bank of Montreal, and how much *ready cash* will redeem it?

$600.00.   MONTREAL, Que., June 13th, 1889.

Eighteen months after date, I promise to pay Samuel Collins or order, at the Bank of Montreal in Winnipeg, the sum of six hundred dollars, with interest at the rate of six per cent. per annum, for value received.   THOMAS W. TAME.

4. An inn-keeper buys 10 gallons of spirits at $2.40 a gallon, 15 gallons at 90 cents a gallon and 18 gallons at $1.15 a gallon. At what price per gallon must he sell the mixture to gain $8.45 on his outlay?

5. Simplify: $1\frac{1}{4}$ of $5\frac{1}{4} + \dfrac{4\frac{1}{2} - \frac{3}{10}}{1\frac{1}{15}} - \dfrac{6\frac{3}{4}}{\frac{1}{2} \text{ of } 2\frac{2}{3}}$

FOURTH CLASS.

6. Divide $2464 among A, B and C, so that A's money put out for a year at 7 per cent., B's at 5 per cent., and C's at 3½ per cent., will each accumulate the same yearly interest.

7. Make out the following bill :
    2 barrels of fish, 60 doz. each, at $1 a dozen.
    14 lbs. raisins at 13 cents a lb.
    10 lbs. bacon at 18 cents a lb.
    3 cheeses, 70 lbs. each, at 12 cents a lb.
    180 eggs at 13 cents a dozen.
    500 lbs. sugar at 20 lbs. for $1.
    20 lbs. 4 ozs. butter at 20 cents a lb.
    5⅓ ozs. ginger at 54 cents a lb.

8. Thirty-five women can do as much work as 20 boys, and 16 boys as much as 7 men ; how many women can do the work of 33 men ?

9. Bought cherries at eight cents a quart and sold them at $3.37½ cents a bushel, by which I gained $34.23 ; find the number of bushels bought ?

10. Find the cost of 85 tons, 1660 lbs., of pease at 45 cents a bushel.

11. What will it cost to fence a lot 60 ft. front and 60 yds. depth at $.87½ a foot ?

12. Bought barley at 60 cents a bushel, and sold it at $1·5625 a cental ; what was my gain per cent.?

13. (a) Fifty per cent. added to a number, and 40 per cent. of the result added to that, gives the number 1764. What was the original number ? (b) What must be the width of a box 4 ft. long by 3 ft. deep in order to hold ⅛ of a cord of cordwood ?

Exercise XLVIII.

1. An estate is divided among A, B and C, so that A has $\frac{5}{16}$ of the whole estate, and has 4½ times as much as C, who has 17800 acres less than B. What is C's share worth in dollars at £15 Sterling an acre ?

2. A, B and C agreed to dig a well 80 feet deep for $112. At the depth of 30 feet A left, and at the depth of 50 feet C left, and B finished the digging alone. How should the money be divided among them ?

3. The map of a county is drawn on a scale of 6 inches to a mile. What area on it will represent a township of 36000 acres ?

56 EXERCISES IN ARITHMETIC.

4. One vessel, A, contains 30 gallons of wine; another vessel, B, contains 20 gallons of water. Five gallons are taken from each and poured into the other. This is repeated *three* times. How much wine and how much water will the vessels then respectively contain?

5. By selling $1\frac{3}{5}$ of my sheep for $2600, I gain 25 cents a head more than by selling them for $2437.50. How many sheep have I?

6. A had $10 less than B, and B had $4 less than C. A gave $6 to B and $8 to C. How many dollars had C more than A then?

7. A sum of money was divided among A, B and C, so that A received $\frac{2}{5}$ of the sum; B $10 more than $\frac{1}{5}$ of what was then left, and the remainder, which was 4 times B's share, was given to C. Find the sum and the share of each.

8. Reduce to its simplest form:

$$\left\{ \frac{2+\frac{2}{5}}{2-\frac{2}{5}} - \frac{2-\frac{2}{5}}{2+\frac{2}{5}} \right\} \div \frac{2-\dfrac{2}{2\frac{2}{3}}}{3} - \frac{2}{5}.$$

9. A bin is 40 feet long, 10 feet wide, and 4 feet high. How much more or less will it cost to fill it with oats at 40 cents a bushel than to fill it with potatoes at 50 cents a bushel?

10. A dealer buys pork at $4.20 a cwt.; at what price per stone must he sell it to gain 25 per cent.?

11. A lump of lead is 5 inches long, 4 inches wide, and 3 inches thick; what does it weigh assuming it to be 8·64 times as heavy as water?

12. If 4 men and 5 boys earn $54.50 in 5 days, and 6 men and 7 boys earn $47.70 in 3 days, how much will 6 men and 6 boys earn in 6 days?

13. (*a*) Find the number of steel rails, each 22 feet long and weighing 20 lbs, 4 ozs. per foot, that can be made out of 112 tons, 532 lbs. of steel. (*b*) From £($\frac{7}{8}$ of $\frac{4}{5}$ of 21$\frac{3}{7}$) Sterling take $52.40, and invest the balance in cotton at 4 cents a yd.

Exercise XLIX.

1. A bin 8 feet long, 4 feet wide, and 4 feet high, is filled with wheat. Find the value of it at $1.20 a bushel.

2. A gives B 6 yards the start in a race of 206 yards. B gives C 20 yards the start in a race of 100 yards. How many yards could A give C in a race of 515 yards?

FOURTH CLASS.

3. A speculator bought a number of horses at $80 a head, and 9 times as many sheep at $5 a head, paying for the lot $1500. Had he bought the whole number at $12 a head all round, he would have paid $60 less than he did. Find the number of each bought.

4. There are four casks of different sizes. The first is full of water; the rest are empty. The second is filled from the first, leaving the first $\frac{1}{4}$ full; the third is then filled from the second, leaving the second $\frac{3}{5}$ full; the fourth is then filled $\frac{8}{15}$ full from the entire contents of the third. The third and fourth casks, together, hold 5 gallons less than the first. How many gallons does the second cask hold?

5. A certain sum amounts to $733,20 in 6 months, and to $789,60 in eighteen months, at simple interest. What is the rate per cent.?

6. What number, diminished by $\frac{2}{7}$ of $\frac{4}{9}$ of itself, leaves a remainder of 580?

7. The sum of two fractions is $1\frac{1}{11}$; one of the fractions is $\frac{1}{5}$; find the quotient of the greater divided by the smaller.

8. Square the quotient of $\dfrac{\frac{5}{7} \text{ of } 2\frac{2}{3}}{6\frac{2}{7} \text{ of } \frac{3}{11}} \div \dfrac{1\frac{1}{8}}{9}$.

9. Trees are planted, 7 feet apart, around the edge of a circular pond, having an area of $\frac{3773}{5080}$ of an acre. Find the number of trees required. ($\pi = 3\frac{1}{7}$).

10. Sold a lot, which cost me $800, gaining $11\frac{1}{4}$ per cent. of the selling price; and also a second lot, which cost me $700, gaining $12\frac{1}{2}$ per cent. of the selling price. Find my gain or loss per cent. on the total investment.

11. If a lump of gold 18 carats fine, contains 81 ounces of alloy, how many ounces of alloy are there in a lump of gold of equal weight, only 14 carats fine?

12. How many times does a wheel, whose circumference is 18 ft. 4 in., turn in going the distance of $2\frac{7}{24}$ miles?

13. How much tea, worth respectively 60 and 70 cents a lb., must be mixed with 50 lbs., worth 84 cents a lb., in order to make a mixture worth 75 cents a lb.?

Exercise L.

1. A person asked, for a lot of land, 40 per cent. more than it cost him; but finally reduced his price 15 per cent., gaining on the whole lot $1900. For how much did he sell the land?

2. Simplify: $\left\{\dfrac{18\frac{2}{5}}{3\frac{3}{5}} \div \dfrac{22\frac{1}{3}}{8\frac{2}{5}} \times 41\frac{7}{8}\right\} - \left\{\dfrac{\frac{1}{2}+\frac{3}{3}+\frac{1}{4}+\frac{1}{5}+\frac{1}{20}+\frac{2}{3}}{6\frac{2}{3} \text{ of } 8 + 4\frac{2}{5} \text{ of } 5 + 5\frac{1}{2} \text{ of } 4} \times 20\frac{1}{25}\right\}$.

3. The quotient of two numbers is 879, and 5 times the smaller number is 40475; find the greater number.

4. Find the cost of 3660 lbs. cranberries at $2 a bushel.

5. Find the cost of 36 bushels dried apples at 15 cents a lb., and 5628 lbs. of dried peaches at $8 a bushel.

6. Make out the following bill:

    13 dozen hinges, 4 lbs. each, at 8 cents a lb.
    45 gals. seal oil at 90 cents a gallon.
    25 gals. coal oil at 11 cents a quart.
    96 dozen lamp wicks at 2 cents each.
    45 yards wire screening at 25 cents a yard.
    20 score bolts at 30 cents a dozen.

7. If 20 per cent. be gained by selling a horse for $210, what per cent. would be lost by selling it for $160?

8. A man sold 36 bushels of flax-seed at 8 cents a lb. How many boxes of figs can he purchase, with the money received, at $4.50 a dozen boxes?

9. A retail tradesman professes to charge 20 per cent. above the wholesale price, but he has adulterated his goods with 25 per cent. of an inferior kind, costing only half as much. What is his real rate per cent. of profit?

10. Find all the prime factors of 6349, 4500 and 6400.

11. What is the *sum* of all the prime factors of 172800?

12. Two men start to go round a circular race-course, 1197 rods in circumference, one at the rate of $3\frac{1}{2}$ and the other at the rate of 7 miles an hour. How long will it take each one to make the circuit?

13. Find the total cost of 600 lbs. rape seed at 55 cents a bushel; 380 lbs. red-top grass-seed at $5 a bushel; 1760 lbs. lime at $3 a barrel; 960 lbs. millet at $4 a bushel.

FOURTH CLASS. 59

Exercise LI.

1. Three graziers, A, B and C, hire a pasture for their common use for which they pay $124. A puts in 9 horses for 4 months, B 12 colts for 6 months, and C 8 horses for 5 months. How much of the rent should each pay, 2 horses being equal to 3 colts?

2. What is the cost at 5 cents a square yard of painting the roof of a barn, each side of which is 60 feet long and 24 feet wide from the eave to the ridge?

3. Simplify $\frac{9}{7}$ of $\frac{7}{15} \div \frac{9}{7}$ of $1\frac{4}{13} \times \frac{5}{6} \div \frac{3}{8}$ of $\frac{19}{27}$.

4. A shaft, 90 feet deep, is sunk through the clay, sand and rock. Two feet more than $\frac{1}{4}$ of the distance through the rock is $\frac{1}{3}$ of the distance through the clay which is $\frac{5}{8}$ of the distance through the sand. Find the distance through each stratum, the distance through the clay and sand together being 72 feet.

5. If 4 smiths earn as much as 5 fitters, and 5 smiths earn $135 in 15 days, how long will it take 13 fitters to earn $243.36?

6. A person begins to distribute $14.56 among a number of children, giving each one 50 cents; but, after having given this sum to the half of them, he finds that he has enough money left to give the others each 54 cents. How many were there in all?

7. Divide the L. C. M. of 24, 48, 96, 120, 42 and 72 by the G. C. M. of all the *even* numbers between 241 and 247.

8. If 2 men cut 16 cords of wood in 2 weeks, how long will it take 12 men to cut 40 cords?

9. (a) Name the two kinds of fractions, and state the difference between them:—(b) Compare the difference between the two kinds of fractions, with the difference between the Simple and the Compound rules of Arithmetic; (c) Simplify:—(I.) $\frac{1}{2} + \frac{2}{9} - \frac{3}{11} + \frac{7}{18} - \frac{17}{33}$ (II.) $\left\{ \frac{\cdot 2 - \cdot 09}{1 \cdot 3 + \cdot 02} \right\}$ of $3 \cdot 27 \div \cdot 00436 \} - .5$; (d) (I.) Divide the difference between twenty hundred hundred, and nine hundred and ninety-nine hundred and ninety-nine by eleven; (II.) Multiply 20 ac., 85 rods, 19 yds., by 15, and divide the product by 5.

10. If $\frac{5}{8}$ of a ship be worth $\frac{7}{8}$ of her cargo, and half the difference between them be $11500, find the value of the ship and her cargo.

11. It costs $38·40 to carpet a room 24′ × 16′, with carpet of a certain quality. What will it cost to carpet a room 6 feet longer and 4 feet wider with a carpet of the same width, 20 per cent. better in quality?

60   EXERCISES IN ARITHMETIC.

12. Divide $1640 between A and B, so that A's share is to B's as 3 : 5.

13. A quantity of coffee has chicory added to it, so that the chicory is $\frac{1}{8}$ of the whole mixture. If the mixture is worth 36 cents a lb., and the chicory 8 cents a lb., what is the price per lb. of the pure coffee?

Exercise LII.

1. A man, having a farm, sold part of it. He then bought 7 times as much land as he sold, when he found he had 1120 acres, or 75 per cent. more land than he had at first. How much land did he buy?

2. If I buy six bushels of raspberries at $2 a bushel, and sell them again at 8 cents a lb., what do I gain per cent., assuming that a quart of berries weighs $1\frac{1}{4}$ lbs.

3. Simplify : $\dfrac{7\frac{1}{2}-(3\frac{2}{3}+\frac{3}{5}-1\frac{1}{4})\times \frac{2}{5}}{7\frac{1}{2}-(3\frac{2}{3}+\frac{3}{5})-1\frac{1}{4}\times \frac{2}{5}} - \dfrac{109}{415}.$

4. How many lbs. of tobacco at 60 cents a lb. must a tobacconist mix with 3 lbs. at 80 cents a lb., in order to make a profit of $11\frac{1}{9}$ per cent. by selling the mixture at 75 cents a lb.?

5. What is the financial standing of a man who owns $\{\frac{2}{5}-\frac{1}{3}+\frac{1}{5}-\frac{15}{27}\}$ of $270?

6. (a) Find the H.C.F. of 5680, 4615 and 5609. (b) Find the L.C.M. of 26, 91, 180, 240, 95, 133, 380.

7. A and B build a wall in 45 days, and B does one-third of the work that A does; how long will it take each to build it?

8. Find the value of : $\cdot 1590 \times \cdot 472 \div 2\cdot 7.$

9. If 10 per cent. be lost on a horse sold for $90, what was the cost of the horse?

10. How often does a hoop, 2 yards, 16 inches in circumference, turn in going 4 miles?

11. A bookseller sells 7000 copies of a book at $2.14, and takes in exchange a note for one year for the amount. What would he gain or lose by selling them instead for cash at $1.80, interest being at 7 per cent. per annum?

12. A room, 11 feet high, is half as long again as it is wide, and its cubical contents 4768·5 feet. Find its length and breadth.

13. (a) What will it cost, at 66 cents a perch, to put a wall 9 feet high under a barn, 56 feet long by 36 feet wide, the wall being 18 inches thick, and the corners being counted both on the side and end walls, but an allowance of half being made for 5 doors each 8 ft. by 4 ft. 6 in., and 12 windows, each 3 ft. by 2 ft. 6 in., a perch being 16½ cubic feet? (b) Lifted a note whose face value was $330, and which had been at interest for 73 days at 8 per cent. per annum, in order to pay a grocery bill of $335. What had I left out of the proceeds of my note after paying the bill?

Exercise LIII.

1. How much per cwt. is 75 cents a bushel for wheat?

2. What is the value of $\frac{6}{11}$ of a pit of apples, if $\frac{9}{10}$ of it be worth $330?

3. Find the total value of 4 piles of cord-wood of the following dimensions at $4.12½ a cord : (a) 20 ft. long, 12 ft. wide and 7 feet high ; (b) 33 ft. long, 8 ft. wide and 6 feet high ; (c) 45 ft. long, 21 ft. wide and 9 feet high ; (d) 140 ft. long, 12 ft. wide and 5 ft high.

4. Find the cost of a strip of carpeting 8 miles, 40 rods long and 2 ft. 6 in. wide, at 64 cents for 10 sq. feet.

5. If ⅜ of a loaf of bread weighing 6 ounces is worth 2 cents, what is bread worth a lb.?

6. A fisherman had 32 tons, 1120 lbs. of trout to barrel. He used 2⅔ lbs. of salt to each barrel of fish, which he sold at $6 a barrel, net. Find his gain, if the fish cost him 2 cents a lb.

7. Find the cost of 440 lbs. of charcoal at 15 cents a bushel, and 7210 lbs. of bituminous coal at 25 cents a bushel.

8. A man exchanges 7200 lbs. of potatoes, worth 45 cents a bushel, with another man for 960 lbs. of apples at 75 cents a bag, and the balance in money. How much money did the latter receive?

9. What is the value of 3206 lbs. of orchard grass seed at $2 a bushel, and 1428 lbs. of blue grass seed at 75 cents a peck?

10. A man bought 16 tons of lime at $7 a ton, and sold it again at 99 cents a barrel ; find his gain.

11. A corn-crib, 6 ft. wide at the top and 5 ft. wide at the bottom, 24 ft. long, and 6 ft. high, is filled with corn on the cob. How many bushels does the crib contain?

EXERCISES IN ARITHMETIC.

12. A bin is 45 ft., 3 inches long, 6 ft. wide and 4½ feet deep, and is divided into three equal compartments (by partitions) the first of which is filled with wheat, the second with oats and the third with potatoes. Find the value of the entire bin, when wheat is 80 cents, oats 34 cents and potatoes 52 cents a bushel, 3 inches being allowed off the length of the bin for the partitions.

13. A drover bought an equal number of sheep and hogs for $1482; he gave $7 for a sheep and $6 for a hog. How many of each did he buy?   *114*

Exercise LIV.

1. A man lost 6¾ per cent. of his property in an unfortunate speculation. He then invested $5000 in a farm which rented for $280 per annum, and put the remaining $9000 of his property out at interest, at 6 per cent. per annum. By how much is his income less per annum than it would have been, had he put it all out at interest before he went into speculation?

2. I gained $765 in a week on the sale of goods, marked 9 per cent. above cost. What value in goods did I sell that week?   *$8500*

3. Simplify: (a) $\frac{1}{2}$ of $\frac{3}{8} \div 1\frac{2}{7} + \frac{1}{10} \times \frac{5}{8} - \frac{5}{7} \div 1\frac{5}{7}$ of 3; (b) $\frac{1}{2} \div \frac{3}{8}$ of $1\frac{2}{7} + \frac{1}{10}$ of $\frac{5}{8} - \frac{5}{7} \div 1\frac{5}{7} \div 3$.   *1/8 & 4 1/108*

4. Ten men can do $\frac{1}{5}$ of a piece of work in 2 days. Eight of the men work at it for 5 days, when they are then joined by the other two men. How long did the work last?   *17*

5. Two boys and a man contract to do a certain work in 8⅝ days; but the man works alone at it for 4 days before the boys join him, and the contract occupies 10⅔ days. In what time would a boy have done it working alone?

6. If $\frac{5}{8}$ of a barrel of apples is worth 60 cents, what is the price of 200 barrels?   *$192*

7. Divide $840 between A and B, so that as often as A gets $4, B will get $3.   *$480 + $360*

8. If $\frac{1}{11}$ of a cheese is worth $4, what is the value $\dfrac{1}{3\frac{2}{3}}$ of it?

9. Divide the least of the following fractions by the greatest: $\frac{7}{11}$, $\frac{4}{7}$, $\frac{21}{44}$ and $\frac{87}{178}$.   *29/44*

10. Find the compound interest on $550 for 3½ years at 8 per cent.

FOURTH CLASS. 63

11. How many barrels of flour at $5 a barrel should be received for 3740 lbs. of oats at 35 cents a bushel, 4260 lbs. wheat at $1.10 a bushel, 540 lbs. clover-seed at $3.60 a bushel, and 510 lbs. of beef at $10 a cwt.?

12. Simplify: $\dfrac{\frac{3}{3} \times \frac{2}{4} + \frac{1}{2} \div 2\frac{1}{2}}{4\frac{7}{10} \text{ of } 5\frac{9}{11} \text{ of } 2\frac{1}{2}} - \left\{ (1\frac{9}{10} - \frac{7}{8}) \times \frac{7}{17} \text{ of } 2\frac{1}{21} \div \frac{3}{8} \right\}$

13. (a) What will it cost to feed 16 horses on oats for 6 weeks, giving each horse 3 pecks daily, when oats are worth 37½ cents a bushel? (b) Bought 40 gross pencils at 3 cents a dozen; sold ¼ of them at 4 for 5 cents, and the rest at 6 for 10 cents; find my gain.

Exercise LV.

1. A and B were partners in a business in which they gained $363.15. A put in $800 for 9 months, and B 60 per cent. of the entire capital for 3 months. How should the gain be fairly divided?

2. What multiple of 450 divided by 18 will give 225 as quotient?

3. At what rate, simple interest, will a sum become 4 times itself in 40 years?

4. How many soldiers will consume 269 tons, 1000 lbs. bread in 4 weeks, giving each man 11 ounces of bread daily?

5. Sold 7260 lbs. pease at 78 cents a bushel, 2400 lbs. apples at 75 cents a bushel, and bought cotton with the proceeds left, after losing 88 cents. Find the number of yards bought, cotton being 12½ cents a yard.

6. If 64 lambs cost $448, what will a flock of 4 score be worth at the same rate?

7. Sold two houses, getting 1⅖ as much for the second as for the first. On the first I gained 15 per cent. and on the second I lost 20 per cent., losing on the whole $10. Find the cost of each house.

8. A box, 8 feet long, 7 feet wide and 5 feet high, is filled with shelled corn. How many bushels does the box contain?

9. A wagon-box, 14 feet long, 3 feet 2 inches wide, and 14 inches deep, is filled with dry sand; what is the weight of the load in tons and lbs.?

10. Find the L.C.M. of 8, 64, 128, 70, 4, 3, 18, 64; and the H.C.F. of 4123, and 351386.

11. Find the cost of 6 bales of hay, 430 lbs. each, at $12 a ton.

64 EXERCISES IN ARITHMETIC.

12. If ¾ of an acre of land will produce 171 bushels of potatoes, what will 2 acres produce?

13. (a) If $44·2425 is the cost of 6940 lbs. of hay, what is hay a ton? (b) A boy takes 1320 steps, each 2 feet 6 inches long, in going round a rectangular field 60 rods long; how many acres does the field contain?

Exercise LVI.

1. How often is the L.C.M. of (⅔ of 11/22) and (⅞ of 9/14) contained in 9 × 9 ? 18

2. A car forty feet long and six feet wide is loaded to the depth of four feet, six inches, with mineral coal. How many tons are there, assuming a cubic foot to contain a bushel of coal?

3. A cylindrical tank, 8 feet in diameter, is filled with plastering hair, to the depth of seven feet. If a cubic foot contains 16 lbs. of hair, how many bushels of hair are there in the tank?

4. Fill in the following statement of seven weeks' cash receipts, and prove the correctness of your work by adding horizontally and vertically:

DAYS OF WEEK.

WEEK.	MON.	TUES.	WED.	THUR.	FRID.	SAT.	TOTAL.
1st.	$65.91	$88.64	$41.82	$33.60	$44.18	$29.41	
2nd.	54.36	71.29	36.42	84.70	63.19	86.24	
3rd.	81.27	29.82	26.71	21.90	29.14	24.71	
4th.	54.77	86.41	21.86	90.82	81.26	36.82	
5th.	81.29	44.82	87.91	21.44	24.33	20.07	
6th.	29.04	63.84	27.68	86.92	36.81	84.71	
7th.	40.01	28.42	72.84	27.34	27.42	64.13	
TOTAL..							

5. If cheese is 9½¼ per cent. of the milk used in its manufacture, how many tons of cheese will 42000 lbs. of milk produce?

6. Find the cost of sowing a field of 18 acres with wheat at 90 cents a bushel, if it requires ⅔ of an ounce of wheat for every square yard of land.

7. If $4\frac{1}{3}$ of $(A - \frac{1}{8} A) = 3\frac{1}{4} (B + \frac{1}{4} B)$, what is the ratio of A to B?

FOURTH CLASS.

8. A man bequeathed $35000 to his family. He gave to his wife $\frac{1}{4}$ of his property, half of the remainder to his son, and the rest he divided equally among his three daughters. Find the share of each of the daughters.

9. Find the cost of $6 \left\{ \dfrac{\frac{1}{4}+\frac{1}{8}}{2\frac{1}{8}} \right\}$ lbs. of tea at $·70 a lb.

10. Simplify: $\dfrac{\frac{1}{28}-\frac{1}{15}+\frac{2}{21}+\frac{1}{110}-\frac{3}{83}}{(\frac{1}{8}+\frac{1}{12})\times(\frac{1}{4}-\frac{2}{8})}-\frac{1}{4}$.

11. Find the cost of 18 tons, 325 lbs. of hay at $15 a ton, and 96 bushels of potatoes at 15 cents a peck.

12. A man bought 27 cows at $30.75 a head, and paid for them with 630 bushels, 15 lbs. wheat at $1.12½ a bushel, and the rest in cash. How much cash did he pay?

13. Bought three boxes of soap, each containing an English cwt.; kept it all summer, during which time it dried away ¼ in weight. I then sold it at 13 cents a lb. Find my gain, if the soap cost me 23 cents for 3 lbs.

Exercise LVII.

1. A flock of sheep, worth $8 a head and $120 in money, were taken in exchange for 2 horses worth $120 a head and 8 cows worth 25 per cent. as much per head as a horse. How many sheep were in the flock?

2. A person owned ¼ of ⅞ of a market-garden, and sold 50 per cent. of his right for $35. What was the value of the garden at this rate?

3. The proceeds of a debt of $98.50, given into the hands of an attorney to collect, amounted to $94.56 for the creditor. What per cent. did the attorney take for his services?

4. What is the value of the hay in a mow, 70 feet long, 34 feet wide and 18 feet deep, at $10 a ton?

5. A bin 20 feet long by 6 feet wide is filled with potatoes to the depth of 5 feet. What are they worth at 75 cents a bag?

6. Simplify: $\left\{ \dfrac{\frac{1}{2}+\frac{1}{8}}{\frac{7}{10}+\frac{3}{5}} \right\} + \left\{ \dfrac{\frac{1}{8} \text{ of } \frac{7}{9} \div \frac{40}{63}}{\frac{9}{10} \div \frac{1}{3} \text{ of } \frac{5}{12}} \right\}$.

7. A field of hay is 40 rods long and 20 rods wide, and averages 1 ton, 14 cwt. per acre. What is the crop worth at $9.60 a ton?

8. Sold 60 loaves of bread for $4.20, which was 60 cents less than cost. Find the cost price of 100 loaves.

9. Find the H.C.F. of 621 and 1472 ; and the L.C.M. of all the *prime* numbers from 201 to 220.

10. Find the cost of a pile of cord-wood 33 feet long and 5 feet high at $3.84 per cord, and also the cost of a pile of eighteen-inch wood, 75 feet long and 9 feet high, at $1.60 a cord.

11. At what fraction of the cost price are goods marked which, when lowered 20 per cent., still leave a profit of $6\frac{2}{3}$ per cent. ?

12. Bought a piece of property for $9000, and agreed to pay for it in 9 months with interest at 6 per cent. per annum. What amount will be due at the expiration of that time ?

13. (*a*) A piece of ground, 88 rods long, contains 22 acres ; find the cost of fencing it with a straight rail fence, the rails being 12 feet, 6 inches long and costing $15 a thousand, the fence to be 6 rails high and 1 foot, 6 inches, per rail-length, to be allowed for overlapping. (*b*) Bought 70 lbs. of tea for $31.50 ; sold it, so as to gain $7. Had I bought to the value of $81, and sold it at the same price per lb., what would I have gained ?

Exercise LVIII.

1. A stationer gained $\frac{2}{3}$ of the purchase money on pens, sold at 6 for 10 cents. What fraction of the purchase money would he have gained by selling 8 pens for 10 cents ?

2. It required $31.20 to redeem a note, given seven years ago, with interest at 8 per cent. per annum. What was the face of the note ?

3. Simplify : (*a*) $\frac{215}{440}$. (*b*) $\frac{5}{12}$ of $\frac{9}{18}$ of $2\frac{2}{11}$. (*c*) Add the results of (*a*) and (*b*) together.

4. A stream increased 40 per cent., in volume, during a freshet. What per cent. must it then decrease to be again at its former volume ?

5. A cut, $\frac{1}{4}$ of a mile long, 66 feet wide and 20 feet deep on an average, is made through a clay hill ; find the weight, in tons, of the earth removed.

6. A block of marble is 9 feet long, 4 feet wide, and 8 inches thick ; find its weight.

7. A man spent $\frac{1}{3}$ of his money, then $\frac{1}{4}$ more than $\frac{3}{8}$ of the remainder, when he found that he had still left $16. How much money had he at first ?

8. A man bought 6 turkeys and 12 geese for $10.80. If each goose cost 50 cents, what was the cost price of the turkeys?

9. A, who has just sold ⅛ of his farm to B, increasing the latter's land property 10%, has now 210 acres less than B. What is the value of both farms at $70 an acre?

10. A plot of ground, 360 feet long and 132 feet wide, has a woodshed 60 feet long and 16 feet wide built on it, which can be filled to the height of 12 feet with cordwood. If 20 per cent. of the plot, not occupied by the shed, is closely piled with cordwood to a depth of 4 feet, what fraction of the pile will fill the shed?

11. The G.C.M. of two numbers is $\frac{1}{15}$; their L.C.M. is 42; one of the numbers is $\left\{\dfrac{2}{1+\dfrac{3}{3+1\frac{1}{2}}}\right\}$; what is the other number?

12. If a road is 1 chain, 50 links wide, how many miles of it will contain 240 acres?

13. A stock-raiser found that by selling his horses at $70 a head he gained half as much as he would have lost at $40 a head. Find his profit on every 100 head of horses sold.

Exercise LIX.

1. If I can have the use of $700.00 for 5 years for $210.00, what will the use of $500.00 cost me a year?

2. One bricklayer charges $2.40 a day of 8 hours: another charges $3.00 a day of 9 hours. Which had I better employ, and what would I save, by employing the cheaper man, to do a job of work lasting six weeks, working 5 hours a day?

3. Find the L.C.M. of:

$$\dfrac{1-\frac{2}{3} \text{ of } \frac{4}{5}}{1-\frac{1}{3} \text{ of } \frac{1}{5}},\quad \dfrac{9\div 1\frac{4}{7}}{8\frac{3}{11}\times 2\frac{7}{13}},\quad \text{and}\quad \dfrac{2\frac{1}{2}\times \frac{3}{5}}{2\frac{1}{2}-\frac{3}{5}}.$$

4. If 15 men require 6¾ days to mow 300 acres, how long will 3 men require to mow 315 acres?

5. Find the cost of papering the walls of a room, 20 feet, 9 inches long, 11 feet 6 inches wide and 12 feet, 3 inches high, with paper, 22½ inches wide, at 15 cents a yard.

6. A borrows $450 for which he pays $2.25 a month. In what time will the interest thereon be 60 per cent. of the principal? At what rate per cent.?

7. A bushel of coarse salt weighs 50 lbs., and a salt merchant buys 13 tons of salt for $180, which he sells again at 9 cents a peck; find his gain per cent.

8. A gentleman's income is 5 per cent. of his capital. He pays annually $22.50, at $1\frac{1}{2}$ per cent., as an income-tax. What is his capital?

9. A merchant in New York bought 20 quintals of coffee in Guatemala for which he was to pay $560. On weighing it, however, he found each quintal to be 5 lbs. short in weight. What should he pay for it?

10. If 7 lbs. of tea and 4 lbs. of coffee cost $7.00, and 3 lbs. of tea and 7 lbs. of coffee cost $4.85, what is the value of 12 lbs. of each?

11. At $70 an acre, a farm is worth $5950. It is 170 rods long. What will it cost to enclose it with a fence at 70 cents a rod?

12. If 5 men, 10 women or 15 boys can do a work in 33 days, in what time will 30 men, 30 women and 30 boys do the same work, if they all work together at it? [redacted]

13. One-fifth and $\frac{1}{8}$ of a number increased by 8 is equal to half the number; find the number.

Exercise LX.

1. A wagon, loaded with hay, weighs 38 cwt., and the wagon alone weighs 960 lbs.; what is the hay on it worth at $12 a ton?

2. A farmer sold 3 pits of potatoes, consisting in all of 700 bushels, for $306. The first pit sold at 35 cents a bushel, the second at 40 cents, and the third at 50 cents. How many bushels were there in each pit?

3. Simplify: $\frac{1}{2}$ of $\frac{3}{4} \div \frac{4}{5} \times 1\frac{1}{5} + \frac{1}{8}$ of $\frac{9}{10}$ of $\frac{80}{18} + \frac{1}{4}$.

4. Bought 640 yards cloth at $1.37\frac{1}{2}$ a yard; $62\frac{7}{8}$ yards at $1.28 a yard; and $46\frac{5}{8}$ yards at $1.92 a yard. At what price per yard must I now sell it all in order to gain $14\frac{22}{105}$ per cent. on the transaction?

5. Find the L.C.M. of $(\frac{1}{7} + 1\frac{1}{4} + \frac{2}{3})$ and $\frac{1}{2} + \frac{1}{3}(\frac{1}{2} - \frac{1}{7})$.

6. In an election $15\frac{5}{13}$ per cent. of the voters refused to vote. Of the total votes in the electoral division A got $\frac{8}{13}$, and was elected by a majority of 500 votes over B, the defeated candidate. How many votes were polled for each?

FOURTH CLASS. 69

7. A gives $4.87½ for bran at $15 a ton, and B gives $5.82 for some at 60 cents a cwt. What fraction of a ton does one get more than the other?

8. Find the L.C.M. of all the *even* numbers between 41 and 101.

9. A and B agreed to do a piece of work for $62. A worked 12 days of 8 hours each, and B worked 9 days of 10 hours each. How much of the money should each receive?

10. If a bushel of wheat makes 40 lbs. of flour, how many barrels of flour can a miller put up out of 127 tons, 17 cwt., 80 lbs. of wheat?

11. A barters 60 bushels, 48 lbs. of beans at $1.60 a bushel; 26 bushels, 14 lbs. rye at 80 cents a bushel; and 7200 feet of lumber at $15.80 a thousand, with B, for a village lot worth $58.01 per acre. Find the size of the lot.

12. Simplify: $\cdot 6$ of $3 \cdot 3 + \dfrac{1\frac{3}{4}}{2\frac{3}{5}}$ of $17 + \cdot 4$ of $5 \cdot 75$.

13. The interest on a certain sum of money for 3 years at 7 per cent. is less by $39.20 than the interest on the same sum for 7 years at 5 per cent. What is the sum?

Exercise LXI.

1. If 3 horses, 4 oxen or 5 cows can be pastured for one month for $4.80, what should be paid for pasturing a horse, 2 oxen and 3 cows for 5 months?

2. A person owning $\frac{3}{8}$ of $\frac{2}{9}$ of $1\frac{2}{13}$ of a factory which is worth $39000 sells $\frac{1}{3}$ of his share, what fractional part of the factory has he left, and what is it worth?

3. If 40 women do a piece of work in 20 days, in how many days will 15 men do the same work, the work of 5 women being equal to that of 3 men?

4. A and B rented a farm together; they grew 850 bushels of grain, which they divided in such a manner that $\frac{2}{5}$ of the number of bushels A received was equal to $\frac{3}{4}$ of the number of bushels B received. How many bushels did each receive?

5. Tom has $400. He gives away $\frac{3}{8}$ of his money and then $\frac{1}{2}$ of the remainder. How much has he left?

6. How much hay can I buy with $35 at the rate of $\cdot 25$ of a cent for 3 ozs.?

EXERCISES IN ARITHMETIC.

7. If 1 bushel, 20 lbs. of wheat will sow 1 acre, 80 sq. rods of land, what will the wheat cost for 27 acres of land at $1·6125 per bushel?

8. What will be the cost of building a stone dyke 80 ft. long, 10 ft. wide and 15 ft. high at $16\frac{23}{25}$ pence, Sterling, per perch? (a perch $=16\frac{1}{2}$ cubic ft.)

9. A merchant lost $\frac{2}{5}$ of his capital and then gained $500; after which he was worth $2600. How much did he lose?

10. The sum of 4 numbers is 2; the first number is $\frac{2}{3}$, the second is $\frac{2}{5}$ of $\frac{6}{8}$ of $\frac{7}{12}$, and the third $\frac{27}{150}$; find the fourth.

11. A man buys an article and sells it so as to gain 50 per cent. If he had bought it at 20 per cent. less and sold it for $5 less, he would have gained $71\frac{7}{8}$ per cent. Find the cost price of the article.

12. A boy buys oranges at the rate of 4 for 3 cents and sells them at the rate of 6 for 5 cents. How many must he buy and sell again to make a profit of 80 cents?

13. (a) By selling cloth at $1.90 per yard a merchant loses 5 per cent. What per cent. does he gain or lose by selling at $2.20 per yard? (b) One bell tolls 5 times in 8 minutes, and another bell tolls 4 times in 5 minutes; how often will they toll together in 18 hours?

Exercise LXII.

1. A man owing $\left\{ \dfrac{1\frac{1}{2}}{2\frac{1}{3}} + 2\frac{1}{5} \text{ of } 1\frac{1}{8} - 4\frac{3}{4} + 2\frac{1}{3} \right\} - \frac{23}{30}$ of a mine sold out $\frac{3}{4}$ of his share by which he decreased his property $60,000. How much was the mine worth?

2. Divide $1280 among A, B and C, so that A may have three times as much as B, and that C may have as much as A and B together.

3. Two lbs. of tea and 5 lbs. sugar together cost $2; but if tea were to rise 25 per cent., and sugar were to rise $12\frac{1}{2}$ per cent. in price, they would together cost $2.45. Find the value at this rate, of a barrel of 300 lbs. of sugar.

4. What will carpeting, 30 inches wide, at $1.15 a yard, cost for a hall 60 feet long by 8 feet wide?

5. How many flag stones, each 2 feet $2\frac{3}{4}$ inches square on the surface, will be required to pave a rectangular court-yard, 60 links long, by 45 links wide?

FOURTH CLASS. 71

6. Find the following bill of produce:—588 lbs. dried peaches at $4.20 a bushel, 8 bushels of cranberries at 3 cents a lb., 7 cwt. of onions at $3 a bushel, 9 bushels of timothy seed at 5 cents a lb., 66 lbs. of parsnips at $1.50 a bushel, and 79 lbs. of new potatoes at $1.50 a bag. Four cents off the dollar for cash. Find amount paid.

7. How many dollars will a tract of land, 75 chains square, cost at £10 Sterling per acre?

8. A room, 72 feet long, 60 feet wide and 10 feet high, contains 2 doors each 7 feet by 4 feet, 6 windows each 5 feet, 6 inches, by 4 feet, and one window 2 ft. square. How many yards of paper 2 ft. wide will be required to cover its walls?

9. A seed merchant bought one-eighth of a ton of orchard grass seed at $7 a bushel, 2 cwt. of English blue grass seed at $15 a bushel. He mixed it and sold the whole at 60 cents a lb. Find his gain per cent.

10. Divide $42.84 among 12 boys and 15 girls, so that each girl may have twice as much money as a boy, and find the share of each.

11. A barrel holds somewhere between 42 and 48 gallons. It can be filled by an exact number of 3 or 5 quart measures. Find its capacity in gallons.

12. When an ounce of gold is worth $18.75, what is the value of ·38 of a lb.?

13. What relative quantities of sugar at 7, 8, 11 and 14 cents a lb. must be sold, in a mixture, in order to realize an average of 10 cents a lb.?

Exercise LXIII.

1. Simplify $3\frac{1}{5}$ of $\frac{4}{7}$ of $8\frac{1}{3}$ of $2\frac{3}{7}$ of $2\frac{1}{63}$ of $\frac{45}{251}$.

2. Hay is worth $8 a ton and lambs are worth $4.50 a head. How much hay should be given for 144 lambs?

3. A man, after paying 3 cents on the dollar of his income and spending $1.20 a day, is able to save $823 a year. Find his annual income.

4. A tradesman adds 40 per cent. to the cost price of his goods, and allows his customers a reduction of $14\frac{2}{7}$ per cent. off their bills. What per cent. profit does he still make?

5. A bought 20 hogs from B at $4.50 a head, and 80 from C at $4.75 a head. He then sold 75% of his entire drove to E at $4.80 a head. At what rate per head must he then sell the remainder, so as to gain $150 by the transaction?

72   EXERCISES IN ARITHMETIC.

6. Two men travelled a certain distance on bicycles. The drive-wheel on one is 6 feet in diameter, and the drive-wheel on the other is 7 feet 6 inches in diameter. How far are they on the road when the drive-wheel on the smaller machine has made 3360 revolutions more than the drive-wheel on the larger?

7. A rectangular field, whose length is to its breadth as 8 : 7, contains 35 acres. What will it cost to enclose it with a hedge at $1.20 a rod?

8. A can do a piece of work in 2 days and B can do it in 3 days. In how many days can they both working together do $\frac{5}{6}$ of it?

9. If the divisor be $\frac{1}{8}$ of the quotient and 5 times the remainder, and twice the half of the sum of the three be 1008, find the dividend.

10. A rectangular plot of ground, 20 rods long and 16 rods wide, is surrounded by a gravel walk 12 feet wide, and on the outside of this walk a platform, 20 feet wide, is built of two-inch plank, surrounding the grounds. Find the value of the plank, in the platform, at $25 a thousand feet, inch measure.

11. The less of two numbers is $(\frac{7}{25} \div 5\frac{1}{5} + 1\frac{23}{30})$, and their difference is $\{10\frac{1}{2} - (2\frac{3}{4} + \frac{3}{8})\}$; what is the greater number?

12. If the time past noon is $\frac{1}{5}$ of the time till midnight, what is the time?

13. Find the areas of the following annuli whose radii are respectively: (a) 18 and 17 inches; (b) 26 and 16 inches; (c) 57 and 50 inches.

Exercise LXIV.

1. The diameter of a circle is 14 inches; find its area.

2. The circumference of a circle is 66 feet; find its radius.

3. The area of a circle is 2464 sq. yards; find its diameter.

4. The radius of a circle is 24 yards, 1 foot, 6 inches; find its area.

5. What is the area of a circular plot of ground whose radius is 112 yards?

6. Find the area of an annulus whose radii are 80 and 60 inches respectively.

7. What is the volume of a a solid cylinder 7 inches in diameter and 28 inches long?

FOURTH CLASS.

8. Find, to two decimal places, the area of a circle 28 inches in diameter from which a triangular piece, 16 inches to a side, is cut.

9. Find the solid contents of a circular piece of lead 18 inches in diameter, and $3\frac{1}{2}$ inches thick.

10. The drive-wheels of a locomotive engine are each 7 feet, 4 inches in circumference and the piston shaft is fastened 4 inches from the circumference of the wheels. Find the length of the piston-stroke.

11. The area of a circle is 1386 sq. rods; what is its diameter?

12. The solid contents of a circular plate of metal is 1 cubic foot, 472 cubic inches; what is its radius, the plate being $1\frac{3}{4}$ inches thick?

13. (a) A solid piece of metal, 31 feet long, $5\frac{1}{2}$ inches wide and 4 inches thick, is melted and cast into a hollow cylinder whose external diameter is 17 inches, and whose thickness is $1\frac{1}{2}$ inches. Find the length of the cylinder. (b) Reduce $\frac{5}{8}$ of an acre to sq. rods, etc., and $\frac{2}{3}$ of a sq. rod to sq. yds., etc., and subtract the results.

Exercise LXV.

1. A farmer took to market 2 hogs, 160 lbs. each; 14 bags pease, 150 lbs. each; 60 dozen eggs; and 70 lbs. butter. He got $5 a cwt. for pork, 72 cents a bushel for pease, 10 cents for 15 eggs, and 20 cents a lb. for butter. How much money did he receive?

2. What is the value of 72716 lbs. of flour at $3.40 a barrel?

3. Find the cost of 13 tons 1520 lbs. hay at $12 a ton.

4. Find the freight rates on two railroads, one of which charges $20 for the carriage of 40 cwt. 50 miles, and the other $70 for the carriage of 160 cwt. 70 miles.

5. A gold ornament, weighing 3 lbs., 2 ozs., cost $600. If it is made of gold worth $15 an oz. what is charged for manufacture?

6. (a) In which order should the signs "of," "×," and "÷," be taken, in bracketing an expression in fractions?
(b) Simplify: $\frac{4}{7}$ of $1\frac{1}{2}\frac{1}{4} \div \frac{5}{6}$ of $\frac{3}{8} \times \frac{9}{10} \div \frac{1}{2}$ of $\frac{5}{8}$.

7. Simplify: (a) $\frac{1}{3}$ of $\frac{5}{8} \times \frac{3}{7} \div \frac{9}{10}$.
(b) $\frac{1}{3} \times \frac{5}{8} \div \frac{3}{7}$ of $\frac{9}{10}$.
(c) $\frac{1}{3} \div \frac{5}{8}$ of $\frac{3}{7} \times \frac{9}{10}$.

8. If 80 men dig 5 acres, 80 rods in 15 days, how long will 45 men require to dig 10 acres, 40 rods, 605 yards?

74   EXERCISES IN ARITHMETIC.

9. A and B in 9 days make 45 chairs, A and C in 8 days make 28 chairs, B and C in 12 days make 54 chairs. How many dozen chairs could A, B and C together make in 500 days?

10. A horse-dealer sold 16 horses at $140 a head. On half of them he gained $16\frac{2}{3}$ per cent. and on the other half he lost $12\frac{1}{2}$ per cent. Did he gain or lose on the lot and how much?

11. In making a drain, the material cost $1\frac{1}{2}$ times as much as the labor for digging it. But had the former cost $12\frac{1}{2}$ per cent. more, and the latter $16\frac{2}{3}$ per cent. more, the total cost would have been $137. Find the actual cost.

12. Change to equivalent fractions having the least common denominator $\frac{23}{80}$, $\frac{29}{120}$ and $\frac{15}{72}$, and add.

13. How long must $540.20 be on interest to amount to $810.30 at 5 per cent. per annum?

Exercise LXVI.

1. Simplify: (a) $\left\{ \dfrac{\frac{2}{3} \times 1\frac{1}{2}}{\frac{1}{18} \times 5\frac{1}{2}} + \dfrac{7 + 3\frac{3}{8}}{1\frac{5}{12}} \right\}$;

   (b) $\left\{ \dfrac{3\frac{1}{4} \text{ of } 4\frac{1}{3}}{(2\frac{1}{2}-\frac{1}{3}) \text{ of } (3\frac{1}{2}-\frac{1}{4})} \right\} \times 4\frac{3}{4}.$

2. The net proceeds of a sale of 999 barrels of flour, after deducting a commission of 5 per cent. for selling and $200.30 for other expenses, are $5494. What is the price per barrel?

3. In which direction from Woodstock might you travel and your watch keep correct time?

4. Find the total cost of 75 bushels apples at 3 cents a quart, 45 lbs. barley at 96 cents a bushel, 12 pecks of clover seed at 12 cents a lb., 18 gallons vinegar at 5 cents a pint, and 2 barrels sugar of 140 lbs. each, at $3\frac{1}{2}$ lbs. for 25 cents.

5. How many miles can a man travel in 312 days of 10 hours each, going at the rate of 800 rods in an hour?

6. Multiply 15 acres, 88 rods, 0 yards, 2 feet 36 inches by 9 and divide the product by 15.

7. How much more will 120 barrels of flour weigh than ·5 of 14 barrels of water?

8. If $\frac{2}{3}$ of $\frac{1}{5}$ of a cheese cost 24 cents, what would a car-load of 470 cheeses cost?

9. If 20 cords of wood cost $36, what will 74 cords cost?

FOURTH CLASS.   75

10. Divide 1640 marbles among 11 boys as follows : Give to the first ⅛ of them ; to the second ¼ of them ; and divide the rest equally among the other boys.

11. Find the cost of 6428 lbs. of Hungarian grass seed at $1.20 a bushel.

12. A drover bought 50 head of cattle at $34 each, and sold them, gaining on all $250. What did he get for 10 of them ?

13. (a) Simplify $\left\{ (4 - 2\tfrac{1}{4}) \text{ of } (6\tfrac{1}{2} - 2\tfrac{1}{7}) + (2\tfrac{1}{2} + \tfrac{1}{6}) \div (3\tfrac{1}{2} - \tfrac{1}{8}) \right\} + \tfrac{55}{63}$.
(b) Bought 8 lbs. of tea and 13 lbs. coffee for $9.04, paying 8c. a lb. more for the tea than for the coffee ; find the price of each.

Exercise LXVII.

1. Simplify : $\dfrac{\tfrac{5}{8} - \tfrac{3}{4}}{\tfrac{3}{4} - \tfrac{1}{8}} \text{ of } \dfrac{\tfrac{3}{4} - \tfrac{1}{3}}{\tfrac{7}{12} - \tfrac{2}{5}} \div \dfrac{\tfrac{5}{12} - \tfrac{1}{4}}{\tfrac{1}{2} - \tfrac{1}{5}}$.

2. What is the selling price, per bushel, of wheat, when an advance of 5 per cent., on the cost, raised the price $6 on a 100 bushels ?

3. A grocer gives 8 lbs. of prunes for a dollar, and thereby gains 25 per cent. He afterwards reduces his gain on prunes to 10 per cent. How many lbs. by the latter arrangement does he give for a dollar ?

4. Five more than ⅓ of A's sheep were stolen ; five less than ⅔ of the remainder strayed ; 10 more than ⅓ of what then remained died ; and he then sold 2 more than ₃⁄₁₀ of what was still left, when his flock still numbered 5 sheep. How many were in the flock at first ?

5. A and B start in opposite directions, away from each other, from two points C and D, on a circular course 960 rods in circumference, and they pass each other when A has gone 400 yards farther than B. How many yards will B be from C (A's starting point) when A has reached D (B's starting point), the shorter distance between these points being 160 rods ?

6. A can dig a trench in 8 hours, B in 12 hours, and C in 20 hours. How long will it take A and B to finish the trench after C has worked in it for 2½ hours ?

7. A dairyman buys milk at 5 cents a quart and dilutes it with water, so that, by selling it at 6 cents a quart, he makes a profit of 80 per cent. on his outlay. How much water does he mix with each quart of milk ?

8. A and B start at opposite corners of a rectangle, whose perimeter is 2600 yards, and sides are to each other as 8 : 5, and walk round it in the same direction. A walks 20 yards, while B walks 15 yards. At what point will they be together, and how many times will each have passed his corner ?

9. A man bought a horse and carriage for $640 ; the horse cost $\frac{2}{3}$ as much as the carriage ; what was the cost of each ?

10. A man, after spending $20 less than $\frac{2}{3}$ of his money, had $60 more than $\frac{5}{14}$ of it left. How much money had he at first ?

11. One-fifth of the difference between two numbers is equal to the thirtieth part of the larger number. The smaller number is 525 ; find the larger.

12. By selling wine at $3 a gallon, I gain 6 per cent. What should I gain, per cent., if I sell at 3.39\frac{3}{5}$ a gallon ?

13. A block of stone, $11'' \times 7'' \times 5''$ is placed in a cylindrical tub, 14 inches in diameter, and 12 inches deep. The tub is then filled with water, and the block is removed. How deep will the water then be in the tub ?

Exercise LXVIII.

1. (a) Distinguish between *multiple* and *factor*; find the L.C.M. of 156, 170, 272, 273, 378, and 455. (b) Of what number are 111, 148, 185, 222, 259, 296 and 333 *multiples*? Which *multiples* are they ?

2. (a) Define : *policy, insurance, premium,* and *rate per cent*. (b) A's barn is insured for $2300 at $\frac{5}{8}$ per cent. Find the premium. (c) If a merchant gain $1.44 on an article sold for $7.20, what is his gain per cent. ?

3. (a) Define : *barter, ratio, proportion, complex fraction, principal* and *interest*. .(b) A barters flour at $5.50 a barrel with B for 36 cwt. 30 lbs. of dried apples at $5 a bushel. How many barrels of flour should B get ?

4. A grocer mixes tea at 45 cents a lb. with tea at 50 cents a lb. in the ratio of 5 lbs. of the former to 3 lbs. of the latter. At what price per lb. must he sell the mixture to gain 60 per cent. ?

5. On May 1st, 1890, I lent $1460 at 5 per cent. per annum. On what date will the amount due me be $1474.60 ? (365 days — a year).

6. A and B can do a certain work in half a day, B and C in one-fourth of a day, and A and C in one-fifth of a day. In what time could B do the whole work alone ?

7. Divide the *sum* of $\dfrac{\frac{1}{2}-\frac{1}{3}}{\frac{1}{3}-\frac{1}{4}}$ and $\dfrac{\cdot25-\cdot2}{\cdot2-\cdot1\dot{6}}$ by their *difference*.

8. State the rule for adding repetends. Add $1\cdot7\dot{8}+340+16\cdot46\dot{2}\dot{1}+17\cdot\dot{4}5\dot{3}$, so as to *exhibit* the whole work.

9. A can do as much work in 5 days as B can do in eight days, and together they are occupied 40 days in digging a ditch for which $52 is paid. (*a*) What share of the money should A receive? (*b*) How long would the work have occupied B alone?

10. If my railway fare from Toronto to Port Arthur be $25.95 at the rate of 3 cents a mile, and my steamboat fare, returning to Toronto by water, be $33\frac{1}{3}$ per cent. per mile cheaper, find my ticket for the round trip, the distance by boat being 20 per cent. farther than the distance by rail.

11. In a basket of oranges and lemons, the oranges numbered $\frac{3}{8}$ of the lemons; but when another dozen of lemons were put into the basket, the oranges numbered $\frac{1}{4}$ of the whole basket; how many dozen, in all, were there in the basket at first?

12. How many miles will a man, who drives 11 chains 11 feet in a minute, drive in 8 hours?

13. Divide $146 among A, B and C, so that $\frac{1}{2}$ A's = $\frac{2}{3}$ B's = $\frac{5}{8}$ C's.

Exercise LXIX.

1. Twelve men can do a certain work in 15 days; but owing to 3 of the men leaving a certain number of days after the work was begun, it was prolonged $3\frac{1}{3}$ days. How many days did the three men work?

2. A train from Winnipeg to Moosejaw, 399 miles, is due in 21 hours; for one-third of the distance it makes 40 miles an hour, and for the remainder of the way 20 miles an hour; how many hours, minutes and seconds is it *ahead of time* at Moosejaw?

3. A, B and C together have $7.50. A has $\$\frac{3}{4}$; B has as much money as A and $\frac{1}{3}$ as much as C, and C has $1\frac{1}{2}$ times as much as A and B together. How much money has C?

4. The hind wheel of a carriage is 13 feet, and the fore wheel 10 feet in circumference. How far has the carriage gone, in miles, when the fore wheel has made 1584 revolutions more than the hind wheel?

78   EXERCISES IN ARITHMETIC.

5. How much tea at 45 cents a lb. must be mixed with 10 lbs. at 52 cents a lb., in order to make a mixture which, sold at 60 cents a lb., gives a profit of 20 per cent. ?

6. A fruiter bought oranges at the rate of $5 per hundred, but found that by mistake he had got 110 oranges instead of one hundred for the $5. He now raised the cost price of oranges 15 per cent. and sold out the whole lot ; find his gain per cent.

7. Bought a portion of land, in the form of a rectangle, 90 by 80 rods. at $75 an acre. I gained $1305 by selling it off in lots at $13 each. What fractional part of an acre did each lot contain ?

8. Reduce 16 lbs., 4 ozs., 17 dwt., 12 grs., *troy*, to lbs. and ozs., *avoirdupois*.

9. A rectangular farm is 360 rods long, and its perimeter is 4 miles, 80 rods. Find its value at $60 an acre.

10. (*a*) How many seconds were there in February, 1860 ? (*b*) One bell tolls 6 times in 8 minutes, and another bell tolls 5 times in 7 minutes ; how often will they toll *together* in 3 hours, 16 minutes ?

11. A's money is $\frac{7}{8}$ of B's ; but B gives A $35, after which A has $1\frac{1}{2}$ times as much as he had at first ; how much money had each at first ?

12. How much heavier will 9 bbls. of flour and 12 bbls. of pork weigh than 2 cubic yds., 2 cubic ft. of water ?

13. A owns *four* rectangular plots of land ; the *first* 161 by 80 rods, the *second* 14 by 5 chains, the *third* 56 by 14 chains, and the *fourth* 90 chains by 13 chains, 40 links. What is the value of A's *four* plots of land at $56 an acre ?

Exercise LXX.

1. At 13 cents a square yard, it cost $20.80 to pave the surface of a rectangular court, whose width was 6 feet ; find its length.

2. The dimensions of a rectangular farm are as 9 : 8, and it costs $74.80 to fence it at 4 cents a yard. Find its size in acres.

3. Equal weights of rye at 70 cents, peas at 75 cents, and millet at 60 cents, are chopped together ; what is the value of the mixture per bushel, given that the mixture increases $7\frac{18}{25}$ per cent., in bulk, in the grinding process ?

4. A man spent $\frac{1}{3}$ of his money, after which he gained 5 times what he spent ; he then had $5600 ; what was his money at first ?

5. A has $657, and B, his brother in Melbourne, has £1755 Sterling. How many dollars should A receive from B that their sums may be equal?

6. Three lbs. tea and 4 lbs. coffee, cost together $3.60, and 10 lbs. tea and 3 lbs. coffee, cost together $7.35; find the value of 1 cwt. of tea.

7. Divide $500 among A, B and C, so that B shall receive $50 more than A, and that C shall receive as much as A and B together.

8. A man earns $525 every $3\frac{1}{2}$ months, and spends in 9 months what he earns in 4 months. What will he save in 13 years and six months?

9. Four persons form a partnership; the second puts in twice as much as the first, the third half as much as the first and second together, and the fourth as much as the other three. They gain in business $5400. How should this be divided?

10. Simplify: $\dfrac{3\frac{1}{2}}{7}$ of $\frac{1}{8}$ of $\frac{5}{8}$ of $\frac{3}{4} \div \frac{7}{8} \times \frac{5}{8}$ of 720 dollars.

11. A has 16 ac., 18 sq. in. of land; B has 117 sq. rods, 2 sq. ft., 18 sq. in.; C has 17 ac., 15 sq. rods, $3\frac{1}{2}$ sq. feet; D has 175 sq. rods, 2 sq. feet, 108 sq. in., and E has enough to finish out a fifty-acre lot. How much land has E less than A?

12. How often does the L. C. M. of $\dfrac{9\frac{1}{8} \times 4\frac{1}{8}}{7\frac{3}{10}}$ and $\frac{1}{4} \div \frac{5}{8}$ of $\frac{7}{12} \times \frac{7}{12}$ contain their H. C. F.?

13. Find the total cost of 2 cwt., 13 lbs., 12 ozs. butter at 18 cents a lb., 16 gals. 2 qts. syrup at 40 cents a gallon, 183 eggs at 16 cents a dozen, 15 bushels, 1 peck of apples at 60 cents a bushel, 45 lbs., 4 ozs. tea at 40 cents a lb., 70 bunches braid at $12.96 a gross, and 45 yds. cotton at $12\frac{1}{2}$ cents a yard.

Exercise LXXI.

1. A wholesale dealer sells goods to a retail dealer at 60 per cent. profit; but the retail dealer fails, paying his creditors with 80 cents on the dollar. What per cent. does the wholesale dealer gain or lose?

2. The difference in weight of two chests of tea is $12\frac{1}{2}$ lbs.; the value of both, at 54 cents a lb., is $47.25. How many lbs. are there in each chest?

EXERCISES IN ARITHMETIC.

3. Find the interest on $650 for 4 years, 3 months, at 8 per cent. per annum. *$221*

4. Find the amount of $720 for 3 years, 2 months, at 8 per cent. per annum. *$902.40*

5. A farmer lost ·02 of his sheep by disease; ·68 by theft, and sold $\frac{2}{3}$ of the remainder, after which he had 30 sheep left. What was the number of his flock of sheep? *300*

6. Bought pencils at 80 cents a gross, and sold them at a cent each; find my gain per cent. *80%*

7. Bought 16 crates of eggs of 40 dozen each, at 15 cents a dozen; lost two out of every score, and sold the remainder at 25 cents a dozen, paying a commission agent $7.70 for selling them; find my gain on eggs. *$40.30*

8. A man owned $\frac{1}{2}$ of $\frac{3}{4}$ of a square mile of land in Shoal Lake County; $\frac{2}{3}$ of $\frac{7}{8}$ of $\frac{3}{4}$ of 1210 square rods in Marquette County, and $\frac{2}{3}$ of $\frac{5}{6}$ of $\frac{7}{10}$ of a thousand square yards in Winnipeg. How many acres, square rods, square yards, etc., of land did he own altogether?

9. Divide $840 among A, B and C, so that A shall receive $\frac{7}{12}$ of the whole sum, and that B shall receive $\frac{1}{3}$ as much as C. *$490, 87.50*

10. Simplify (a) $\left[\left\{\dfrac{3\frac{1}{2} \text{ of } 3\frac{2}{3} \div \frac{1}{4}}{\frac{1}{4} \div \frac{4}{5} \text{ of } \frac{5}{17}} \div \dfrac{1\frac{1}{2}}{4\frac{1}{3}} \text{ of } 8\frac{2}{3}\right\} \times \dfrac{72}{175}\right]$ of $12; (b) Add £2$\frac{2}{3}$, 6$\frac{1}{8}$s., 5$\frac{2}{3}$d. *$10*

11. Joseph lost $\frac{4}{5}$ of $\frac{1}{5}$ of his money and had $15 more than $\frac{1}{4}$ of it left. How much money had he at first? *$18.90*

12. Find the difference between $\left\{3\frac{1}{4} \times \frac{2}{13} + 1\frac{1}{13} \div 5\frac{1}{2} - \frac{7}{20}\right\} \times 52$ and $\left\{3\frac{1}{4} \times (\frac{2}{13} + 1\frac{1}{13} \div 5\frac{1}{2}) - \frac{7}{20}\right\} \times 78.$ *37*

13. (a) Divide the L.C.M. of 4, 6, 18, 27, 54, 72 and 99 by the H.C.F. of $\left\{\dfrac{\frac{5}{6} \text{ of } \frac{1}{9}}{27} \div \dfrac{25}{486}\right\}$ of $\dfrac{75}{12}$ and $\frac{7}{8}$ of 1$\frac{1}{3}$. *2851*

(b) (I) In the Arabic system of Notation, what is meant by the '*local value*' of a digit? (II) In the number 5760, what two values has the figure 7? (III) To the sum of all the *even* numbers between 915 and 925, add 7282; square the sum; and write the product in Roman numerals.

Exercise LXXII.

1. (*a*) Name and define the two kinds of fractions, giving an example of each ; (*b*) simplify $\left\{ \dfrac{\frac{4}{5}}{\frac{5}{6}} \div \dfrac{\dot{5}}{18} \text{ of } 1\frac{1}{4} \div \dfrac{1}{89\frac{2}{7}} + \frac{1}{7} \right\}$;

(*c*) $\dfrac{\cdot 6 \text{ of } \cdot 8\dot{3}}{3 \cdot 5}$.

2. (*a*) Name the different kinds of decimals ; and, without using the denominators of the following fractions as divisors, state which kind of decimal each will produce : $\frac{77}{100}$, $\frac{5}{81}$ and $\frac{227\frac{1}{3}}{355\frac{2}{3}}$; (*b*) Simplify each of the following by changing it to a vulgar fraction : (i) ·48125; (ii) ·054945 ; (iii) ·456056.

3. Sold a pair of fur mitts for $3.50, gaining thereby 14⅔ per cent. of my selling price ; what fractional part of the cost would I have lost, had I sold the mitts for $2.40 ?

4. A fuel-dealer's sales, for the year 1890, amounted to $3500 ; on coal, which formed ⅔ of his sales, he realized 16⅔ per cent. profit; on wood, which formed ¼ of his sales, he realized 25 per cent. profit, and on coke, which formed the balance of his sales, he realized 11¼ per cent. profit. Find his total yearly profit.

5. A merchant's cash price, which is 20 per cent. in advance of his cost price, is 20 per cent. below his marked price. Find his cost price for an article marked $15.

6. A man's farm is 160 rods long and 12 chains 50 links wide ; what decimal part of a square mile of land does he own ?

7. One-fifteenth of a man's money is in the Bank of Commerce at 5 per cent. per annum ; ⅗ in Canada Pacific Railway debentures at 10 per cent. per annum ; the rest in farm property, paying 8 per cent. per annum. Find his total yearly income, if farm property, alone, yields him $100 half-yearly income.

8. Find the H.C.F. and the L.C.M. of 4305, 1722, and 1640.

9. Express, in Roman numerals, four times the difference between the sum and difference of $\overline{\text{XIII}}\text{XIII}$ and $\overline{\text{VII}}\text{CDIII}$.

10. If eight bushels of wheat will sow 4 acres, 80 sq. rods of land, what will the wheat, necessary for sowing a "quarter-section" of land, cost at $1.35 a bushel ?

11. B lost ⅔ of ⅜ of 1¼ of his money on Monday, and 75 cents more than ½ of the remainder on Tuesday, after which he had $13 left ; how much money had he it first ?

82   EXERCISES IN ARITHMETIC.

12. If 4 lbs. of wheat make 3 lbs. of flour, how many bbls. of flour can be made from 439 bushels, 54 lbs., 10¾ ozs. of wheat?

13. A gentleman's estate consists of 50 square fields, each 14 chains, 40 links to a side; how many acres, rods, etc., of land does he own?

Exercise LXXIII.

1. At 20 per cent. a merchant pays $1512 duty on 700 puncheons of molasses. If the cost price per gallon of molasses is 15 cents, what is the size of a puncheon in gallons?

2. A grocer, by selling 15 lbs. of sugar for a dollar, gains 10 per cent.; what per cent. does he gain by selling 12 lbs. for a dollar?

3. Which is the greater rate of interest, and by how much per $100—$14.40 on $60 for 3 years, or $18 on $40 for 5 years?

4. Sold two tubs of butter weighing together 80 lbs., 2 ozs.; the larger tub brought 24 cents, and the smaller one 20 cents a lb. If the larger tub weighed 9 lbs. 2 ozs. more than the smaller, find the total receipts for both tubs of butter.

5. The hands of a clock indicate 10 a.m. What o'clock is it when the hands are 36 degrees apart?

6. At 13 cents a square yard, it costs $7.02 to paint the floor of a room; and it costs $19.50, at 15 cents a square yard, to paint its four walls. Find the dimensions of the room, if its breadth is ⅔ of its length.

7. When wheat is $1.60 a bushel, a barrel of flour costs $5; what should be the cost of a barrel of flour when wheat is $1.28 a bushel, the cost of making a barrel of flour being 35 cents?

8. Find the value of a pile of wood, 6 rods long, 9 ft. wide and 12 ft. high, at $2.88 a cord.

9. An elevator's capacity is 18000 bushels, and three elevating spouts, A, B and C, fill it in 6 hours, when working together. If A fills 500 bushels per hour more than B, and C fills 100 bushels per hour less than A, what fractional part of the elevator does A fill in the *given time?*

10. When 36 eggs are worth $2.19, what is the price of eggs per dozen in shillings Sterling?

11. Two boys together walk 7 miles, 160 rods, in 1 hour, 30 min., one walks 120 chains in 30 min.; how many miles per hour does the other walk?

FOURTH CLASS. 83

12. A cistern holds 33 bbls. 10½ gals. of water; its upper surface measures 6 ft. by 4 ft.; how deep is it?

13. At 5 cents each board, it costs $72 to build a board-fence, four boards high, around a rectangular field 40 rods wide, the boards being 11 ft. long; what will it cost to plough and sow the field at $5 an acre?

Exercise LXXIV.

1. The selling price of a horse was $81, and the gain at which it was sold was 12½ per cent. of the cost. Find the cost price of the horse.

2. Find the total of the following by adding, *horizontally* and *vertically*:

706	30	44	864	9	16	341	
41	641	2	71	14	41	146	
3	142	19	1	216	244	684	
28	673	416	13	31	687	127	
604	457	614	41	4	709	741	
71	681	582	264	72	907	382	
200	168	281	7	28	871	281	
							Total.

3. Reduce $\tfrac{1}{10}$ lb. troy + $\tfrac{1}{10}$ lb. avoirdupois to ozs., dwt., grs., troy.

4. The interest on a certain sum for 6 years at 7 per cent. is greater than the interest on the same sum for 8 years at 5 per cent. by $26.26; find the sum.

5. Bought 50 tons of coal at $4.50 per *long ton*, and sold it at $45 for every seven *short tons*; find my gain per cent.

6. Simplify: (a) $1694 \times 5 + 38691 \div 9 \times 3 - 5342 \times 4 + 1 + 606 \times 6$.
(b) $\{ 2\tfrac{1}{2} \times \tfrac{3}{4} \div \tfrac{9}{10}$ of $\tfrac{19}{27} - \tfrac{3}{4} \times \tfrac{5}{8}$ of $\tfrac{3}{10} \div \tfrac{1}{4} + 6\tfrac{1}{2} \div \tfrac{1}{8}$ of $16\tfrac{1}{2} \times 1\tfrac{2}{13} \} + 78\tfrac{373}{764}$.

7. A, B and C, together, bought 150 sheep. A invested $270, B, $180, and C, $300. How should the sheep be divided, and what is the *average* cost price per head?

84 EXERCISES IN ARITHMETIC.

8. A did ¼ of a certain piece of work, B ⅙ of it, and C finished it in 11 days. Of $40, paid for the work, how much should each one get? What were C's *daily* wages? (10, 8, 22,) C $2 a d

9. Divide sixty-six and two tenths by four and four tenths, and reduce the quotient to a decimal. 15·045

10. A has 16 acres, 150 sq. rods, 3½ sq. yds. of land; B has 70 sq. rods, 3 sq. ft., 18 sq. in., and C has 11 acres, 27·5 sq. yds. How much less than ·15625 of a square mile of land have they together?

11. What fraction of a mile and a half is four-elevenths of ninety-nine rods?   3/40

12. Sold 62 cwt., 40 lbs. wheat at 87 cents a bushel; 28 tons 720 lbs. hay, at $15 a ton; 120 lbs. butter, at 37½ cents a lb., to pay a note of $520 which had run from May 31st, 1889, until Jan. 5th, 1890, at 6 per cent. per annum; what had I left after paying the note? $22.16

13. A boy gave away 40 cents more than ⅓ of his money to his sister, who then had ¼ more money than she had at first. If, after the donation, the boy had still 60 cents, how much had both together at first?

Exercise LXXV.   8 cord ft = 1 cor

1. Find the value of a pile of cordwood, measuring 864 cord-feet, at $5.60 a cord. $604.80   cord ft = 16 cu ft

2. A and B together weigh 287 lbs., 14 ozs, and A's weight is ¾ of B's; find the weight of each. 123 - 6 - 164 - 8

3. A farmer sold 15 bushels, 15 lbs. of wheat at $1.25 per cental, 41·493 lbs. fine wool at 37·5 cents a lb., and 129 lbs., 3 ozs. coarse wool at $·0075 an ounce. With the proceeds of his sales he bought carpeting, 21 inches wide, at 75 cents a yard, to cover the floor of a room 18 feet long, 15 feet, 9 inches wide. If the strips ran lengthwise of the room, how many yards did it take, and how much money had he left out of his sales?

4. Bought a puncheon of beer at 8 cents a gallon, and sold it off in half-pint bottles at 30 cents a dozen; find my gain on the puncheon.

5. A has 40 acres, 40 sq. rods of land, and B has a rectangular field 14 chains long by 5 chains wide. What is the value of both pieces of ground at $56 an acre?

6. Bought 15 barrels flour at $5 a barrel, and put it up in bags, holding 25 lbs. each, which I sold at 80 cents each. Find my gain or loss on the whole quantity? $19.08 gain

FOURTH CLASS. 85

7. A and B working together can dig a drain in 56 hours, B and C in 35 hours, and A and C in 40 hours. In what time would they all working together dig the drain? *28 hrs.*

8. Find the value, in acres, sq. rods and sq. yards, of 34·5 acres + 475·4 sq. rods − 50060·85 sq yards. *27 - 20 - 15*

9. A can walk 4 and B 5 miles an hour; how many minutes' start must B give A in an eighteen-mile race, so that they may come out evenly? *54 min.*

10. James walks 120 chains in 30 minutes, and George walks 160 rods in 15 minutes. How many miles apart will they be, in 3 hours, walking from the same point, and in *opposite* directions? *15 mls.*

11. A farm of 105 acres, 125 sq. rods, 15 sq. yards, is divided into 5 fields; the first contains 10 acres, 15 sq. rods, 17 sq. yards, the second 3 times as much as the first, the third half as much as the second, and the fourth half as much as the third; what does the fifth contain?

12. To 41 add $\frac{1}{2}$ and $\frac{1}{8}$ of $\frac{9}{10}$, and divide the result by $83\frac{1}{8}$. (N.B.—Write out the question in *fraction form*, so as to show that you understand it; then solve it). *1/2*

13. Find the *product* of the L.C.M and H.C.F. of 450 and 525. *2j*

Exercise LXXVI.

1. A farmer sold 1248 lbs. of Hungarian seed at 3.12\frac{1}{2}$ a bushel, and with the money bought carpeting at $37\frac{1}{2}$ cents a yard. How many yards and feet did he receive?

2. A and B can do a work in 4 days, A and C in 3 days, and B and C in 5 days. In what time can B finish the work alone, after he works at it with A for half a day? *15 dys.*

3. A merchant throws off 20 per cent. of the cost price of an article, and then is paid with 50 per cent. of the remainder; what per cent. of the cost has he *actually* lost? *60 %*

4. When apples are selling at $\frac{2}{3}$ a peck, how many lbs. can I buy with $\left\{ \frac{5}{8} \div \frac{4}{5} \text{ of } \frac{3\frac{1}{2}}{12} \times \frac{5}{8} \right\}$ times $2.88?

5. I ordered 5 lbs. of cheese, but the grocer weighed out 4 lbs., 12 ozs., to fill the order. What *per cent.* was I cheated? *5 %*

6. In question 5, what would the grocer gain on the sale of 19 lbs. cheese (by "*filling orders*" as stated therein) at 13 cents a lb?

7. The area of a vineyard is 4860 square rods, and its length is to its breadth as 5 : 3 ; find the cost of enclosing it with a fence at 15 cents a rod. *$432.0*

8. If 4 men *or* 6 boys can do a work in 12 days, how long will 4 times the work occupy 4 men *and* 6 boys? *24*

9. Bought a quantity of coal oil at 20 cents a gallon ; one-third of it was lost by leakage ; at what price per quart must I now sell the remainder to gain 20 per cent. on the whole quantity? *9*

10. Bought 15876 pounds of flour at $4.20 a barrel, and gained $136.08 on the whole quantity, by selling it off in paper bags at 90 cents each. How many pounds did each bag contain? *30*

11. A has as many sheep as B ; but B steals 10 per cent. of A's, and finds that he has then 99 sheep. What is the value of both flocks at $5.37½ per head? *$967.50*

12. A has $120, and B has $105 ; what per cent. is B's money of the whole? *46⅔*

13. Bought pencils at 80 cents a gross, and *cleared* 440 per cent. on selling them ; what was my selling price per pencil?

Exercise LXXVII.

1. I sell 45 tons of coal for $281.25, thereby gaining 25 per cent.; find the cost price of coal per cwt. *25 cts.*

2. A miller sold $\frac{7}{8}$ of his stock of flour at $5.50 a barrel, realizing thereby $3080 ; what would he have realized on the sale of his entire stock, had he sold it a week sooner, when flour was 10 per cent. dearer? *$3872*

3. A merchant sold 145 barrels of apples, part at $4.50, and the remainder at $5.00 a barrel, realizing altogether $709. How many barrels did he sell at each rate? *32 and 113*

4. A, B and C have together $800. If A gives his money to B, B will have ¼ as much as C, but if A gives his money to C, C will have 10⅔ times as much money as B. How much money has each?

5. Simplify $37 \left\{ \left(6 + \dfrac{1}{6 + \frac{1}{6}} \right) \text{ of } \frac{1}{8} \right\} + 61.$ *99*

6. A and B throw dirks at marks, both beginning at the same time, and each throwing 21 dirks. A can throw 4 dirks in 5 minutes and B can throw 14 dirks in 15 minutes. How many dirks will A have to throw after B has thrown his last one? *3*

FOURTH CLASS. 87

7. A cistern has three pipes, A, B and C. It can be filled by A in 10 hours, and it can be emptied by B and C in 20 and 30 hours respectively. If the cistern is $\frac{2}{3}$ full and all the pipes are opened, in what time will it be $\frac{1}{4}$ full, it being found that the cistern has sprung a leak $\frac{1}{5}$ the size of pipe A ?   *175 hrs*

8. A man, who can row 6 miles an hour in still water, is occupied 1 hour, 30 minutes in rowing that distance up a stream; how long will he be occupied in rowing down again ?

9. Divide $560 among A, B and C, giving B $10 more than half as much as A, and C as much as A and B together.   *$180, 100, 2*

10. A grocer buys a barrel of sugar weighing 315 lbs. for $18. What per cent. does he gain or lose by selling $\frac{3}{5}$ of it at the rate of 18 lbs. for a dollar, and the remainder at 12 lbs. for a dollar ?   *16⅔ %*

11. Tom has $\left\{ \dfrac{\frac{4}{5}}{\frac{4}{5}} \div \dfrac{5}{18} \text{ of } 1\frac{1}{4} \div \dfrac{1}{89\frac{3}{4}} + \frac{1}{7} \right\}$ cents more than Bob in a purse of $9.35 ; find the share of each.   *5.91   3.44*

12. A miller bought 156 cwt. of wheat at 87 cents a bushel; he ground it into flour, getting 38 lbs. of flour and 22 lbs. of bran and shorts from a bushel of wheat; he sold the flour at $4.90 a barrel, and the bran and shorts at 60 cents a cwt.; find his gain.   *55.12*

13. Divide 250 acres, 83 rods, 23 yds., 2 ft., 36 in. by 6.

Exercise LXXVIII.

1. What will it cost to carpet a floor 24 feet long, by 18 feet wide, with carpeting 30 inches wide at 75 cents a yard ?   *$43.20*

2. At what time after 9 o'clock p.m. are the hands of a watch equidistant from the figure IX ?

3. Divide the sum of $305 among 12 men, 16 women and 45 children, so that each man shall receive as much as 3 women, and each woman as much as 5 children.   *each $15, $5, $1*

4. Find the simple interest on $3285 for 150 days at 6 per cent. per annum.   *$81*

5. A boy spent $1 more than $\frac{1}{2}$ of his money on Monday; $5 more than $\frac{1}{3}$ of the remainder on Tuesday; then $15 more than $\frac{1}{4}$ of the remainder on Wednesday; after which he had $30 left. How much money had he at first ?

6. Bought 4 boxes of biscuits at 15 cents a lb., paying therefor $13.80; how many lbs. were there in a box ?   *23 lbs*

7. Simplify : $\left\{ 3\frac{1}{2} + 2\frac{1}{4} \times 3\frac{1}{3} - 1\frac{1}{2} - 1\frac{1}{4} \right\} \times 4$.   *33*

88   EXERCISES IN ARITHMETIC.

8. Find the total cost of :
   6834 lbs. of oats at 32 cents a bushel.
   8 tons, 116 lbs. hay at $16 a ton.
   582 lbs. cheese at $0.01 an ounce.
   480 ounces tea at 62½ cents a lb.
   1097 yards. 23$\frac{7}{25}$ inches cotton at 5 cents a yard.

9. A speculator bought a certain number of mules for $3300; he sold ⅓ of them for $1386, gaining thereby $13 per head on his sales. What did he pay per head for his mules?

10. A and B agreed to divide their travelling expenses in the ratio of 3 : 2 ; but A paid $4 and B paid $3.50 ; how much must one pay and the other receive to settle accounts?

11. Find the value, in lbs. and ozs., of ·243 of a ton.

12. Simplify: $\left\{\dfrac{3\frac{1}{2}}{7}+\dfrac{2}{10\frac{1}{2}}-\tfrac{5}{18}\text{ of }\tfrac{4}{5}\right\}\times 1\tfrac{2}{3}\times 72.$

13. John can dig 14 bushels of potatoes in 3 hours, and Tom can dig 3 pecks in 5 minutes. How many bushels would they both together dig in a week, working 6 hours a day? What fractional part of the whole does John dig in a week?

Exercise LXXIX.

1. What sum will amount to $38.78 in 3 years, 2 months, 15 days at 12 per cent. per annum?

2. The cloth from a certain loom is 20 per cent. cotton, 80 per cent. of the remainder is worsted, and the rest silk ; what is the silk, in a web of 80 yards, worth at $3.80 per yard?

3. In a certain school the boys were to the girls as 3 : 2; but when 5 more girls were admitted, the girls numbered $\tfrac{5}{11}$ of the whole school ; find the number of girls in the school at first.

4. How many yards of carpet, worth 87½ cents a yard, must be given in exchange for 253 yards, 2 ft. of carpet worth $5.25 a yard?

5. A man lost ⅔ of his money in an adventure. He then gained $800 ; after which he had $9800 ; how much money did he lose?

6. The fore and hind wheels of a carriage are 12 and 15 feet, respectively, in circumference ; how far must the carriage travel in order that the fore wheels may *each* **make 572 revolutions** more than the hind wheels *together?*

7. If 40 oranges sold for $1.20, and the gain thereby be 20 per cent., find the cost price of oranges per dozen.

8. A merchant sells 20 yards of cloth at 28 cents a yard, gaining thereby 40 per cent., and takes eggs, at 14 cents a dozen, in payment. What per cent. profit does he make if 3 eggs in a dozen are bad?

9. Find the cost of papering a room 30 ft., 4 in. long, by 20 ft., 8 in. wide, with paper 21 inches wide, worth 40 cents a single roll, allowance being made for 3 doors, each 3 ft. wide, and 5 windows, each 2 ft., 10 in. wide.

10. A man borrows $480 for 2 years, 8 months and 15 days at 8 per cent. per annum, simple interest. Draw a note to secure the payment of *principal* and *interest* at the time the note is due.

11. A floor is 36 × 24 feet; what sum of money will carpet it with 27-inch carpeting worth 87½ cents a yard?

12. Bought 16 sheep at $5.37½ each; sold ¼ of them at $3.75 each, and the rest at $12 each; what did I gain?

13. (a) Find the value, at $38.37½ an acre, of a piece of land of rectangular shape, 160 chains long by 60 rods wide. (b) Simplify, $\frac{7}{10} \times \frac{7\frac{2}{3}}{5\frac{1}{4}} \times \frac{3\frac{2}{5}}{5\frac{3}{4}}$, (1) without cancellation, by multiplying the numerators together for a new numerator, and the denominators together for a new denominator, and then dividing the *terms* by their H.C.F. (2) By dividing the terms of the new fraction by 7, then by 8, then by 16. (3) By cancellation; and so that your cancellation shall correspond *with* the *second method*.

Exercise LXXX.

1. A cistern loses, by leakage, 4 gallons, 3 quarts, 1 pint in 7 hours 48 minutes; what is its hourly loss?

2. Find *a multiplier* which will give *the amount of any sum* at simple interest for 5 years at 4 per cent., and use it to find the *amount* of $500 for the said time and rate.

3. Express as the fraction of a pound troy, $\frac{1}{53}$ of a pound troy + $\frac{1}{57}$ of a pound avoirdupois.

4. An agent charged $15 for selling a sewing machine for $75; what per cent. commission did he collect?

5. Simplify :— $\left[\left\{ \frac{\frac{9}{10}}{3\frac{1}{4}} \text{ of } \frac{5\frac{1}{6}}{7\frac{1}{7}} \times \frac{1}{4} \div \frac{4\frac{1}{3}}{3\frac{2}{7}} \right\} \text{ of } \frac{91 \times 49}{11 \times 31} \right]$ × $\left[\left\{ \frac{7\frac{1}{2}}{15} \text{ of } \frac{2}{3} \div \frac{1}{4} \times \frac{4}{5} \right\} \div \frac{1}{12\frac{1}{4}} \right]$.

90   EXERCISES IN ARITHMETIC.

6. If $\frac{1}{4}$ of $\frac{2}{3}$ of $\frac{19}{20}$ of 4 stacks of hay is worth $12, when hay is selling at $7 a ton, how many tons does the stack contain?

7. A man has a certain sum of money in the Savings' Bank, drawing 5 per cent. per annum, simple interest. He withdraws $1155 at the end of 13 years; find the original sum deposited in the Bank.

8. Lemons bought at $1.20 per 2½ dozen, are sold so as to give a profit of 16⅔ per cent. How many lemons are sold for $5.60?

9. (a) Of what does the L. C. M. and H. C. F. of *any two* numbers consist? (b) Find the H. C. F. and L. C. M. of 2340 and 2520, by resolving each into its *prime* factors, and *selecting from these factors* the H. C. F. and L. C. M. (c) The H. C. F. of *two* numbers is 31; their L. C. M. is 28520; one of the numbers is 713; find the other. (d) Divide the L. C. M. of 760, 204, 190, and 510, by the H. C. F. of 1938 and 2261.

10. Find the *product* of the L. C. M. of 5980, 2730, 2484, 3105, 1680, 1960, 2800 and the H. C. F. of $7\left(\dfrac{\frac{1}{6}-\frac{1}{7}}{\frac{2}{84}}\right)$ of $1\frac{3}{5} \div \frac{7}{10}$ and $9\,\dfrac{\frac{1}{4}-\frac{1}{8}}{\frac{1}{4}+\frac{1}{8}} \div 13\frac{2}{3}$ of $\frac{3}{7}$.

11. A laborer agreed to dig a certain ditch at 12 cents a rod. The first week he dug 25 rods more than the half of it, and the following week he finished the remaining 215 rods of the ditch. (I) What were his *daily* wages the *first* week? (II) What were his *daily* wages *throughout* the work?

12. Divide $200 among A, B and C, so that $\frac{1}{3}$ A's = $\frac{1}{2}$ of B's = $\frac{2}{5}$ of C's.

13. (a) Divide $490 among A, B and C, so that B shall receive $\frac{4}{5}$ of A's share + $22, and that C shall receive $25 more than half as much as A and B together. (b) Divide $66 among A, B and C, so that A shall receive 1½ times as much as B, and that C shall receive $13 more than $\frac{8}{15}$ of the remainder.

Exercise LXXXI.

1. A man leaves $\frac{1}{3}$ of his property to his wife, and $\frac{1}{4}$ of it to his son, who gets $800 more than each of his three sisters, among whom the rest is equally divided. Find the value of the property.

2. A certain contract is to be completed by 16 men in 12 days, but every 4 days 4 of the men leave and the remainder work on; this is continued until the work is abandoned; how many days is the contract under way, and how much work remains unfinished at the end of that time?

FOURTH CLASS.

3. A merchant sells, to a pedlar, goods at 80 per cent. advance on cost; the pedlar becomes bankrupt, and pays 50 cents on the dollar. What per cent. does the merchant really lose?

4. A man mixes 45 gallons of ale at 25 cents a gallon, with 55 gallons of beer at 18 cents a gallon; at what price per pint must he now sell the mixture to gain $13\frac{87}{141}$ per cent. on the whole?

5. The price of coal rises $11\frac{1}{9}$ per cent.; by how much per cent. must the consumer reduce his consumption of coal, so as not to increase his expenditure?

6. A rectangular plot of ground contains 153679680 square inches; its length is to its breadth as 5 : 4. Find its length and breadth in rods.

7. *Bracket* the following; then re-write in a more *concise form* and simplify: $4\frac{1}{8} \div \frac{3}{4}$ of $\frac{13}{42} + \frac{5}{8}$ of $\frac{3}{4} \div 2\frac{8}{16} - \frac{1}{8} \times \frac{9}{10} \div 1\frac{7}{10} - \dfrac{5\frac{1}{4}}{7}$.

8. The sum of $66.50 was divided among 33 persons; a certain number of them received $3 each, and the rest 50 cents each; how many were there at each rate?

9. If sea-water contains $2\frac{3}{4}$ per cent. of salt, how many tons of sea-water must be evaporated in order to obtain 1 ton, 1300 lbs. salt?

10. A pile of cordwood contains 128 cords; it is $1\frac{1}{2}$ times as long, and $\frac{1}{3}$ times as high as it is wide; find its dimensions in feet.

11. Eight men contracted to do a piece of work in 20 days; but, owing to three of the men leaving a certain number of days after the work was begun, it was under contract $24\frac{1}{4}$ days. How long did the three men work?

12. A tank contains 300 gallons of water after a certain quantity of water has been added which increased its volume 25 per cent.; how many gallons must now be withdrawn, so that the water may find its former level?

13. Find the value of 728 lbs. of rye and barley mixed equally by measure, when rye is 70 cents, and barley is 80 cents, per bushel.

Exercise LXXXII.

1. The sum of $118.75 was paid for a certain piece of work. A and B worked together at it for a certain time; after which B finished it alone in $7\frac{1}{2}$ days. If A and B, when working together, received $5 a day, how many days did each work? (*Note.*—A = B in work, throughout.)

92   EXERCISES IN ARITHMETIC.

2. Simplify $\left\{\frac{1}{7}\left(\frac{1\frac{1}{3}}{\frac{4}{5}} \text{ of } \frac{7\frac{1}{2}}{4\frac{5}{16}}\right) \div \left(\frac{9\frac{1}{4}}{14\frac{2}{3}} \times \frac{24}{25}\right) \text{ of } \left(2\frac{1}{3} \text{ of } \frac{2\frac{1}{4}-1\frac{1}{2}}{16}\right)\right\} + \frac{10}{27}.$

3. Two cogged wheels work together; one wheel has 90 and the other 40 cogs; the larger revolves 100 times in a second; how often will the wheels be in contact, in the same position, every second?

4. A has $3 more than $\frac{1}{8}$ of a certain sum of money; B has $12 more than $\frac{5}{16}$ of the same sum, and C has $10 less than $\frac{1}{2}$ of it; find the sum.

5. Bought fruit for $120; sold 60 per cent. of it at 80 per cent. of the cost price, and the rest at 20 per cent. advance on the cost price. Find my gain or loss per cent. on the whole.

6. A boy has 9 coins in his purse; there are twice as many twenty cent pieces as five-cent pieces, and half as many ten-cent pieces as fives and twenties together. How much money has the boy in his purse?

7. A and B have together $420; and 20 per cent. of A's is $4 less than $16\frac{2}{3}$ per cent. of B's. How much money has each?

8. Wheat weighs 48 lbs. to the cubic foot; find the value of a bin of wheat, 40 feet long, 20 feet wide and 4 feet 6 inches deep, at $1.05 a bushel.

9. A does $\frac{2}{5}$ of a piece of work in 16 days, and then B joins him. They work together at it for $1\frac{1}{4}$ days when B leaves, and A finishes the work in $4\frac{3}{4}$ days more. How long would it have taken B to do the whole work alone?

10. A has $7\left\{\dfrac{7\frac{1}{2}\times\frac{1}{3}\text{ of }\frac{4}{9}}{13\frac{8}{17}-12\frac{7}{9}}-\frac{1}{13}\right\} \times \left\{\dfrac{\frac{7}{6\frac{1}{8}} \times \frac{2\frac{1}{2}}{9} \text{ of }\frac{36}{40}}{\frac{3}{5}\div\frac{7}{8}\text{ of }\frac{32}{35}\times\frac{1}{7}}\right\}$ times as much money as B, and together they have $495; how much money has A more than B?

11. A vat, 45 ft. long, 16 ft. wide, and 2 ft., 6 in. deep, is filled with syrup; what is it worth at $57.60 a puncheon?

12. Find the net cash proceeds of the following bill of produce, 8 per cent. being allowed off for ready payment:

    76 bushels, 20 lbs. buckwheat at 60 cents a bushel.
    29 bushels, 12 lbs. wheat at 90 cents a bushel.
    72 bushels, 16 lbs. barley at 63 cents a bushel.
    92 bushels, 24 lbs. millet at $1.72 a bushel.
    53 bushels, 30 lbs. Hungarian at $2.40 a bushel.

FOURTH CLASS. 93

13. A circular reservoir, having a diameter of 98 rods, is half-full of water, and 891666·015625 gallons are admitted; how much will it raise the surface of the water in the reservoir?

Exercise LXXXIII.

1. Of what does the L.C.M. and H.C.F. of *any two* numbers consist? The L. C. M. of two numbers is 1194830, and their H.C.F. is 34138; one number is 238966; what is the other?

2. What is the difference between the *simple* and the *compound* rules of arithmetic? The product of two numbers is 11352418227, and their quotient is 307; find the numbers. Reduce $\frac{11}{10}$ of a ℔. troy + $\frac{11}{10}$ of a ℔. avoir. to ℔s., ozs., dwts. and grs. *troy*.

3. What is the difference between *vulgar* and *decimal* fractions? Simplify: $[\frac{7}{8} \text{ of } \{\frac{3\frac{1}{3} + 2\frac{1}{5} \text{ of } 2\frac{1}{2}}{7\frac{1}{4}}\} + \frac{2\frac{1}{2}}{3} \text{ of } \frac{2}{3}] + \frac{1}{4}$. Find the sum of 6·2$\dot{3}\dot{8}$, 4.62$\dot{7}$ and 2·134$\dot{5}$.

4. Find the total cost of papering the walls and painting the ceiling of a church, 120 ft. long, 70 ft. wide, with a ceiling 18 ft. high, the paper to be 21 inches wide, worth $1.30 a double roll, and 37 strips to be allowed for openings, the bordering to cost 9 cents a yard, and the painting 15 cents a square yard.

5. What would be the cost of carpeting the church in question 4, with 45-inch carpeting, laid down lengthwise of the church, and costing $1.87½ a yard?

6. A rectangular field, whose length is to its breadth as 5:4, contains 12 acres, 80 sq. rods. A strip 30 rods wide and running the length of the field, is sown with barley at a cost of $1.60 an acre, and the remainder is sown with wheat at a cost of $2.40 an acre. Find the entire cost of sowing the field.

7. A owned $\frac{7}{11}$ of a lot, and was offered $1800 for $\frac{4}{7}$ of his share. B bought the whole lot at this rate, and paid a year's back taxes amounting to 1$\frac{1}{35}$ per cent. of the value of the lot. Find B's total investment.

8. In a mixture of 50 gallons of liquid, the wine is 40 per cent. of the whole; how much wine added will make the wine 90 per cent. of the whole?

9. Divide $270 among A, B and C, giving B $\frac{1}{3}$ as much again as A, and C $\frac{1}{4}$ as much again as B.

EXERCISES IN ARITHMETIC.

10. A grocer bought $660 worth of tea, and by using a false weight gained $44 on the sale of the lot; how many ozs. did he sell for a ℔.?

11. How often does $\{(30\frac{7}{30} - 22\frac{5}{18}) - \frac{331}{360}\} \times \{10\frac{1}{5} \times \frac{5}{13} \times \frac{24}{17} \times 1\frac{1}{5}\}$ contain $13\frac{1}{2}$ times $1\frac{5}{9}$?

12. If 6 horses and 4 oxen can consume the pasture on a field in 27 days, and 9 horses and 12 oxen can consume the pasture on the same field in 12 days, compare the appetite of the horse with that of the ox.

13. When 1830 ℔s. of hay sells for $16.47, what is hay per ton?

Exercise LXXXIV.

1. Simplify: $\frac{1}{2} \div \frac{3}{4} \times \frac{1}{3} \div \frac{4}{5}$ of $\frac{5}{8}$.

2. Have a certain sum of money of which I spend $\frac{1}{4}+$$5$; then $\frac{5}{9}$ of the remainder all but $5; I have then left $10; find my money at first.

3. Reduce 144 lbs. avoirdupois to ozs. troy, and express the result as the fraction of 350 lbs., troy.

4. Sold $\frac{3}{4}$ of a ton of coal gaining 8 per cent.; what fraction of the cost did the $\frac{3}{4}$ of a ton cost me?

5. Bought 50 lbs. of tea and coffee for $14.60, paying 40 cents for the tea and 25 cents for the coffee per lb.; how many lbs. of each were in the mixture?

6. Sold a pile of cordwood measuring 80 feet long, by 6 feet high, getting $4.50 a cord for 10 cords of it, and $3.75 a cord for the rest; how much did I get altogether for the pile?

7. If $2666\frac{2}{3}$ lbs. of sugar cost £$462\frac{2}{3}$, how much will $\frac{7}{16}$ of a ton of sugar cost?

8. Divide the L.C.M. of 1380, 1960 and 1386 by the H.C.F. of 1470, 4907 and 567.

9. Divide $190 among A, B and C, so that B may have $1\frac{1}{2}$ times as much as A, and C $1\frac{1}{2}$ times as much as B.

10. Divide $\dfrac{18}{\frac{3}{7} \text{ of } \frac{4\frac{5}{8}}{12\frac{1}{3}} \text{ of } 3\frac{4}{11}}{11\frac{5}{7}}$ by $\dfrac{\frac{5}{6}}{2\frac{1}{2}} + \dfrac{35}{3\frac{2}{14}} + \frac{7}{8}$

11. If $\frac{4}{5}$ of a barrel of flour costs $1.12, what will two bags, one holding $\frac{3}{14}$, and the other $\frac{27}{28}$ of a barrel, cost me?

FOURTH CLASS. 95

12. Twelve calves are equal in value to 4 goats, and 2 calves equal to 4 pigs, and 10 pigs cost $80; find the value of a drove of 7 animals of each kind.

13. Find the *product* of the *sum* and *difference* of $8\dfrac{\frac{1}{8}+\frac{1}{9}}{\frac{1}{8}-\frac{1}{9}}$ and $9\left[\dfrac{\frac{1}{6}+\frac{1}{7}}{\frac{1}{6}-\frac{1}{7}}\right]$.

Exercise LXXXV.

1. Find the value of $5\frac{1}{3}$ yds. cloth at 8/6d. a yard, $7\frac{1}{4}$ yds. lace at 7/8d. yard, and 8 qrs. 5 bushels wheat at 44/8d. a quarter.

2. One hundred bushels of wheat and barley together cost $70.80; the wheat was 87 cents, and the barley was 60 cents a bushel; how many bushels of each were there?

3. A farmer sows $\frac{480}{6887}$ of an ounce of wheat to the square foot in sowing a rectangular field, 90 rods long by 80 rods wide; what does it cost him to sow the field when wheat is worth $1 a bushel?

4. It costs $5.25 to sow a field, 40 rods long, with oats at 35 cents a bushel, putting on 2 bushels to the acre; how wide is the field?

5. A merchant mixes 16 lbs. tea, at 60 cents, with 14 lbs., at 50 cents a lb.; at what rate per lb. must he sell it to gain $24\frac{28}{33}$ per ct.?

6. Divide $225 among A, B and C, so that B may have $\frac{1}{4}$ as much again as A, and C may have $\frac{1}{3}$ as much again as B.

7. Find the simple interest on $470 for $5\frac{1}{2}$ years at 5 per cent. per annum.

8. The cost of building a tight board fence, 40 rods long, with inch-lumber, worth $10 a thousand, is $39.60; how high is the fence?

9. A lady wishes to carpet a floor 20'8" × 18'6" with 30-inch carpeting worth 90 cents a yard, the strips to run lengthwise of the room and 4 inches per strip to be allowed for waste in cutting; find the cost.

10. Express $\frac{5}{8}$ of $\frac{4}{10}$ of a dollar as the fraction of £30 Sterling.

11. The gain at which an article is sold is 20%, and the sum of the gain, cost, and selling price is $108; find the cost price.

12. A merchant sold a suit of clothes for $54, gaining thereon $\frac{1}{4}$ of the selling price; find the cost of 13 dozen such suits.

13. A has 14 acres, 15 sq. rods, $8\frac{1}{4}$ sq. yds. of land, which he sells at $22 an acre; find his receipts.

Exercise LXXXVI.

1. A can do $\frac{1}{3}$ of a piece of work in 5 days, B can do $\frac{2}{4}$ of the remainder in 10 days, and C can finish it in 4 days. A and B work together at it for 5 days ; how long will it take C to finish it alone ?

2. Find the amount of $450 for 657 days at 10 per cent. per annum, simple interest.

3. If 5 men or 8 women or 12 boys can do a piece of work in 40 days, how long will it take 20 men, 2 women and 9 boys working together to do it ?

4. Find the total cost of painting the outside of a box, (with lid), 4 ft. long, 3 ft. wide and 4 ft. deep, with paint at 18 cents a square yard, and of lining it inside with lead worth $4.50 a cwt., given that 2 lbs., 4 ozs. of lead lines a square foot of surface, and that the box is 90 per cent. as large inside as outside.

5. A boy harrows, lengthwise, a rectangular field containing 15 acres ; if the field is 60 rods long, and the harrow is 15 ft. wide, how far does the boy walk in going once over the field ?

6. Simplify : $9\left\{\dfrac{1\frac{1}{7}}{1\frac{8}{21}} \text{ of } 6\frac{2}{3} + 10\frac{1}{2}\right\} \div 7 \dfrac{\frac{1}{4}+\frac{1}{3}}{\frac{7}{10}+1\frac{1}{11}} \text{ of } 5\left[\dfrac{\frac{1}{6}+\frac{1}{3}}{\frac{19}{18}}\right]$

7. Find the value of a mixture of 15 gallons of brandy, wine and whiskey, mixed in the ratio of 3 : 2 : 1 respectively, when brandy is $8, wine $3, and whiskey $1.60 a gallon.

8. A produce dealer sells 16 cwt., 30 lbs. flour at $2.60 a cwt., 4 tons, 150 lbs. hay at $12 a ton, 4 cwt. 42 lbs. oats at 33 cents a bushel, and 50 lbs. corn. at $8.86 a cwt. Find the cash receipts on the sale, there being 10 per cent. off for cash.

9. Show that ·4 of an acre + ·3 of a square rod + ·45 of a square yard + 39·6 square inches — ·2 of 2 acres, 1 square rod, 17 square yards, 4 square feet, 108 square inches.

10. A and B start together from M. and travel directly *east*, A at 4 miles and B at 3 miles an hour. C starts, at the same moment, from N., 54 miles directly east of M., and travels *west* at 2½ miles an hour. In how many hours will C be midway between A and B ?

11. Find the quotient of the L.C.M. and the H.C.F. of 444, 1480 and 1665.

12. By how much does the sum of the following numbers exceed their product ?— $\frac{3}{8}$, 1, $2\frac{1}{6}$, $\frac{2}{3}$ of $1\frac{9}{12}$, $\dfrac{2\frac{1}{2}}{3\frac{1}{4}}$, $7\frac{1}{3}$.

FOURTH CLASS.

13. B has $99, which is 90 per cent. of C's money, which is $91\frac{2}{3}$ per cent. of D's. Find the sum total of their money.

Exercise LXXXVII.

1. A can do a piece of work alone in 10 days, B in 12 days, and C in 20 days. A and B work together at it for 2 days; then B and C work together at it for 3 days; after which all three work together at it until the work is finished; how long is the work under contract?

2. A man receives $37.50 per day for working 10 hours a day for 15 days; what is the *unit* of work used in the computation?

3. A, B and C are joint owners of a rectangular piece of land, 70 chains long by 40 rods wide; it has on it a standing crop of wheat estimated at 35 bushels per acre, C sells the land with the crop as it stands, receiving $60 an acre for the land and 80 cents a bushel for the wheat. He retains 5 per cent. of the receipts for his commission as salesman, and the balance is then divided as $1.3 \cdot 3 : 5$, respectively. Find each man's share.

4. A clothier buys 15 cases of ready-made clothing of 20 suits each; he sells $\frac{2}{3}$ of the lot at an advance of 20 per cent. on cost, and the remainder at 30 per cent. discount. What is his gain or loss per cent. on the whole lot?

5. A tank is fed by an inexhaustible supply of water which flows out through an opening, 7 inches in diameter, at the rate of 10 miles an hour. How many barrels, gallons, pounds and ounces of water pass through the opening every 15 minutes?

6. Nine bushels of rye and nine bushels of barley together cost $11.34; the rye cost 70 cents more for every 5 bushels than the barley; find the value of each per bushel.

7. Simplify: $\left\{ \dfrac{31 \cdot 6 \div \cdot 042}{\cdot 378 \times 426 \times 12\frac{3}{8}} \right\}$ of $\left\{ \dfrac{(2\frac{1}{2}+\frac{1}{6}) \div (3\frac{2}{3}-\frac{1}{8})}{1\frac{8}{17}} + \cdot 4 \right\}$.

8. Nine bells which toll at intervals of 3, 9, 12, 15, 18, 21, 24, 27 and 30 seconds respectively, all begin tolling simultaneously with the hour of one o'clock, p.m., as struck by a clock which strikes the hours and half-hours. What o'clock is it when the bells all toll again simultaneously with the striking of the clock?

9. In a bag of 341 marbles, Tom's share is to Will's as $\left\{ \frac{1}{3} \text{ of } 13\frac{1}{2} \text{ of } \frac{2}{3} \text{ of } 4 \right\} : \left\{ 1\frac{1}{3} \text{ of } \dfrac{6\frac{2}{3}}{1\frac{1}{7}} \right\}$. How many marbles has Tom more than Will?

EXERCISES IN ARITHMETIC.

10. Find the *square root* of the L.C.M. of $1\frac{1}{3}$, $16\frac{1}{2}$ and 9.

11. A man spent $100 and had still left 40 per cent. of what he spent, which was $2 less than $\frac{3}{10}$ of what he had at first. How much had he at first?

12. A man buys apples at the rate of 3 for 5 cents, and sells them at the rate of 4 for 10 cents; what is his gain on the sale of 144 dozen apples?

13. A, B and C together, have $279. B has $\frac{5}{6}$ as much money as C, and for every $4.50 that A has, B and C together have $11. How much money has each?

Exercise LXXXVIII.

1. If 20 men, 32 women *or* 40 boys can do a piece of work in 15 days, how long will it take 11 men, 24 women *and* 8 boys to do it?

2. Divide the sum of $\left\{\dfrac{\frac{1}{2}-\frac{1}{3}}{\frac{1}{3}-\frac{1}{4}}\right\}$ and $\left\{\dfrac{\frac{1}{4}-\frac{1}{5}}{\frac{1}{5}-\frac{1}{6}}\right\}$ by their difference.

3. Divide $96.60 among A, B and C, so that A shall get twice as much as B, and C as much as A and B together.

4. Find the cost of lathing the walls and ceiling of a room $16' \times 12' \times 9'$, an allowance being made for one door $6' \times 3'$ and for two windows $5' \times 3'$, the lath being worth $12\frac{1}{2}$ cents a bunch.

5. The roof of a building is 40 feet long, and each side, from the eave to the ridge, 15 feet wide; find the cost to shingle at $3.20 a thousand shingles.

6. It costs $720 to build a bridge at 18 cents a square foot of surface; the bridge is 13 ft., 4 inches wide; how long is it?

7. Find the value of the following crop: 16 acres, 120 square rods of oats, 19 acres, 100 square rods of wheat, and 10 acres, 76 square rods of barley; the oats yielding 60 bushels to the acre, worth 36 cents a bushel, the wheat 45 bushels to the acre, worth $1.12 a bushel, and the barley 50 bushels to the acre, worth 56 cents a bushel.

8. Out of a cistern, containing 57 gallons of water, 14 pails were taken. If the pail held 2 gallons, 3 quarts, how much water (in gallons and quarts), still remained in the cistern?

9. Gentlemen's neck-ties are bought at $3.50 a dozen, and sold at 35 cents each. What is the gain on the sale of 300 such ties?

FOURTH CLASS. 99

10. If $39.12 were paid for a load of wheat at $1.60 a bushel, how many bushels and lbs. did the load contain?

11. Find the product of the L.C.M. of 6, 12, 20, 24, 54, 81, 63, 14, and the H.C.F. of 945, 840, and 1365.

12. Simplify: $\left\{1+\tfrac{1}{4}+\tfrac{1}{9}+\tfrac{1}{16}+\tfrac{1}{25}+\tfrac{1}{36}\right\} \times \left\{\tfrac{3}{13}-\tfrac{1}{7}+\tfrac{8}{59}\right\}$.

13. Divide 1330 among A, B and C, so that for every $5 that A gets, B shall get $6 and C $8.

Exercise LXXXIX.

1. A man earns $640 a year and spends $400; how long will it take him to pay for a rectangular plot of ground, 40 by 36 rods, worth $80 an acre?

2. Find the *net* receipts of the following bill, 5 per cent. being allowed off the face value for cash:

    13 bushels, 1 peck grass-seed at $6 a bushel.
    20 lbs., 15 ozs. cheese at $16 a cwt.
    50 lbs. hay, at $18 a ton.
    39 ozs. gold dust at $200 a lb.
    5 lbs. lead at $0.13 a lb.
    81 lbs. nails at $0.05 a lb.

3. Paid $22.50 for buckwheat at 60 cents a bushel; how many bushels and lbs. did I buy?

4. If $78.75 are paid for flour at $3.75 a barrel; how many cwt. and lbs. are there?

5. A sells land for $310.10 at $22 an acre; how many acres, rods, yards, feet, and inches does he sell?

6. Divide $108 among A, B, and C, so that A shall have $\tfrac{3}{4}$ as much as B, and that B shall have $\tfrac{4}{5}$ as much as C.

7. A merchant sold velvet at $6.50, and lost thereby $7\tfrac{1}{7}$ per cent.; find the cost price of the velvet per yard.

8. The cost price of a rectangular piece of land, 40 by 18 chains, was $4250. It was sold at $80 an acre; find the gain on the sale of the land.

9. How often does the *square* of 890040 contain $873 \times 441 \div 63$?

10. Simplify: $\left\{ \dfrac{\tfrac{3}{5} \times \tfrac{1}{9} \times \tfrac{3}{4}}{\tfrac{5}{13} \text{ of } \tfrac{1}{25} \text{ of } \tfrac{1}{5}} \right\} \times \left\{ \dfrac{\tfrac{2}{3}-\tfrac{1}{2}}{\tfrac{1}{3}-\tfrac{1}{4}} + \tfrac{3}{8} \text{ of } \tfrac{4}{9} \text{ of } \tfrac{3}{4} \right\}.$

EXERCISES IN ARITHMETIC.

11. Bought pencils for $57.60 at 3 cents a dozen; if $\frac{3}{4}$ of them were sold at the rate of 20 for 5 cents, what did the balance sell for per dozen, so as to incur neither gain nor loss?

12. If a loan of $640 brings in 4.26\frac{2}{3}$ interest a month, what is the rate per cent. at which the money is loaned?

13. Find the sum of the *three* quotients arising from the division of the L.C.M. of 3864, 4830 and 4554 by each of the given numbers.

Exercise XC.

1. Simplify: $\left\{ \dfrac{\frac{1}{2}+\frac{1}{3}}{\frac{1}{2}-\frac{1}{5}} + \frac{1}{3} \right\} \times \left\{ (\frac{4}{11} \times 1\frac{4}{5}) + \frac{7}{8} + 15\frac{23}{24} \right\}$.

2. Find the L. C. M. of (a) 462, 534, 623, 693, 728 and 936; and (b) $\frac{2}{3}$, $\frac{3}{10}$ and $\frac{4}{5}$.

3. A certain number of lbs. of coffee cost $32. It was sold again at 52 cents a lb., giving a profit of 30%; find the number of pounds bought.

4. The amount of a certain sum at interest for 8 years at 9 per cent. is $464.40; find the sum.

5. An article is sold at 12$\frac{1}{2}$ per cent. advance on the cost price, and the *sum* of the gain and selling price is $1050; find the selling price.

6. Nine men receive $633.60 in 16 days, working 8 hours a day; what are each man's *hourly* wages?

7. The amount of a certain sum is $655.20, the time 7 years, and the interest $\frac{273}{820}$ of the sum; find the rate per cent.

8. Find the amount of $500 for 16 years at 4% simple interest.

9. A farmer sold an equal number of horses, cows and pigs for $1755, receiving $32 for each cow, $90 for each horse, and $13 for each pig. Find the total number of animals sold.

10. A has a farm $\frac{3}{4}$ of a mile long and 20 chains wide. What is it worth at $63 an acre?

11. Divide $67.10 among four boys, giving each one $\frac{1}{8}$ less than the one before him.

12. Divide $25.20 between two boys, so that one may receive 60 cents more than twice what the other receives?

13. A cart-wheel makes 2640 revolutions in going 11 miles; how many inches is the wheel in diameter?

FOURTH CLASS.

Exercise XCI.

1. Simplify $\left\{\dfrac{1\frac{1}{8} \times \frac{7}{6} \div \frac{1}{6}\frac{1}{4} \times \frac{4}{7}}{1\frac{1}{7} \text{ of } \frac{4}{6}\frac{9}{4} \div 2\frac{1}{7} \text{ of } 3\frac{1}{3}} \times 5\right\}$ of £3, 16 sh., 8d.

2. A board is 18 feet long and 15 inches wide; what is it worth when lumber is selling at $16 a thousand feet?

3. It required 55296 sods, each $2\dfrac{3\frac{1}{2}}{12}$ feet by $\dfrac{8\frac{1}{4}}{12}$ feet, to turf a certain plot of ground; find the value of the plot at $145 an acre.

4. Eggs cost 13 cents a dozen, and 16 of them are sold for 20 cents; how many dozen sold will produce a gain of $1.65?

5. Brown's farm consists of 10 uniform, rectangular fields, each $53\frac{1}{3}$ rods long by 30 rods wide; how many acres of land has Brown?

6. Simplify $\left[\left\{6\frac{1}{2} \text{ of } 4\frac{1}{2} - 2\frac{1}{4} \text{ of } 3\right\} \div \left\{\dfrac{20\frac{1}{2}}{5\frac{2}{7}} \times \frac{1}{3} \div 2\frac{1}{3}\right\}\right] - \frac{1}{8}.$

7. Divide $1200 among A, B and C, so that B shall receive $\frac{3}{4}$ as much as A, and that C shall receive $\frac{7}{8}$ as much as B.

8. A merchant bought sugar at $150 a ton, and sold it out at 4 lbs. for 33 cents; find his gain per cent.

9. A room, $31\frac{1}{3}$ feet long and 15 feet, 9 inches wide, will require how much less than 100 square yards of carpet to cover its floor?

10. How often does the L.C.M. of 2, 4, 21, 36, 45, 91 and 180 contain the H.C.F. of 5642 and 7462?

11. When the minute hand has travelled 330° on the dial-plate of a clock since 3 o'clock p.m., what time is it?

12. Find the L.C.M. and the H.C.F. of the following numbers by *resolving* each of them into its *prime factors*, and then selecting the L.C.M. and H.C.F. from these factors: 7560, 8820, and 44100.

13. (*a*) Tom's age 5 years ago is to his age 3 years hence as 2:3. How old is Tom now? (*b*) A owes a grocery bill of $759.90, payable in 3 months. What sum should A now put out at interest so that the sum, together with the interest thereon at 8 per cent., shall exactly meet the bill?

Exercise XCII.

1. If $13.50 buy ⅜ of a ton of flax, what fraction of a ton will $30 buy?

2. A piece of land costs $4080 at $80 an acre; it is 20 chains, 40 links wide, how long is it in rods?

3. How many 2½ inch cubes can be cut out of a block of stone 5 ft. long, 3 feet, 1½ inches wide, and 10 inches deep?

4. The remainder, 9, is ⅛ of the divisor and ⅜ of the quotient; what is the dividend?

5. Find the L.C.M. of:
   (a) 4, 28, 16, 72, 96 and 108.
   (b) 8, 9, 27, 64, 39, 45 and 52.

6. The cost to fence a road on both sides, at 15 cents a rod, is $2880.00. How many miles long is it?

7. At what rate, in miles and rods per hour, will 62 miles, 200 rods be travelled over in 9 hours, 16 minutes, 40 seconds?

8. Divide the L.C.M. of 18, 48, 64, 72, 28, 96, 132 and 244 by the H.C.F. of 275781 and 276025.

9. Find the total cost of:
   32 tons, 900 lbs. middlings at $15 a ton.
   7944 lbs. barley at 56 cents a bushel.

10. A person bought 4 bushels, 12 gallons of wheat at 2 cents a lb. and 5 bushels and a certain number of gallons of oats at 9 cents a peck, paying for the whole $9.12. How many gallons of oats did he buy altogether?

11. When 20 lbs. of potatoes cost 25 cents, what is the value of 75 bushels?

12. Divide the L.C.M. of 21, 42, 18, 36, 9, 45, 180, 90 and 640 by the G.C.M. of 3232 and 1952.

13. Simplify $\left\{ \left(\tfrac{7}{18}+1\tfrac{3}{24}+1\tfrac{5}{12}+\tfrac{5}{6}-\tfrac{27}{72}\right) \times \left[\dfrac{4\tfrac{1}{6}+10\tfrac{2}{8}}{\tfrac{1}{8} \times \tfrac{9}{80} \times \tfrac{3}{6}} \right] \right\} \div (48\tfrac{1}{8} \times 9)$.

Exercise XCIII.

1. If six score is a "*long*" hundred, how many dozen herrings are there in 132 boxes of 2 "*long*" hundreds each?

2. Simplify: $\dfrac{\left\{\tfrac{7}{6}\left(\tfrac{1}{3}\times\tfrac{2}{8}\right) \text{ of } \tfrac{5}{8} \times \tfrac{7}{6}\right\} \div 61\tfrac{1}{4}}{\tfrac{3}{4}+\tfrac{7}{8}+1\tfrac{3}{16}+\tfrac{23}{28}} \text{ of } \dfrac{81 \times 31}{12 \times 4}$.

FOURTH CLASS. 103

3. If 40 rods of a telegraph line cost $50, find the value of 40 miles of the same line.

4. It costs $189 to feed 16 horses on oats for 6 weeks, giving each horse 3 pecks daily; find the price of oats per bushel.

5. How many barrels of flour, at $5 a barrel, should be exchanged for 3740 pounds of oats at 35 cents a bushel, 4260 pounds of wheat at $1.10 a bushel, 540 pounds of clover seed at $3.60 a bushel, and 510 pounds of beef at $10 a hundred weight?

6. A boy takes 1320 steps, each 2 ft., 6 in. long, in going round a rectangular field 60 rods long. How many acres does the field contain?

7. Out of a sum of $2655.00, $762.20 are allotted to a charitable institution, and of the remainder B gets 20 per cent. more than A, and C 20 per cent. more than B. Find C's share.

8. Divide $396 among James, Andrew and Robert, giving Andrew $13 *less* than James, and $13 *more* than Robert.

9. Find the cost of papering a room 40' 2" by 16' 4" with paper worth 95 cents a single roll, allowing, for windows and doors, 9 strips.

10. What will it cost to paper the walls of an opera house, 60' x 40', with paper worth $1.00 a double roll, allowing for 13 windows, each 4' wide and 3 doors each 8' wide, the ceiling being *27 feet high*?

11. Find the cost of carpeting the opera house, in question 10, with 45 inch wide carpeting at $1.20 a yard, the strips to run lengthwise of the house.

12. Find the cost of papering a room 70 by 30 feet, with paper worth 85 cents a double roll, allowing 14 strips for windows and doors.

13. Have a certain sum of which I spend $\frac{1}{3}+$2$, then $\frac{1}{4}$ remainder $+ 3; after which I have still left $3. How much was the original sum?

Exercise XCIV.

1. Sold 80 yards cotton at 12 cents a yard, gaining $\frac{1}{5}$ of the selling price: Show that 20 per cent. of the number of yards at cost price is equal to the gain at which the cotton was sold.

2. Find the sum of all the odd numbers from 781 to 797, inclusive.

3. A, B and C can do a work in $18\frac{18}{19}$ days working together. A and B together can do it in 24 days. In what time can C do it alone?

104 EXERCISES IN ARITHMETIC.

4. A merchant buys 640 yards of cloth at 80 cents a yard. He sells ¼ of it at 12½% advance on cost, and the rest at 10% advance on cost; find his entire gain.

5. Simplify: $4\left\{\dfrac{9\frac{1}{4} \text{ of } \frac{6}{7\frac{1}{7}} \times 7\frac{1}{3}}{\frac{1}{6} \times \frac{3}{8} \text{ of } 1\frac{9}{2\frac{1}{7}}} \text{ of } 1\frac{1}{2}\frac{6}{9}\right\}$ of 111 shillings, Sterling, and reduce the result to dollars and cents.

6. A rectangular farm contains $\frac{7}{8}$ of a square mile of land. It is 93¼ chains long; how many rods wide is it?

7. A house and lot together cost $990, and the house cost 25% more than the lot; find the cost of each.

8. A merchant sold 3 tons, 120 lbs. of yarn in 7-lb. and 10-lb. packages, selling an equal number of each, and getting $37.50 a dozen for the larger packages, and $27.50 a dozen for the smaller packages. How much did he receive for the yarn?

9. A pile of 20-inch wood, 80 feet long, and 4 ft. 6 in. high, is sold at $2.40 a cord; find the receipts for wood.

10. Find the total value of 15 bushels 12 lbs. wheat at $1.20 a bushel, 16 gallons peas at 70 cents a bushel, 24 pounds of potatoes at 35 cents a bushel, and 72 pints of rye at 72 cents a bushel.

11. The amount of a certain sum of money for 5 years, at 9 per cent., is $263.90; find the sum.

12. Multiply the difference between 67 × 85 and 50 (67 + 85) by $\{(896 \text{ times } 987) \div 141\}$.

13. (a) Find the product of the sum and 20% of the sum of 402 and 63. Divide the product thus obtained by $156\frac{1}{4}\left\{\dfrac{9\frac{1}{8}}{22\frac{13}{18}} \div \dfrac{10\frac{1}{4}}{1\frac{7}{2}}\right\}$ of $\frac{25}{28}$. (b) In 1892 a merchant's profits were ⅛ of his receipts. At what rate per cent. profit were his goods marked?

Exercise XCV.

1. On what sum is the interest for 8 years at 5 per cent. equal to the interest on $202.50 for 20 years, at 4 per cent.?

2. If ⅓ of a number *plus* 3 is equal to $\frac{1}{12}$ of the same number *plus* 8, what is the number?

FOURTH CLASS. 103

3. (a) What must we do with fractions before we *can compare* them? (b) By how much does the *greatest* of the following fractions exceed the *least?*—$\frac{72}{135}$, $\frac{3\frac{1}{4}}{}$ and $\frac{7}{13}$. (c) Arrange them in order of magnitude.

4. The quotient is 16 times the divisor, and the latter is 17 times the remainder, and the sum of the three is 9280; find the dividend.

5. The sum of $2304 is divided among A, B and C, so that B shall receive 5 times as much as A, and that C shall receive 7 times as much as A and B together. How many times A's money is B's and C's together?

6. The amount of $621 for 9 years is $900.45; find the *yearly rate of interest*.

7. On $512, $716.80 is due at the end of a certain time at 5 per cent. per annum; find the time.

8. When 60 tons, 870 lbs. of hay sold for $966.96, what was hay per ton?

9. A farmer sold 6 tubs of butter of 36 lbs. each at 30 cents a lb., and 56 dozen eggs at $37\frac{1}{2}$ cents a dozen; he then bought with the money, 98 lbs., $\frac{2}{3}$ of an oz. butter; what was butter per lb.?

10. One man travels 16 miles, 120 rods per hour for 8 hours a day, and another man travels 140 miles, 30 rods per day. How much longer will it take one man than the other to complete a journey of 587273 miles, counting 6 days to a week?

11. Find the *square* of the sum of all the odd numbers between 780 and 798.

12. Sold fifty-four dollars' worth of eggs at 10 cents a dozen; if I had bought the eggs at 9 for 10 cents, find my loss.

13. (a) What is the total amount of the following bill: 72 dozen fish at 3 for 5 cents; 21 oranges at 20 cents a dozen; 114 lbs. sugar at 19 lbs. for a dollar. (b) What is the balance due on a note for $250 at 6 per cent. interest for two years, on which a *partial payment* of $65 is made every six months?

Exercise XCVI.

1. What is 25 per cent. of $640? Invest it in oranges at 3 for ten cents, and find the number of dozens bought.

2. Three-fourths of a dollar is what fraction of 340 cents?

3. A boy takes 5420 steps in going from X to Y. If 6 steps are equal to one rod, how many miles, rods, yards, feet and inches is it from X to Y?

EXERCISES IN ARITHMETIC

4. Forty per cent. of a barrel of 96 dozens of eggs was sold at 3 for 10 cents, and the rest at 15 cents a dozen. Find receipts.

5. If 13 dozens suits of clothes cost $7488, and the selling price of a suit is $54, find the gain per cent.

6. If 5 lbs. tea at 78 cents a lb. be mixed with 8 lbs. at 65 cents a lb. and the mixture be sold at 80 cents a lb., find the gain per cent.

7. Cloth, which cost $1.50 a yard, is marked 40 per cent. below cost; find the selling price of 700 yards.

8. Subtract $(\frac{2}{4}+\frac{2}{3}+\frac{7}{12}+\frac{5}{36}+\frac{13}{100})$ from $3\frac{1}{6}$, and multiply the difference by $342\frac{2}{7}$; then, divide the product by $84\frac{11}{21}$.

9. Arrange in order of magnitude: $\frac{5}{8}, \frac{23}{36}, \frac{24}{37}$ and $\frac{7}{8}$.

10. Simplify: $15 \left\{ \dfrac{3\frac{1}{12} - \frac{85}{165} + \frac{5}{21} + 1\frac{11}{14} + 2\frac{1}{8} + \frac{1}{3}}{2\frac{7}{8} \times 7\frac{1}{5} \times \frac{3}{8}} \right\}$.

11. Find the intermediate fraction between $\frac{123}{247}$ and $\frac{512}{837}$, whose denominator is 2613.

12. By how much does a barrel of water exceed a barrel of fish in weight?

13. (a) A stationer bought 20 bales of paper at $20 a bale; he then sold it again at $12\frac{1}{2}$ cents a quire; find the gain per cent. (b) How much tea at 30 cents a lb. must I mix with 18 lbs. at 45 cents a lb. in order to produce a mixture of tea worth 39 cents a lb?

Exercise XCVII.

1. In going from A to B a man takes 5,400 steps, each 2 feet $3\frac{1}{4}$ inches long. How many miles, rods, yards, feet and inches does he travel?

2. Divide 3 acres, 240 square rods by 2 square feet, 36 sq. inches.

3. At 20 cents a rod, it costs $92.40 to enclose a circular plot of ground with a fence; find the value of the plot at $3.20 an acre.

4. Divide $7098 among A, B and C in the proportion of 2, 5 and 7.

5. A boy has 91 coins in his purse, made up of 5-cent, 10-cent and 25-cent pieces. He has twice as many 10's as 25's, and 5 times as many 5's as 10's. How much money has he?

FOURTH CLASS.

6. A rectangular farm is 50 chains long by 50 rods wide; a strip 40 rods in width is sold off the entire length of the farm. (a) How many acres and square rods are sold? (b) What is the remainder of the farm worth at $65 an acre?

7. Find the value of $\left\{\dfrac{1\frac{1}{15} \div \frac{1}{8} \text{ of } \frac{9}{10}}{74\frac{2}{3}} \text{ of } \frac{28}{40}\right\}$ of a square mile of land at $69 an acre.

8. Find the cost of 29 lbs., $0\frac{1}{4}$ of an ounce of tea at 60c. a lb., and 45 lbs., 2 ozs. butter at 20c. a lb.

9. If $800 amounts to $1161 in 5 years, at what rate per cent. per annum is it loaned?

10. Find the value of $29040 \times 30405 - 100002045 \div 6081$.

11. A can walk 3 miles an hour, and starts on a journey at 6.30 a.m. B starts 2 hours, 45 minutes, afterwards for the same place, and along the same road, and they, together, arrive at their destination at 4.45 p.m. How fast did B walk per hour, if they both stopped 1 hour, 30 minutes for dinner?

12. Find the value of $\frac{1}{8}$ of 2 pecks of beans at $3 a bushel, $\frac{7}{15}$ of 4 quarts of onions at $6 a bushel, $\frac{7}{12}$ of 8 gallons of beets at $1.80 a bushel, and 7 lbs. of potatoes at $23\frac{1}{3}$ cents a lb.

13. A can do a work in 5 days, B in 6 days, and C in 15 days. They work together at the work until it is finished. If $13.26 is paid for the work, find each man's share.

Exercise XCVIII.

1. Find the total cost of 16 bush., 18 lbs. peas at 70 cents a bushel, 42 lbs., 12 ozs. butter at 28 cents a lb., 13 bush., 15 lbs. parsnips at 36 cents a bushel, and 6 bush., 40 lbs. onions at 90 cents a bushel.

2. Simplify: $\left\{\left(\dfrac{3\frac{2}{3} \times 9}{\frac{5}{6} \text{ of } \frac{7}{8}} \div \dfrac{\frac{9}{10} - (\frac{1}{2} + \frac{1}{3})}{\frac{1}{3} - \frac{7}{18}}\right) + 1\frac{2}{7}\right\} \div 13.$

3. Divide $609 between John and Robert, giving John $(3\frac{22}{30} \times 2\frac{11}{13} \times \frac{9}{17} \times 2\frac{1}{31})$ times as much as Robert.

4. Had a certain sum of money of which I gave away $3 more than $\frac{1}{7}$; then $1 more than $\frac{5}{17}$ of the remainder; then $5 less than $\frac{4}{9}$ of what now remained; after which I had still left $15. How much money had I at first?

5. A farmer sells 40 geese and a certain number of turkeys at the average price of 96 cents each. He receives 75 cents each for the geese, and $1.20 each for the turkeys. How many turkeys does he sell?

6. A merchant buys 60 webs of cotton of 42 yards each at 6 cents a yard; he then sells ¼ of it at 25 per cent. advance on cost and the rest at 8 cents a yard; find his total gain on the sixty webs.

7. A speculator bought 5 acres of land on the confines of a city at $100 an acre. He divided it into lots, each 12 rods long and 2 rods, 3 yards, 2 feet wide. He then sold the lots at $75 each; find his gain, if it cost $75 to survey the lots.

8. Simplify: $\left\{ \dfrac{3\frac{1}{16} \times \frac{5}{6} \times 1\frac{1}{3} \times \frac{2}{7}}{6\frac{5}{18} \text{ of } 1\frac{2}{25} \text{ of } 16\frac{2}{3} \text{ of } \frac{3}{4}} \times \dfrac{113 \times 81}{14} \right\}$.

9. Find the distance, in miles, rods, yards and feet, that a man travels in 13 days, 13 hours, 40 minutes, at the average rate of 3·5 miles an hour, 8 hours constituting a day's walk.

10. Find the value of $5 \dfrac{\frac{1}{2}+\frac{1}{3}}{\frac{1}{3}+\frac{1}{4}}$ yards of sealette at $7 $\left\{ \dfrac{\frac{1}{6}-\frac{1}{7}}{\frac{1}{7}-\frac{1}{8}} \right\}$ a yd.

11. Find the L.C.M. of 14, 15, 20, 12, 30, 7, 8, 4, 21, and divide it by the H.C.F. of 30 and 75.

12. Find the *product* of the L.C.M. of 3, 9, 17, 81 and the L.C.M. of 6, 7, 8, 9, 56, 252; increase it by 36 and divide the result by the L.C.M. of 13, 39, 12 and 78.

13. The amount of a certain sum for 5 years at 6 per cent. simple interest is $191.10; find the sum.

Exercise XCIX.

1. Simplify: $\left\{ \dfrac{7\frac{1}{4}+6\frac{1}{3}+1\frac{5}{12}}{7\frac{3}{4} \div 2\frac{1}{16} - 2\frac{5}{8}} \right\} \div \left\{ \dfrac{\frac{1}{13}+\frac{1}{26}+\frac{2}{39}}{\frac{2}{7} \times \frac{3}{5} \times \frac{1}{4} \times 2\frac{5}{8}} \right\}$.

2. A man owns ⅜ of a potato plot, and B the rest, and ⅓ of the difference between their shares is 42 bushels, 2 pks. Find the value of the potatoes in the plot at 60 cents a bag.

3. When 2860 lbs. of hay sells for $11.44, what is hay per ton?

4. Find the L.C.M. and G.C.M. of $(7\frac{2}{3} \div 4\frac{3}{17})$ and $(14\frac{3}{7} \div 9\frac{1}{4})$.

5. How many square rods in ¾ of ·1 of an acre?

FOURTH CLASS.

6. If $133 gives 5 per cent. gain, what is the gain per cent. at $158½ ?

7. Divide $540 among A, B and C, giving B half as much as C, and A ¾ as much as B.

8. It takes A and B 1⅔ days to mow a certain field. A alone can mow it in 4 days. How long will it take B alone to do it ?

9. It required 359424 sods, each 2 ft., 3½ inches long by 8¼ inches broad, to turf a certain lot ; find the size of the lot in acres.

10. The amount of a certain sum for a certain time at 7 per cent. is $508.20, and the amount of the same sum for the same time at 12 per cent. is $571.20 ; find the sum and the time.

11. If 20 boys or 15 men can do a work in 19 days, in how many days could 24 boys and 20 men do it ?

12. Find the cost of papering the walls, and painting the ceilings of a room 36 ft. 2 in. by 24 ft., 4 in., there being 3 doors, each 3 ft. wide, 6 windows, each 2 ft., 8 in. wide, the paper costing 8 cents a single roll, and the painting 18 cents for every ⅞ of a sq. yard.

13. Find the amount of the following bill of goods :
   24 yards, 9 inches carpeting at 80 cents a yard.
   52 yards, 2 feet carpeting at 90 cents a yard.
   36 yards, 2 ft., 6 inches linen at 30 cents a yard.
   73 yards, 4 inches hemp carpet at 18 cents a yard.

Exercise C.

1. Find the *greatest* factor common to 299 and 312 and the *least* number into which they will each divide without a remainder.

2. At 3¾ cents a square yard for material and labor to hang, what will it cost to employ a paper-hanger to hang 50 double rolls of Canadian wall-paper, each roll 16 yards long and 21 inches wide?

3. Using the *mean* between 8750 and 3392 as a *co-factor* of 11466 find the *result* and write it out in *words*.

4. A man bought a farm for $13000, paying for it with ten-dollar and twenty-dollar gold pieces. If he paid in all 825 coins, how many were there of each ?

5. Simplify: $\left\{ \dfrac{5\frac{5}{11} \times 4\frac{8}{9}}{7\frac{3}{13} \div 1\frac{8}{39}} + \frac{5}{9} \right\}^2 \times \left\{ \dfrac{10\frac{7}{8} \times 2\frac{11}{12}}{6} \right\}^2 .$

6. Have 30 gallons ale worth 20 cents a gallon ; how much water must I add to lower the price to 15 cents a gallon ?

110 EXERCISES IN ARITHMETIC.

7. Hay is worth $5 a ton and oats 35 cents a bushel, and a horse eats 20 lbs. of hay and 2 gallons of oats *daily* from February 13th, 1892, till July 31st in the same year, both days inclusive. Find the total cost of feeding the horse during that time.

8. Two-fifths of a *section* of land is sown to wheat, ½ of the remainder to oats, and the remaining 192 acres to barley. (*a*) Find the value of the whole section for land and crop thereon, at $40 an acre. (*b*) If the land cost $1792 more than the crop, what is the land worth per acre?

9. Find the *difference* between $98 \times 46 - 8 \div (91 - 46)$ and $40 \times 35 + 2025 \div 5$, and square the fifth part of it.

10. Sold 80 bushels of apples at 60 cents a bag, and gained thereby $16; what did I pay per bushel for them?

11. (*a*) Write a fraction that will express the Figure A C D B as a part of H C D F, as a part of E G D F, referring to the following diagram :—

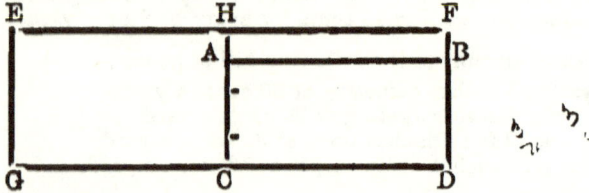

(*b*) What kind of a fraction have you? (*c*) Show that the Fig. A C D B is *three-eighths* of the Fig. E G D F.

12. Divide $100 among A B and C, giving A ⅓ as much as B, and B 3 times as much as C.

13. Find the cost of carpeting a room 31'6" by 24'10", with 30-inch carpet, laid down lengthwise of the room, and costing $1.20 a yard, nothing allowed for waste in cutting.

Exercise CI.

1. A debt of $368.35 is due at the end of nine months. What sum of money put out immediately at 8 per cent. interest, will at the end of the nine months liquidate the debt?

2. Bought a certain number of cows and sold them again at $40 each, thereby gaining $135 on the lot; but, had I sold them at $21 each, I would have lost $378 on the lot. How many cows did I buy, and what did they cost me per head?

FOURTH CLASS.   111

3. Find the cost of papering the walls of a room, 48 ft. by 32 ft., at $1.05 a double roll, an allowance being made for 8 windows each 2' 7" wide, and for 2 doors each 3' 2" wide.

4. What is the balance due on a note for $250 to run for 2 years at 6 per cent. per annum, a *partial payment* of $65 being made on the note every six months?

5. A and B together can do a piece of work in $8\frac{1}{2}$ hours. A and C can do it in 10 hours, and B and C can do it in 12 hours. Out of $9 paid for the work, what is the share of each, when they all work together at it?

6. When the sum of $500 amounts to $710 in 7 years, what is the rate per cent., per annum, at which it is loaned?

7. (a) Draw a note for $205 at nine months payable by yourself to A. T. Moody or order and bearing interest at 5 per cent. per annum.

(b) B does $\frac{2}{3}$ as much work as A when they work together, and they both together take $2\frac{2}{3}$ days to do a piece of work. How long would it take each one working alone to do it?

8. A man spent $\frac{1}{4}$ of his money + $10 and he then lacked $20 of having the half of his money left. How much money had he at first?

9. I bought goods for $240, and sold them again at 15 per cent. advance on cost. What did I get for the goods?

10. When 16 lbs. of tea cost $6.80, what is the value of $9\frac{1}{17}$ ozs. of tea?

11. When 18 bushels of wheat cost $15.93 more than 18 lbs. of wheat, what is wheat per bushel?

12. If $\frac{1}{4}$ of A's money = $\frac{2}{3}$ of B's in a purse of $132, find the share of each.

13. If 10 caps are exchanged for 25 hats, what per cent. are caps dearer than hats?

Exercise CII.

1. Bought 45 bushels, 2 pks., 1 gal. wheat for $47.45, and sold 16 bushels, 1 peck, 3 qts. of it for $20.92. Find my gain per bushel on all I sold.

2. Find the L.C.M. and H.C.F of $130\{ 7\frac{5}{8} \times 1\frac{1}{5} \times \frac{3\frac{1}{3}}{8} \times 4\frac{2}{13} \}$ and $\frac{1}{2}$ of $\{ 15\frac{3}{5} \times 1\frac{3}{5} \times 2\frac{3}{37} \times 6\frac{8}{11} \times 22 \}$.

3. A and B rent a pasture for $82. A puts in 16 cows for 4 months, and B a certain number for 5 months; B pays $50 of the rent; how many cows had he in the pasture?

4. What number bears the same relation to 31, as 51 does to 17?

5. A farmer, "breaking," on the prairie, half the length of a "*quarter-section*," works 18 hours, 45 minutes a day for one week. How much prairie does he turn over in that time if his plow cuts a 14-inch furrow, and his team travels 2½ miles an hour, an allowance being made of 1½ minutes every time in turning around?

6. Flour sold at $9.80 a barrel gave a profit of 42⅔ per cent.; find the cost of the flour per cwt.

7. What is the name of the Rule by which "*we take one number as many times as there are units in another*"? Give an example to show that you understand the question. Explain your example.

8. Define interest. Find the simple interest on $320 for 511 days at 5 per cent. per annum.

9. What time past 12 o'clock will the hands of a watch be 240 degrees apart?

10. Reduce 40 cents to the decimal of $2½.

11. Tom lost 2 more than ⅓ of his marbles, and had still left 6 more than ⅔ of them. How many marbles did Tom lose?

12. A can mow 9 acres of hay in 6 days. B can mow 5 acres in 4 days, and C can mow 18 acres in 10 days. How long will they jointly take to mow 136 acres, 80 rods?

13. The net cost of a bill of goods is $367.54, after two successive discounts of 6 per cent. and 8 per cent. have been deducted from the invoiced price. Find the invoiced price.

Exercise CIII.

The *old* par of exchange on Sterling money is $4.44⅔ to the £. What does an Englishman benefit by the *new* par of exchange over the *old*, in exchanging £900 Sterling for Canadian currency?

2. What per cent. is the *new* par of exchange in advance of the *old*?

3. A rabbit is 375 of its own leaps ahead of a dog, and it takes 12 leaps while the dog takes 5, but the dog covers as much ground in 2 leaps as the rabbit does in 6 leaps. How many leaps does the dog take in catching the rabbit?

FOURTH CLASS. 113

4. If a guinea be worth $5.11, and a gentleman has $6285.30 in Canadian currency, what is he worth in English money?

5. By resolution into *prime factors* (no long division to be used) find the L.C.M and the G.C.M. of 10350, 113022 and 169533.

6. Divide $105.30 between A and B (1) so that A shall have twice as much as B, and (2) so that A shall have $30.30 more than *twice the half* of B's ; (3) Which is the better division for A, and by how much?

7. Twelve rolls of carpet, weighing in all 6 tons, 1440 lbs., cover a surface of 2250 square yards. How many cwt. and lbs. of such carpeting would a strip 50 yards long and 2 feet, 3 inches wide, weigh?

8. An egg merchant buys eggs at 9 cents a dozen ; how many ought he to sell for $162.36 to gain 10 per cent. by the transaction?

9. A rectangular gravelled plot is 12 yards, 3 feet, 6 inches long by 3 yards, 1 foot, 9 inches wide. Find its area.

10. Simplify : (a) $5 + \cdot 23\dot{8} + 1\frac{3}{3}\frac{7}{6}$; and (b) $\cdot 23\dot{8} \div \cdot 76\dot{1}$, giving the results in vulgar fractions.

11. If 6 lbs. of tea are worth as much as 20 lbs. of coffee, and 2 lbs. of coffee are worth 4 lbs. of rice, and 8 lbs. of rice are worth 5 lbs. of butter, what is butter a lb., when 50 lbs. of the tea sell for $43.75?

12. (a) A wood dealer buys wood at $3.50 a cord. At what price per cord must he sell it in order to realize a profit of 20 per cent., after allowing $12\frac{1}{2}$ per cent. of his sales as worthless ? (b) A grocer buys sugar at 4 cents a pound. Allowing $16\frac{2}{3}$ per cent. of all the sugar bought for loss by waste and through shrinkage in weight, how many lbs. must he sell for the dollar to ensure a gain of 25 per cent. ?

13. Simplify (a) $\dfrac{9\frac{1}{4} \div 2\frac{3}{17}}{7\frac{1}{2} \times 1\cdot 26} \times 38$; (b) $\left\{ \dfrac{15\frac{3}{8}}{2\frac{1}{4}} + \cdot 1\dot{6} \right\} \times 7.$

Exercise CIV.

1. On a certain day an egg-merchant bought eggs at 25 cents a score, and sold them again at 20 cents a dozen, thereby clearing $40.50 ; how many dozen did he handle that day?

2. A man took a cargo of apples in his boat from Annapolis to Digby. The boat held 75 barrels and $3\frac{1}{2}$ bushels each. Find the weight of his cargo in tons and lbs., if each barrel weighed 18 lbs.

3. Classify: (a) 23; and (b) ⅛ of an inch.

4. A man takes 160 steps per minute, each step being 2 ft. 9 in. long on the average. How long will it take him to walk 36 miles, 80 rods?

5. Make out, neatly and correctly, the following bill, and find the total amount of it: May 1st, 1893, A. B. Burns & Co., Burnside, sold to John A. Bruce, 32 bushels 40$\frac{1}{2}$ lbs. wheat at 62½ cents a bushel; 450 lbs. barley at 37½ cents a bushel; 2 pecks, 3 lbs., 4 ozs. rye at 44⅖ cents a bushel; 17 cwt., 95 lbs., 10$\frac{2}{3}$ ozs. flour at $1.80 a cwt.

Write receipt for payment in full, May 13th, 1893.

6. Divide 4 acres, 10 square rods by 27, using factors, and no reduction before beginning the operation of dividing.

7. A sum of money is made up of 4 times as many crowns as shillings, and there are 75 coins in all. What is the sum?

8. Ten per cent. of a certain sum of money increased by $21 is equal to ½ of 66⅔ per cent. of the sum. Find the sum.

9. Find the cost of carpeting a hall-way, 40 feet long and 7 feet wide, with 30 inch carpeting, laid lengthwise of the room, and worth 75 cents a yard, allowing 4 inches per strip for waste in matching.

10. A field, 20 rods long by 16 rods wide, is bordered by ornamental trees, set 11 feet apart and worth 15 cents each, the trees being included in the area of the field. It is surrounded also by a ditch 7 ft. wide and 3 ft. deep (the ditch being no part of the area of the field) at a cost of 4½ cents a cubic yard to excavate. Find the total cost of the property (including improvements) land being worth $70 an acre.

11. A and B own a farm of 320 acres which they have rented. Of the rent, A gets 50 per cent. and B 40 per cent., the rest going for taxes. A's share is $48 more than B's. Find the amount of the rental per acre, and the number of acres B owns.

12. Two men, A and B, hire a boat for $2.80, to go from X. to Y. and return. One-third of the way to Y. they take in C., who agrees to share the expenses fairly for the distance he goes. C. gets off at Y., paying his share of the fare, and A and B return to X. How much does C pay?

13. Find the amount of $4451 $\frac{11}{16}$ at simple interest for 8 months at 7 per cent. per annum.

Exercise CV.

1. A, B and C undertake a job of work, for which the sum of $14.40 is to be paid. A could do it alone in 6 days, B in 7½ days, and C in 9 days. They all work together at it for 1¼ days, when B and C leave, and A finishes it alone. How much of the money should each receive?

2. If a gill of water weighs $5\frac{99\frac{1}{4}}{6912}$ ozs., and an imperial gallon contains 277·274 cubic inches, how many tons of water would a tank, 48 feet long, 9 feet wide and 4 feet deep, hold?

3. A sells a watch to B at a loss of 20 per cent.; B then sells it to C for $26.88, gaining thereby 5 per cent. Find what the watch cost A.

4. On January 1st, 1892, a depositor placed in the Savings' Bank $262.50. On May 26th, 1892, he withdrew the deposit with interest at the rate of 4 per cent. per annum. What amount did he withdraw?

5. A has £40, 10sh. Sterling, B has £20, 18sh., 6d., Halifax currency, C has 750 York shillings. How many dollars and cents has A more than B and C together?

6. A has $44.97, B 134 York shillings, C £10, 4s., 6d., Halifax currency, and D £15, 18s., Sterling. They put their money together and buy ornamental trees at 75 cents each. How many do they get?

7. Simplify: $\frac{1}{5}\left\{\dfrac{2\frac{1}{4}+1\frac{1}{3}}{2\frac{1}{4}-1\frac{1}{3}} \div \dfrac{\frac{1}{5}-\frac{1}{6}}{\frac{1}{5}-\frac{1}{7}} \text{ of } 1\frac{31}{55}\right\} + 12\frac{9}{14}$.

8. The following question is given at an examination: "How often have I ⅙ of a cent in £21, 15s., 6d."? A works it, using Halifax currency, and B works it, using Sterling money. What is the difference in their answers?

9. A can row a mile in 20 minutes, B in 15 minutes, C in 13 minutes, 20 seconds, and D in 12 minutes respectively. If they all start from the pier at the same time and row directly out into the lake, how far must each go, so that returning they may all reach the pier again together?

10. "Multiplication is the process of taking one number as an addend as many times as there are units in another." (a) What is the one number, here referred to, called? (b) What is the other called? (c) When is this true, if we interchange the numbers? (d) Take two numbers and prove this rule. (e) Indicate the multiplication of "*six times seven.*"

11. If the sum of ·7, ·27 and ·57 of a number be 3076, what is the number?

12. A man sold 660 barrels of apples for $667.80, thereby clearing 5 per cent. of the cost. If he paid $1 a barrel for the Northern Spies, and 90 cents a barrel for the Rhode Island Greenings, how many barrels of each did he buy and sell?

13. What decimal part of ⅔ of a square rod is 121 square inches?

Exercise CVI.

1. (a) Divide the *sum* of 7698 × 2103 and 8496 × 8694 by 2310 by short division, using *all the factors* of the divisor. (b) Find the continued product of: (35568 ÷ 78) (550974 − 446 ÷ 1472) (1699029276 ÷ 4567283) (431135173 − 93 ÷ 738245).

2. How much is { (687139 − 2 ÷ 11) + (768475 − 7 ÷ 12) } ÷ 462? In dividing use (a) long division, and (b) short division by all the factors and explain each *partial* remainder.

3. A, B and C dig a drain for which they, together, receive $93. A works at it for 7½ days and digs 60 rods. B works at it as many days as A digs rods per day, and C works as many days as A and B together. If they all work uniformly, and are paid according to the number of rods each digs, what is each man's share of the receipts?

4. A man, by his will, left his property, which was then valued at $15,300, to be divided among A, B and C., so that B should get $1000 more than A, and C $1300 more than B. On the death of the testator, the property was found to have depreciated in value 16⅔ per cent. What is the *just* apportionment of the balance of the property, after a legal claim of $510 is paid out of it?

5. If 16 eggs weigh 2 lbs., 2 ozs., what will 66 dozen and 8 of the same sized eggs weigh?

6. A man paid $25.80 for 85 dozen oranges and lemons, there being $\frac{5}{12}$ as many oranges as lemons, and the lemons costing 8 cents per dozen *less* than the oranges; find the cost price of each per dozen.

7. An estate consists of 18 rectangular fields, of *uniform* size, each containing 11 acres, 17 rods, 23 yds., 4 ft., 108 inches. How many acres are there in it?

8. I sow 2½ bushels of wheat to the acre, and grow 720 bushels on 18 acres; how many bushels have I for each bushel sown?

FOURTH CLASS. 117

9. A man travels 58 miles, 200 rods, in 11 hours; how many chains and feet does he travel per minute?

10. Find the *average price* per lb. of the following:

$21\frac{3}{4}$ lbs. at 72 cents a lb.
$10\frac{1}{3}$ lbs. at 45 cents a lb.
$8\frac{1}{5}$ lbs. at 35 cents a lb.
$20\frac{4}{15}$ lbs. at 60 cents a lb.
$5\frac{9}{20}$ lbs. at $126\frac{68}{109}$ cents a lb.

11. On a certain day, a merchant gained $13 by buying eggs at 10 cents a doz., and selling them again at 50 cents a score. How many dozen of eggs did he handle that day? 65

12. Simplify: $2\frac{1}{3} \div \frac{4}{5}$ of $\frac{5}{8} \div \frac{9}{10}$ of $\frac{5}{8} \times 1\frac{8}{35}$. $3\,^3/_5$

13. If $\frac{4}{5}$ of a lb. of tea be worth 22 cents more than 40 per cent. of a lb., what would be the value of 70 lbs. of the same tea?

49

Ditch 120 Rods

FIFTH CLASS.

Exercise I.

1. The *product* of two numbers is 324, and their *quotient* is 9; find the numbers.

2. What will it cost to paint the outside walls and both floors of a two-storey cottage, 30 feet, 6 in. long, 26 feet, 6 in. wide, and 18 feet high, at 15 cents a square yard, the walls to be 15 inches thick and no allowance being made for cornices, partitions or openings?

3. Simplify $\left\{\dfrac{5\frac{3}{5} \text{ of } 7\frac{2}{9}}{8\frac{7}{4} - 3\frac{5}{12}}\right\} \div \left\{\dfrac{1\frac{3}{5}}{3 + \dfrac{1}{3\frac{1}{3}}} + \dfrac{1\frac{2}{4} \text{ of } 4\frac{2}{7}}{1\frac{2}{5} \text{ of } 3\frac{4}{7}}\right\}.$

4. Fred gave away $12.60, and had still $\frac{7}{17}$ of his money left; how many pairs of ducks at 34 cents a pair could he have bought with his money before he gave any of it away?

5. A river is 10 feet deep and 125 feet wide, and flows at the rate of 5 miles an hour; how many tons and lbs. of water will flow, over a fall on it, every minute?

6. Bought 8 lbs. tea at 59 cents, 15 lbs. at 58 cents, and 28 lbs. at 65 cents; mixed it together and sold it so as to gain 50 per cent. At what rate per lb. was the mixture sold?

7. The sum of the cost, gain, and selling price, of an article is $90, and the gain at which it was sold is 12½ per cent.; find the *selling price* of the article.

8. If 16 men can split a pile of wood in 10 days, how many men could split *four* times as much wood in *one-third* of the time?

9. A rectangular field, 180 rods long and 8 chains wide, is rented for one year for $72. Seven acres of it are sown to wheat, yielding 30 bushels per acre, worth $1.08 a bushel; 18 acres to oats, yielding 70 bushels per acre, worth 40 cents a bushel; and the rest to barley, yielding 60 bushels per acre, worth 65 cents a bushel. What is the *net* gain on the entire crop, if it costs $87.80 to market it?

10. How fast is a locomotive running when the truck wheel, which is $2\frac{8}{11}$ feet in diameter, makes, every 3 minutes, 440 turns more than the driving-wheel, which is $5\frac{8}{11}$ feet in diameter?

11. B paid $57.60 for 29 lbs. of tea; what was that for every $4\frac{5}{8}$ ounces?

12. Find the L.C.M. and H.C.F. of $(19\frac{13}{18} \div 7\frac{5}{8})$ and $(8\frac{7}{13} \times 1\frac{8}{17})$.

13. How often does the L.C.M. of $(7\frac{1}{4} \div 8\frac{2}{7})$ and $(1\frac{1}{8} \div \frac{2}{9})$ contain their H.C.F.?

Exercise II.

1. How fast is an engine running per hour, when the truck wheel which is $2\frac{8}{11}$ feet in diameter, turns 330 times a minute more than the driving wheel, which is $5\frac{8}{11}$ feet in diameter?

2. How many cubic feet of iron are required for 3 water-pipes, each 30 inches in diameter and 24 feet long, the iron being 2 inches thick?

3. A spent $\frac{3}{8}$ of his money on Tuesday, $\frac{2}{7}$ of the remainder on Wednesday, and $\frac{4}{5}$ of what he had then left on Thursday; after which he had $72. How much money had he at first?

4. Divide $142 among A, B and C, in the proportion of $\frac{1}{3}, \frac{1}{5}, \frac{1}{7}$.

5. The distance between two towns is 840 miles, and is represented on a certain map by 1 ft. 9 inches. Find the distance between two places, if the distance between them on the same map is 3.6 inches.

6. Bought 200 bushels wheat for $173.50, part at 90 cents and the rest at 85 cents a bushel. How many bushels at each rate did I buy?

7. A can do a work in 12 days, and B in 20 days. (a) How long will it take both, working together, to do it? (b) After A has worked alone at it for 3 days, how long will it take B, alone, to finish it? (c) If A's wages are $3.25 a day, and B's are $4.25 a day, how much more does the work cost when A works 3 days and B finishes, than when both work together at it?

8. Rode to town at the rate of 6 miles an hour, and walked back at the rate of 4 miles an hour, which occupied me 5 hours; how far is it to town?

9. A has $\left\{ \dfrac{\frac{4}{5}+\frac{5}{8}}{24\frac{1}{2}} + \frac{1}{2} \text{ of } \frac{3}{4} \div \frac{5}{8} - \frac{9}{20} \right\}$ times as much money as B, who has half as much as C, who has $\frac{4}{7}$ as much as D, and altogether they have $380; how much money has each?

120   EXERCISES IN ARITHMETIC.

10. A can do a piece of work in 15 days, and B in 25 days, A works alone at it for 3 days, then B works alone at it for 5 days, after which they both together finish the work; how long was the work under contract?

11. Bought 120 bushels wheat for $87, part at 60 cents and the rest at 80 cents a bushel; how many bushels at each price did I buy?

12. A man threw 20% off the price of a horse; then, 15% off that again: the next day, he sold another horse of the same value, at the same selling price as the former; what per cent. did he throw off the latter horse?

13. Simplify: $\left\{\left[\dfrac{4\frac{1}{5}}{20} + \dfrac{7\frac{1}{2}}{9} \text{ of } 4\frac{1}{3}\right] - \left[\frac{7}{8} \text{ of } 1\frac{10}{21} - \frac{1}{8}\right]\right\}$
$+ \left\{\dfrac{3\frac{1}{2}}{9} \text{ of } 1\frac{1}{14} - \frac{2243}{5400}\right\}.$

Exercise III.

1. Find the net cash value of bill of merchandise, 8 per cent being allowed off for cash:

    76 bushels 20 lbs. buckwheat at 60 cents a bushel.
    29 bushels 12 lbs. wheat at 90 cents a bushel.
    72 bushels 16 lbs. barley at 63 cents a bushel.
    92 bushels 24 lbs. millet at 172 cents a bushel.
    53 bushels 30 lbs. Hungarian at 240 cents a bushel.

2. Sold a pile of 20-inch wood at $1.45 a cord; the pile was 80 feet long and 6 feet high. Received in payment $11.25 in cash, and the balance in potatoes at 35 cents a bag; how many bushels did I receive?

3. Bought 40 tons coal at $4.32 per "*long ton*," and sold the whole again at $4.25 per "*short ton*"; find my gain.

4. Four-sevenths of a ton of hay cost $28, and $\frac{5}{13}$ of $2\frac{2}{3}$ tons of such hay are exchanged for 7 sheep; what are sheep a head?

5. If $\frac{7}{8}$ of a gross of brooms cost $18.90, how many brooms should be given for $5\frac{1}{4}$ dozen eggs at 3 for 5 cents?

6. Two-sevenths of the vinegar in a cask leaked out, and it was then found to contain 9 gallons more than $\frac{1}{2}$ of the original quantity when full; find the size of the cask.

7. A, B and C can do a certain work in $4\frac{8}{13}$ hours. A and B can do it in $5\frac{5}{11}$ hours. In what time can C do it alone?

8. Divide the L.C.M. of 24713 and 26614 by their H.C.F.

FIFTH CLASS.

9. A boy spent $6 more than $\frac{1}{3}$ of his money, after which he had $6 more than half of it left. How much money had he at first?

10. Divide the L.C.M. of 439101 and 440908 by their H.C F.

11. Had a certain sum of money of which I spent $4 more than the $\frac{1}{4}$, I then had left $20 more than $\frac{3}{8}$ of the original sum; find that sum?

12. Square the quotient of the L.C.M. of 43923 and 45254 and their H.C.F.

13. Invested $60 in hay at ·5 of a cent a lb.; how many tons did I get?

Exercise IV.

1. A mixture of 28 lbs. of chicory and coffee together costs $3.64, the chicory being 9 cents a lb, and the coffee 25 cents a lb. ; find the number of lbs. of each in the mixture.

2. A merchant sold his stock of goods for $5368.90, realizing 6 per cent. more than he would have done, had he sold the week before he did. Find the value of 80 per cent. of his stock the week before he sold.

3. A received $\left\{\dfrac{1\frac{3}{8}}{8\frac{1}{4}} \text{ of } \frac{3\frac{7}{8}}{5\frac{2}{5}} + \dfrac{14\frac{1}{2} \div 6\frac{1}{4}}{12\frac{1}{3} \times 6\frac{3}{5}}\right\}$ of $6105; find the sum which A received.

4. Reduce $[5 \{ 12\frac{2}{3} + 15\frac{2}{3} + 30\frac{1}{3} \} \text{ of } 5]$ to £ Sterling.

5. Find the *product* of the *quotients* of $\dfrac{\text{L.C.M. of } 9, 18, 20}{\text{G.C.M. of } 14, 20}$ and $\dfrac{\text{L.C.M. of } 3, 6, 9, 20.}{\text{G.C.M. of } 14, 22.}$

6. Express as the *product* of the *powers of prime factors*:
$$\frac{1, 2, 3, 4, 5, \ldots \ldots 25, 26, 27, 28.}{1^3, 3^3, \ldots \ldots 9^3, 10^3.}$$

7. (a) A boy ploughed $5 \left\{\dfrac{7\frac{1}{4} \text{ of } \frac{12}{53}}{6\frac{1}{4} - 3\frac{1}{3}}\right\}$ acres of land at 7 mills per sq. rod ; how much did he get for his work ? (b) Sold 75 sheep for what 120 sheep cost me ; what rate per cent. did I gain?

8. Simplify, as the product of the powers of the prime factors arising from :
$$\frac{1 \cdot 2 \cdot 3 \cdot 4 \ldots \ldots 17 \cdot 18 \cdot 19 \cdot 20.}{1^3 \cdot 2^5 \ldots \ldots 4^3 \cdot 5^3.}$$

9. Two wheels of a toy carriage are 3 feet, 8 inches, and 4 feet 10 inches, respectively, in circumference. How far will the carriage have gone when the smaller wheel has gained 7 revolutions on the larger?

10. The price of 60 lbs. of a mixture of black and green tea is $31.20. If the black tea costs $57\frac{3}{11}$ cents and the green tea $37\frac{1}{2}$ cents a lb., how many lbs. of each were in the mixture?

11. If 20 apples = 12 pears and 8 pears = 6 oranges, and 18 oranges = 15 lemons, and 5 doz. lemons = 2 lbs. tea, how many lbs. of tea should be exchanged for 60 doz. apples?

12. A note of $750 amounted to $759 from January 1st, to March 14th, 1892. At what rate of interest was the note drawn?

13. A regiment of 840 men walking 5 abreast and 4 feet apart, takes 13 minutes, $38\frac{2}{11}$ seconds to cross a bridge $\frac{533}{1320}$ of a mile long. If each soldier steps 80 times a minute, what is the length of each step?

Exercise V.

1. Sixty lbs. of tea at 40 cents a lb. and a certain number of lbs. at $56\frac{2}{3}$ cents a lb., averaged 50 cents a lb., when mixed together and sold. Find the total amount received for the tea.

2. At 18 mills on the dollar, a man pays $27 income tax, when 20 per cent. of his income is exempt from taxation. Find his income.

3. John Pines rents a farm for $520 a year. If he does not pay the rent for 3 years, when money is worth 5 per cent. per annum, what will be the sum due then?

4. A Canadian tourist goes to Vienna with $2500.66, which he exchanges for *florins* at 97 cents for 2 florins. He spends 176 florins in Vienna, and thence goes to Santiago, where he exchanges the remainder of his florins for *rials*, at the rate of 2 florins for 7 rials. He spends 2100 rials in Santiago, and thence goes to Paris, where he exchanges the remainder of his rials for *francs*, at the rate of 10 rials for 7 francs. He now spends 511 francs in Paris, and thence goes to Glasgow, where he exchanges the remainder of his francs for *Sterling* money at 73 francs for 55 shillings. He spends £10 in Glasgow, and then exchanges the rest of his Sterling money for Canadian money at the *ordinary rate of exchange*. How much money does he bring home after paying $73 for a ticket to Montreal?

5. A farmer has horses worth $75 each and sheep worth $15. He has 42 head in all, valued at $1470. How many sheep has he?

FIFTH CLASS.

6. A wine merchant bought 70 gallons of wine at $4 a gallon, mixed with it 14⅔ per cent. of itself of water, and then sold the mixture at $4.75 a gallon. Find his gain.

7. A and B have equal shares in a certain sum of money. A spends 60 per cent. of his share and B spends 45 per cent. of his share. Now, one-third of the difference between what they each have left is $28. Find the sum in which both together had equal shares.

8. A tank containing 45 barrels of water is emptied by a pail which holds 10 quarts, 2 pints. (a) How many full pails are removed? (b) How many quarts remain in the tank to be removed after the last full pail is taken out?

9. (a) Simplify $\{(2\frac{1}{3}+1\frac{1}{6}+3\frac{1}{2}) \div \frac{1}{4} \text{ of } \frac{8}{9} \text{ of } 1\frac{5}{9}\} \times 15$. (b) From $\frac{1}{11}$ of a certain number $\frac{7}{10}$ of $\frac{1}{3}$ of it is taken and 43 remains; what is the number?

10. A's apples are worth 3 for 5 cents, and B's pears 2 for 5 cents. Both together they have between 1½ and 2 dozens. They exchange without loss to either party. How many had each at first?

11. Sold 18 lbs., 12 ozs. of butter at 16 cents a lb., and 59109 lbs. of oats at 18¾ cents a bushel. Put the proceeds out at interest for 5 years at 5 per cent.; find the total amount due at the end of that period.

12. Spent ⅛ of my money and $5 more, then ⅝ of the remainder all but $5; after which I had still $10 left. How much had I at first?

13. Using the measure, "*25 quarts to the cubic foot*," for wheat, how many lbs. should be reckoned to the *measured* bushel to make it correct by *weight?*

Exercise VI.

1. What times after 9 o'clock are the hands of a clock 144° apart?

2. (a) Add 760, 240, 516, 829, using the *Roman symbols.*
   (b) Subtract 1725 from 2069, " " "
   (c) Multiply 42 by 95 " " "
   (d) Divide 1825 by 25 " " "

3. A farm of 100 acres runs back ⅞ of a mile across a concession; what is the farm worth at $7.42½½ *per foot frontage?*

4. It takes a boy 21 $\frac{3}{17}$ minutes to walk around a circular racecourse whose radius is 315 yards; how many miles and rods per hour does the boy walk?

5. Find the value of the land, enclosed within a circular hedgerow 1980 yards in circumference, at $88 an acre.

6. At $9.60 an acre, a circular plot of ground costs $3383.11; find the cost of enclosing it with a fence at 55 cents a rod.

7. A does ⅖ of a piece of work, and B, who works half as fast as A, finishes the work in 6 days. Find the value of the work, if A is paid $2.25 a day.

8. How long will it take a man, who travels at the rate of 2 yds., 7·2 inches per second, to complete a journey of 72 miles?

9. A weaver sold 60 per cent. of his stock of cloth at 80 cents a yard, realizing thereon $2784; he then sold the remainder at 20 per cent. advance on his former price; find his entire receipts for cloth.

10. Buy 600 bushels peas at 90 cents a bushel, payable at the end of 8 months. Sell immediately at 85 cents a bushel, and put ¾ of the proceeds out at 6 per cent. and the rest at 12 per cent. per annum. How much do I gain or lose?

11. Had a flock of sheep of which 40 more than ⅓ died; then, 50 less than ¾ of the number left strayed off and I sold ⅓ of what I had still left. I then had 20 sheep; find the original number in my flock.

12. Simplify: $\left\{ \dfrac{52 \div 3\frac{1}{4}}{\dfrac{52}{3\frac{1}{4}} \div 9\frac{3}{5} \text{ of } 4\frac{1}{16}} \times \dfrac{39}{1} \right\} \div (20\frac{3}{20} - 7\frac{1}{8} + \frac{1}{80}).$

13. If 10 bbls. of sugar of 300 lbs. each cost $4.50 a barrel, and the merchant sells it out at 20 lbs. for a dollar, find his gain per cent.

Exercise VII.

1. Had a certain sum of which I spent $2 more than ⅛ and had left $2; find the sum.

2. Had a certain sum; spent $2 more than ¼ of it on Monday, then $4 more than ¼ of the remainder on Tuesday, and had left $20; find the original sum.

3. Of a certain sum, I spent ⅔ *plus* $3; then ½ of the remainder *minus* $1, and have left $13; find the sum.

4. Have the half of my money left, after spending $5 more than $\tfrac{5}{12}$ of it; find my money at first.

5. Had a certain sum of which I spent 50 cents more than $\frac{2}{7}$; then 30 cents more than $\frac{3}{8}$ of the remainder; then 25 cents less than $\frac{1}{2}$ of what was still left. I found I had left $1. How much had I at first?

6. Annie gave away $\frac{1}{3}$ of her apples; then $\frac{5}{8}$ of the remainder; then 2 more than $\frac{3}{4}$ of what she had still left. She found that she now had 4 apples left. How many dozens had she at first?

7. Two gallons more than $\frac{1}{3}$ of all the liquid in a barrel leaked out; then $\frac{3}{8}$ of the remainder and 5 gallons more were taken out; then $\frac{1}{2}$ of the remainder all but 2 gallons evaporated; after which there were 7 gallons left in it. How many gallons of liquid were in the barrel at first?

8. Had a certain sum of which I spent $14 more than $\frac{2}{7}$; then $5 less than $\frac{3}{8}$ of the remainder; then $3 more than $\frac{1}{2}$ of what still remained. I then had left $5; how much money had I at first?

9. Bought goods for 1666\frac{2}{3}$ and sold them for 1866\frac{2}{3}$; find my gain per cent.

10. Divide the difference between $1\frac{1}{4}$ and $\frac{7}{8}$ by their sum, and multiply the quotient by 119.

11. Divide $120 between A and B, so that $\frac{3}{4}$ of A's money is $\frac{1}{2}$ of B's.

12. Out of a certain sum I take $2 more than the fifth; then $10 less than $\frac{2}{5}$ of the remainder; then, $2 less than $\frac{3}{5}$ of what still remained; after which I had left $10; find the original sum.

13. Bought 70 lbs. of green tea at 42 cents a lb., and 80 lbs. of black tea at 63$\frac{1}{4}$ cents a lb., and on selling the mixture I gained 1$\frac{1}{4}$ per cent.; find the selling price, per lb., of the mixture.

Exercise VIII.

1. A circular tank, 6 ft. 1$\frac{1}{2}$ inches in diameter, and of uniform size, is 16 ft. long; how many barrels of water will it contain?

2. Simplify: $60 \left\{ \dfrac{\frac{7}{8} \div 1\frac{1}{4} \text{ of } \frac{9}{15} \times \frac{21}{40}}{\frac{8}{9} \text{ of } \frac{3}{4} \div \frac{16}{21} \times \frac{48}{80}} \times 62\frac{2}{5} \right\} + 36.$

3. Find the exact amount (in quarts) that a bucket 14 inches in diameter, and 14 inches deep, will hold.

4. Divide $325 between A and B, so that 25 per cent. of A's share shall be equal to 40 per cent. of B's.

5. A tank is 9 feet deep, 7 ft. wide and 12½ ft. long, and is filled with water; how many barrels does it hold?   *156¼ bbl.*

6. How many barrels and gallons will a circular tank, 16 feet long and 3 ft. 6 in. in diameter, hold?

7. Spent ⅜ of a certain sum and $2 more, and had left ⅜ of the sum and $10; find the sum.

8. Find the difference between the bank discount and the true discount on $1640 due in 4 months at 7½ per cent.

9. The amount of a certain principal for a certain time at 6 per cent. is $455, and at 8 per cent., the amount is $490; find the principal and the time.

10. When 72 cwt. 15 lbs. wheat brings $144.30, what is wheat (a) per bushel? (b) per cental?

11. What must be the marked price of cloth that cost $1.50 a yard, so that the seller may reduce his price 10 per cent., and still make a profit of 20 per cent.?

12. The amount of a certain principal for certain time at 6 per cent. is $1029.50, and at 9 per cent. the amount is $1181.75; find the principal and time.

13. Divide $108 among A, B and C, so that A shall get ⅔ of B's share, and B ⅔ of C's share.

Exercise IX.

1. If $\frac{4}{7}$ of the value of a house is exempt from taxation, and $21 is the tax levied on the remainder at 4 per cent., what is the value of the house?   *925*

2. Divide $800 into two parts, so that 4 times 6 per cent. of one part shall be equal to 5 times 8 per cent. of the other.

3. Divide $64 into two parts, so that the interest on one part for 5 years at 4 per cent. shall equal the interest on the other part for 4 years at 3 per cent.

4. A chest of tea weighs 90 lbs., and a grocer puts it up into caddies of equal size; the next day he puts up an 98-pound chest into the same sized caddies, and has 13 lbs. left. If the selling price of a caddie is $10.50, what is the value of what he has left, from filling the caddie, the second day?

5. Simplify: $\left\{ \dfrac{4\frac{7}{8} \times 6\frac{3}{7} \div \dfrac{2\frac{1}{2}}{7}}{\frac{3}{4} \times \frac{9}{10} \times 2\frac{2}{3}} \times 38 \right\}$.

6. Find the quotient of the L.C.M. and G.C.M. of 30401 and 12341.

7. A's rope is 3 times $\frac{3}{4}$ of an inch $+ \frac{1}{2}$ of $\frac{2}{3}$ of a yard $+ 6\frac{5}{16}$ ft. $+2\frac{1}{2}$ yards long, and B's is 3 times as long; find the total value of their ropes at 5 mills a foot.

8. If 20 per cent. of the cost of a horse is equal to $12\frac{1}{2}$ per cent. of the selling price, find the gain per cent. at which it is sold.

9. A lodger pays his bill of $29.50 with 25-cent and 10-cent pieces. If there were 160 coins, how many of these were 25-cent pieces?

10. Pure milk is worth 32 cents a gallon, but by watering it the price is reduced to 6 cents a quart. What fraction of the milk is the water in the mixture?

11. Find the value of $\left\{ \dfrac{2\frac{1}{2}+1\frac{1}{4}-2\frac{1}{8}}{3\frac{3}{4}+2\frac{1}{3}-4\frac{1}{4}} + \dfrac{1}{44} \right\} \times \dfrac{33}{40}$ of a yard of cloth at $\$ \left\{ (2\frac{2}{3} \text{ of } 3\frac{3}{4}) \div 3\frac{3}{8} \right\}$ a yard.

12. (a) What is the *least* number which, as a co-factor of 21, will give a product which shall be a multiple of 45? (b) Which *multiple* is it?

13. The diameter of a circle is 3 miles, 77 rods, 1 yard, 1 foot, 6 inches; find the length of a *degree in the circumference* of the circle.

Exercise X.

1. Paid 40 per cent. duty on a horse, and sold it at a loss of 10 per cent.; but if I had sold it for $75.60 more, I would have gained 20 per cent. Find the cost price of the horse.

2. Six boys hired a boat for an hour, but two of them failed to pay, and the expense of each of the others was increased 15 cents. What was charged for the boat?

3. An American grain-dealer paid 20 per cent. duty on Canadian barley, and sold it to a brewer at 5 per cent. loss; but had he received $12\frac{3}{4}$ cents a bushel more for it than he did, he would have gained $12\frac{1}{2}$ per cent. Find the cost price in Canada of 835 bushels of the barley.

4. Simplify: $\left\{ \dfrac{\frac{1}{2} \text{ of } \frac{3}{8} \times \frac{1}{2} \text{ of } \frac{21}{64}}{\frac{3}{4} \div \frac{7}{10} \times \frac{3}{8} \text{ of } \frac{7}{15}} \text{ of } \frac{5}{8} \times 9\frac{1}{7} \right\} \div \frac{1}{10}$

128 EXERCISES IN ARITHMETIC.

5. Find the *sum* of *three quotients* of 37665, 76167 and 61101 and their L.C.M.

6. At 8 cents a lb., all round, C marketed 13 hogs—7 for A, averaging 450 lbs. each, and 6 for B, averaging 210 lbs. each. A, however, claimed that his hogs were worth half a cent a]b. more than B's which B allowed. C then divided the proceeds accordingly. Find the amount that each received and the *actual selling price* of each man's hogs per pound.

7. A and B, in 8 days, can finish a piece of work of which A alone did $\frac{2}{3}$ in 4 days. In what time could B, alone, have done it?

8. A coal-dealer has a bin, 23 feet long, 14 feet wide and 12 feet deep, which he fills with hard and soft coal in the ratio of 2:5 respectively. If the hard coal costs \$6.50 a ton, and the soft coal \$4.75 a ton, find the cost of filling the bin.

9. A and B have certain sums out at interest at 4 and 5 per cent. per annum, respectively, and $\frac{27}{80}$ of A's income is equal to $\frac{2}{3}$ of B's; also, the sum of their incomes is \$40.90. Find the sums out at interest.

10. A and B have certain sums out at 5 and 6 per cent., respectively, per annum and $\frac{2}{3}$ of A's income is equal to $\frac{27}{125}$ of B's; also, the difference between their incomes is \$134; find the sums out at interest.

11. How far may a person ride at 15 miles an hour, so that he may walk back at $3\frac{1}{2}$ miles an hour, and be away 7 hours, 24 minutes?

12. A and B, in 6 days, can finish a work of which A alone did $\frac{3}{10}$ in $4\frac{1}{2}$ days. In what time would B, alone, have done it?

13. Find the product of the thirteenth *multiple* of 603 and the seventh *power* of seven.

Exercise XI.

1. Find the L.C.M. of all the *composite* numbers between 204 and 220 inclusive.

2. Find the L.C.M. of all the even numbers from 67 to 81.

3. A man borrows \$72, on the first day of every month during the year, on which he pays $\frac{1}{2}$ a cent a month on every dollar he borrows How much does he owe at the end of the year?

FIFTH CLASS.

4. Find the *square root* of each of the following numbers:
   (a) 74666881.
   (b) 7045601.
   (c) 9619489541.
   (d) 499849.
   (e) 36493681.
   (f) 8071281.
   (g) 64899136.

5. Extract the *cube root* of each of the following numbers:
   (a) 129554216.
   (b) 23639903.
   (c) 94010175323.
   (d) 67419143000.

6. Find the simple interest on $155 for 2 years at 6 per cent. per annum.

7. Find the amount of $320 for 5 years at 8 per cent. simple interest.

8. What sum of money will amount to $537.60 in 8 years at $3\frac{1}{2}$ per cent., per annum, simple interest?

9. When $116 is the simple interest on $580 for 5 years, what is the rate per cent. at which it is loaned?

10. In what time will $640 amount to $768, at the rate of 4 per cent. per annum, simple interest?

11. What principal will amount to $87.60 in 4 years at 5 per cent. per annum, simple interest?

12. In what time will $154 amount to $294.14 at 7 per cent. per annum, simple interest?

13. A had $11830, B $12740, and C had $13650; they invested their money in city lots at the *highest* price per lot, so as to allow each one to invest all his money. They then sold the lots to D, gaining $5460 on the whole. Find each man's share of the gain.

Exercise XII.

1. The difference between the interest on a certain sum, at 5 per cent. for one year and at 15 per cent. for the same time, is $8.40; find the sum.

2. (a) Increase $740 by 5 per cent. of itself; (b) A has $893, after losing 6 per cent. of his income; what is his income?

3. A man's pay being increased 25 per cent., is thereby increased to $8.75 a week ; what was his former yearly salary ?

4. Divide $981 among A, B and C, giving B three times as much as A, and C twice as much as A and B together.

5. What is the least number which as a *cofactor* of 60 will give a product which shall be a *multiple* of 75 ?

6. In the expression $\frac{4}{5}$ of a lb. : (I.) What does $\frac{4}{5}$ of a lb. express? (II.) What does the 4 express? (III.) What does the 5 express? (IV.) What is the *prime* unit? (V.) Name all the *fractional* numbers in connection with the expression. (VI.) What name is applied to the numerator and denominator of a fraction? (VII.) Is a fraction a *number ?* Give reason for your answer.

7. Find the difference, in inches, between a *minute* on a circle whose circumference is 3 miles, 21 rods, 4 yards, 1 foot, 6 inches, and on one whose circumference is 4 miles, 290 rods, 5 yards.

8. One-fourth of the cost of a horse is $\frac{1}{6}$ of the selling price, and the gain at which it is sold is $180 ; find the cost of three car-loads of 17 such horses each.

9. Bought 6125 lbs. sugar at 4 cents a lb. ; paid $60.60 freight, and 1½ cents a lb. duty. I lost 4% of the entire weight in waste, and sold the remainder so as to gain $3\frac{137}{387}$ per cent. ; how many lbs. did I sell for the dollar ?

10. By how much does $\left\{\dfrac{2\frac{1}{2}+\frac{1}{8}}{3\frac{2}{3}-\frac{1}{8}}\right\}$ exceed $\left\{\dfrac{\frac{1}{4}+1\frac{1}{3}}{\frac{2}{7}+1\frac{5}{14}} \div \dfrac{\frac{1}{6}+\frac{3}{4}}{\frac{1}{3}+\frac{2}{7}}\right\}$?

11. Find the *smallest* cofactor of 3051 which will form a product that shall be a *multiple* of 2938. Which *multiple* is it ?

12. A grocer had two barrels of sugar, one weighing 350 and the other 360 lbs., which he put up into an even number of the largest sized dollar parcels. In putting up the parcels, he found that he had left 8 lbs. in the first barrel, but nothing in the second, the parcels exactly emptying it. How many lbs. did he sell for the dollar ?

13. (*a*) Find the L.C.M. of 24 and 42 by *three* different methods. (*b*) Find the G.C.M. (H.C.F.) of 96 and 240 by *three* different methods.

Exercise XIII.

1. A regiment of soldiers is billeted in three towns as follows : In the largest $\frac{3}{7}$ of the number in the smallest, and in the smallest $\frac{7}{12}$ of the whole regiment, the remaining 380 being quartered in the other town. How many men are in the regiment ?

FIFTH CLASS. 131

2. Three casks of the same size are filled with wine ; in the first cask 80 per cent. of the contents is pure ; in the second 70 per cent., and in the third 95 per cent. From the first cask 60 per cent. of the contents is withdrawn ; from the second 90 per cent. and from the third 40 per cent. What per cent. of the original contents is the pure wine now left in the three casks ?

3. If 1 lb. avoirdupois of gold be coined into £50, 8s., what weight (troy) is a sovereign ?

4. A reservoir, containing 907500 barrels of water, is emptied by a pipe, the section of which is 7 inches in diameter, and through which the water flows with a velocity of 4 miles an hour. In how many days and hours will the reservoir be emptied ?

5. What sum of money will amount to $18375.64½ in three years at 7 per cent. compound interest ?

6. A, B and C, start together from the same point, at the same time, and travel in the same direction, round an island 20 miles in circumference. A goes 4 miles an hour, B 7, and C 12. (*a*) In what time after starting will they all be *first* together again ? (*b*) At what point will this be ? (*c*) How often will each have gone round the island ?

7. Divide 31·6 by ·3̇7̇8̇ without *first* changing the decimals to vulgar fractions.

8. Find correctly to five decimal places the value of the series :
$$1 + \frac{1}{1} + \frac{1}{1\times 2} + \frac{1}{1\times 2\times 3} + \text{etc.}$$

9. A merchant bought two pieces of tweed of equal lengths containing together as many yards as it cost him cents per yard to buy it. He sold it all for $180 at a gain of 25 per cent.; find the number of yards in each piece bought, and the selling price per yard.

10. There is a rectangle whose length is 1¼ times its breadth, and which may be planked either way with planks of lengths 10, 12 or 14 ft. What is the least size of the rectangle ?

11. At what rate per cent. will $1,992 for 2½ years amount to as much as $1,660 for 8 years at 5 per cent. ?

12. A person investing in the 4½ per cents. pays ⅛ brokerage and makes 5 per cent. on his money. In what priced stock does he invest ?

13. *(a)* A conical piece of marble, the diameter of whose base is 2 ft., 4 inches, contains 7 cubic feet, 1456 cubic inches of marble. Required the altitude of the cone. *(b)* If I sell my farm for $1440 and my stock for $600, I shall gain 20 per cent. on the original cost of both; and if I sell the farm for $1710 and the stock for cost, I shall gain 30 per cent.; find the original cost of each.

Exercise XIV.

1. A bill due 4 months hence is discounted at 7 per cent. per annum (true discount) and $3801.00 is received for it. What is its face value?

2. How much money must be invested in stock at $80\frac{7}{8}$, paying an annual dividend of 5 per cent., in order to realize an income of $720 per annum, brokerage being $\frac{1}{8}$?

3. In the middle of a rectangular plot, 348 ft., $2\frac{8}{11}$ inches long by 35 ft. wide, is dug a circular pit 25 ft., 8 inches in diameter and 18 ft. deep., and the earth so removed is then spread evenly over the remainder of the plot. Find by how much the level of the plot is raised? (Area of a circle = $3\frac{1}{7} \times r.^2$).

4. Two drovers, A and B, go to a market and buy together 800 sheep at $10 a head. A takes 500 of the sheep and B the remainder; but upon examination they agree that A's sheep are worth a dollar a head more than B's. How much should each pay for the sheep?

5. If an ounce of pure gold be worth £3, 16 sh. and $\frac{7}{8}$ in weight of a gold coin be pure gold and the remainder an alloy 40 times less valuable, what is the weight of the pure gold in *(a)* a guinea? *(b)* a sovereign?

6. A license to kill game costs $20; a cartridge costs 3 cents and a sportsman kills his bird every fourth shot on an average; when birds are worth 40 cents a brace, how many must the sportsman shoot to pay expenses and buy a license for next season?

7. A speculator buys 371 sheep at $3 a head due a year hence. He immediately sells 271 of them at $2.75 per head for cash, and the remainder at $4.10 a head due in 6 months hence. How much does he gain by the transaction, money being worth 5 per cent.?

8. A snail begins to crawl 12 inches per minute, up a pole, and is followed 21 minutes afterwards by a potato-beetle, whose rate is to that of the snail as 8 is to $\cdot 9$, and they are together 2 ft. from the top of the pole. Find the length of the pole.

9. A railway train travels 40 miles an hour when it does not stop and 35 miles an hour including stoppages. In what distance will the train be 45 minutes late on account of stoppages?

10. A contractor agreed to do a certain work in 6 days. He employed 2 men and 3 boys who did $\frac{3}{5}$ of the work in 4 days. He then put on two more men and one more boy and $\frac{4}{15}$ more of the work was done the next day. He now took off all the men, and employed enough boys to finish the contract on time. How many additional boys were employed the last day?

11. Simplify :— $11 \times \left\{ \frac{9}{28} \text{ of } \dfrac{6 - 1\frac{4}{9}}{3\frac{1}{3} + 2\frac{1}{4}^{\frac{3}{4}}} \text{ of } \dfrac{13\frac{5}{11}}{35\frac{1}{4}} \right) \text{ of } \left(\dfrac{2 \cdot \frac{4}{5}}{4 \cdot 5} \div \dfrac{\frac{2}{\cdot 5}}{1 \cdot 4 + 1 \cdot \dot{4} + 1 \cdot \dot{4}} \right\}$ of 182250 farthings.

12. A garden contains 38,419,920 square inches, and its length is 35 rods. How wide is it? *28 rds*

13. I take 210 steps in walking round the four sides of a rectangular lawn; find the area of the lawn, if 6 steps are equivalent to 5 yards and the shorter side takes 48 steps. *1900 sq. yd.*

Exercise XV.

1. A clock loses 10 seconds every 12 minutes and is set right at 6 a.m., what will be the true time when the clock indicates 5.50 p.m.?

2. A watch loses 36 seconds in 10 minutes, and is set right at 10 o'clock a.m.; what will be the true time when the hands are coincident between 6 and 7 p.m.?

3. A clock which gains 10 seconds in 15 min., is set right at 6 a.m.; what will be the true time when the clock indicates 9·10 p.m.?

4. What is the second time after 4 o'clock that the second hand is midway between the hour and minute hands on a clock having 3 hands all moving about the same centre?

5. What is the first time 5 o'clock when the second hand is midway between the other two hands on a clock with a minute, a second and an hour hand all moving about the same centre?

6. At what time after 9 o'clock will the hour hand be midway between the other two, on a clock having three hands all moving about the same centre?

7. What is the first time after one o'clock that the minute hand is midway between the other two, on a clock with three hands—a minute, a second, and an hour—all moving around the same centre?

8. At what time after two o'clock will the minute hand be first midway between the second and hour hands on a clock, on which there are three hands all revolving round the same centre?

9. At what times after 8 o'clock are the hands of a watch 10 minutes apart?

10. A person started at half-past two in the afternoon and walked to a village, arriving there when the village clock indicated a quarter past three. After staying in the village 25 minutes, he drove home by a road one-fourth as long again, at a rate twice as fast as he had walked, and reached home at 4 o'clock p.m. How much was the village clock wrong?

11. A man left home at 3 o'clock p.m. for a village, arriving there when the village clock pointed to 4.30 p.m. After staying 20 minutes in the village, he returned home by a road ⅓ longer than the one by which he went, and at a rate twice as fast as he went, arriving at home at 6 o'clock p.m. How much was the village clock wrong?

12. A man left home at 2 o'clock p.m. and walked to a village, arriving there when the village clock indicated 4 o'clock p.m. After staying in the village 15 minutes, he returned home by another road, which was half as long again, at a rate three times as fast as he went, and arrived at home at 4.30 p.m. How far was it to the village, if his rate in was 6 miles an hour?

13. At what time after 7 o'clock are the hands of a watch 13 minutes apart?

Exercise XVI.

1. Tea at 50 cents a lb. is mixed with 4 lbs. at 70 cents a lb. and 20 per cent. is gained by selling the mixture at 68 cents a lb. How many lbs. of fifty-cent tea were in the mixture?

2. Sold sugar at $9\frac{1}{5}$ cents a lb., gaining thereby $14\frac{2}{7}$ per cent. of the sales. Find my gain per cent. on cost when the selling price is 10 cents a lb.

3. The road between two villages, A and B, 9 miles apart, is over a mountain, the summit of which is $3\frac{1}{2}$ miles from A, and two persons set out from A and B at the same time, the former walking at the rate of 2 miles an hour up hill and 5 miles an hour down, and the latter 3 miles an hour up hill and 6 miles an hour down. How far from B will they meet?

4. Bought a piece of cloth at $4.50 a yard. It shrank $16\frac{2}{3}$ per cent. in length. Sold it at $7.20 a yard; find my gain per cent. on the whole.

5. A bought an article for $40 and sold it to B at a certain gain per cent., B sold it to C, C to D, and D disposed of it for $82.944. If each gained the same percentage on what the article cost him, find that percentage.

6. A's capital, B's capital and C's capital are to one another as the numbers 3, 4 and 5; and A's time is to B's time as 5:6. A's gain is $700 and C's gain is $900. Find (a) ratio of B's time to C's time, and (b) B's gain.

7. A holds a note against B at 9 months, drawing interest at 8 per cent. per annum. C buys the note at a discount of 5 per cent. off the face of the note. What per cent. per annum does C make on the money invested?

8. At what rate per cent. discount on the face of a note must a broker buy notes bearing interest at 10 per cent. in order to make 25 per cent. on his investment?

9. I sell 40 lbs. of tea at a gain of 25 per cent., and 50 lbs. at a gain of $12\frac{1}{2}$ per cent. Had I sold the whole lot at a gain of 10 per cent., I would have received $2.90 less than I did. What was the cost price per lb?

10. The cost at 14 cents a square yard is $479.16 for gravelling a circular plot. Find the diameter in rods. *12*

11. If the specific gravity of silver is 10·5, and a silver ball 1 ft., 9 in., in diameter is to be considered, find (a) its weight in lbs. and ozs., and (b) its surface in square feet and inches.

12. A fruit-dealer bought a quantity of cherries, apples and grapes, paying for the whole $120.00. The grapes cost him 60 per cent. as much as the cherries, and the apples cost him $44\frac{4}{9}$ per cent. as much as the apples and cherries together. How much did each kind of fruit cost him?

13. A man bought a hide of leather in the United States, and smuggled it across into Canada, where he sold it, gaining $15. Had he paid the import duty of 15 per cent., he would have gained in selling it, $19\frac{13}{20}$ per cent. of the cost to import into Canada. What did it cost him in the United States?

Exercise XVII.

1. Sold a coat for $20, losing thereby 20 per cent. of the proceeds. From this find the cost of 40 dozen coats. *$115.20*

2. A horse cost $6\frac{2}{3}$ times as much as a saddle. By selling the saddle at $11\frac{1}{4}$ per cent. *loss* and the horse at $11\frac{1}{4}$ per cent. *gain*, $224 is realized. Find the cost of the horse. *$150*

3. I take 1452 steps in going round a field in the form of a rectangle. Find the area of the field, in acres and sq. rods, if $6\frac{3}{5}$ steps are equivalent to a rod, and the longer side takes 396 steps.

4. An excursion party of men, women and children purpose going on an excursion, agreeing to pay expenses in ratio, 5:3:2 ; but on account of 10 men, 5 women and 15 children being absent, the ratio of expenses was 10:3:2. How many children purposed going on the excursion, if the whole party who purposed going numbered 90 ? How many children went ?

5. Sold tea at 9 lbs. for a certain sum and gained thereby 50 per cent. I afterwards reduced the gain on tea to $33\frac{1}{3}$ per cent. How many lbs. did I give for that sum ?

6. A person discounts a note due in 15 months so as to make 10 per cent. per annum on his money. What rate per cent. on the face of the note does he exact ?

7. The true discount on a sum of money for one year, at $7\frac{1}{2}$ per cent. is $40. Find the true discount on the same sum at $3\frac{1}{8}$ per cent. for the same time ?

8. Bought cloth at $4 in gold, and sold it at $6 in currency. Did I gain or lose and how much per cent., gold being at 120 ?

9. I received an eight per cent. dividend on railroad stock, purchased at 20 per cent. discount. What per cent. did my investment pay ?

10. How many bricks 9 inches long, $4\frac{1}{2}$ inches broad, and 4 inches thick, will be required for a wall 30 feet long, 20 feet high, and 4 feet thick, allowing the mortar to make up one-sixteenth of the entire wall ? By what per cent. does the mortar increase the volume of each brick ?

11. A company of boys is met by A who gives each boy 25 cents. Afterwards they are joined by 4 more boys and the money equally divided among all the boys, who are then met by B and he gives each boy 25 cents. The boys are then joined by 10 others and the money again equally divided among them, when it is found that each boy has 20 cents. Had all these boys been met by A his donation, divided equally among them, would have been $7\frac{1}{2}$ cents each. How many boys did A meet ?

12. Two numbers are to each other as 13:17, and their sum is 16230 ; find the numbers.

13. For what must I insure property at $1\frac{7}{8}$ per cent. to cover a loss of $4710 ?

FIFTH CLASS. 137

Exercise XVIII.

1. From a uniform cylindrical water-tank, 14 feet in diameter and standing vertically upright, water is drawn, till the surface is lowered 3 feet, 4 inches. Find the number of gallons removed, given that a quart is 60 cubic inches.

2. Into how many *equal* parts must $\cdot 6$ of $3.3 + \dfrac{1.75}{2.625}$ of $17 + \cdot 4$ of $5 \cdot 75$ be divided, so that 13 of such parts may amount to $10 \cdot 83$?

3. Find the L.C.M. of all the *even* numbers between 167 and 181.

4. A contractor employs 5 men to dig a ditch in 40 days, each man doing an average day's work ; but he finds that only one of his men does an average day's work and that two of them do respectively $\frac{1}{4}$ and $\frac{1}{5}$ *less*, and the other two respectively $\frac{1}{10}$ and $\frac{3}{20}$ *more* than an average day's work. How many men, doing an average day's work each, must he employ the 40th day in order to complete the contract on time ?

5. A merchant in Montreal, who wishes to transmit 400 pistoles to Malaga, finds that direct exchange from Montreal on Malaga is \$3.65 for 1 pistole, and that circuitous exchange from Montreal on Malaga, through London and Paris, is as follows :   From Montreal on London \$4.86 for £1 Sterling; from London on Paris $25\frac{1}{4}$ francs for £1 Sterling, and from Paris to Malaga 19 francs for 1 pistole. What course of exchange should he adopt ?

6. How much water must be added to a mixture of 55 gallons of wine $\frac{19}{20}$ pure, to make the mixture 80 per cent. pure ?

7. A feed merchant mixes 40 bushels of oats at 35 cents a bushel, 20 bushels of rye at 60 cents a bushel, with 10 bushels of bran at 15 cents a bushel, and grinds it all together into chop. If the bran decrease 10 per cent. and the rest of the mixture increase 10 per cent. in the grinding, what will be the value and what the weight, by measure, of a bushel of the chop ?

8. A cask contains 7 parts brandy and 5 parts water ; $\dfrac{20\frac{1}{2}}{144}$ of the mixture is now drawn off and it is filled with water ; what is the strength of the mixture then ?

9. A person had a certain capital, $\frac{1}{4}$ of which he invested in 3 per cents. at 90, and the remainder in the $5\frac{1}{2}$ per cents at 110. What was his capital, if his total income is \$286 ?

138   EXERCISES IN ARITHMETIC.

10. The difference between the bank and true discount on a certain sum of money for 5 years at 6 per cent. per annum is $76.05. What is the sum?

11. Divide $720 between A and B, giving A 66⅔ per cent. of both shares.

12. The area of an ellipse is 308 sq. inches, and its major axis is 2 ft., 4 in. Find its minor axis.

13. How many balls, each 7 inches in diameter, can be made from a piece of lead 14 inches long, 11 inches wide and 7 inches thick?

Exercise XIX.

1. A dealer sent his agent to sell 500 bushels of pease at 90 cents a bushel and 800 bushels barley at 60 cents a bushel. The agent sold the pease at $1, and the barley at 75 cents a bushel, took his commission of 2½ per cent. and paid expenses of $30.90, remitting the balance. What per cent. profit did the dealer realize?

2. Find the cost of enclosing a circular park whose area is 85 acres, 99 sq. rods, 21 sq. yds., 5 sq. ft., 130½ sq. inches, with fencing at 65 cents a rod. ($\pi = 3\frac{1}{7}$.)

3. What would a dishonest dealer gain per cent. by using a weight 15 ozs. to the lb.?

4. Water rises 9 inches per hour, in a circular tank 28 ft. in diameter. If the water stand 2 ft., 9 inches deep in the tank, and a pump which empties 1000 cubic feet per hour be set in motion, in what time will the tank be empty?

5. Which is the better investment, to pay $8125, for a farm, due 5 years hence, or to pay $6200 cash, money being worth 6 per cent. per annum?

6. I sold a quantity of Bank of Commerce Stock at 120 and invested in Montreal Bank Stock at 88 which I afterwards sold at 90, and repurchasing my Bank of Commerce Stock which had risen to 125, I found I had lost $180 by the operation. How much Bank of Commerce Stock had I at first?

7. Divide $1875 among A, B, C, D and E, giving D $190 more than E, C $295 less than E and D, B $10 less than E, and A $235 more than B and C together.

8. How many cords of stone will be required to curb 96 circular wells, each 5 ft. 10 inches in diameter, and 30 ft. deep, the thickness of the curb being 1 ft., 2 in.?

FIFTH CLASS.

9. A person sells out $5000 stock in the three per cents. at 96 and invests in Bank stock at 75, which pays an annual dividend of 2½ per cent. What is his increase in income?

10. Divide $2080 among five men, seven women and fourteen boys, so that each woman may have ⅘ of a man's share and each boy ⅔ of a woman's share.

11. At what rate per cent. discount on the face of a note must a broker buy notes bearing interest at 8 per cent. per annum, so as to make 20 per cent. on his investment?

12. A man's income is derived from $4500 at a certain rate per cent., and $7300 at 2 per cent. more than the former rate. His whole income is $1090. Find the rates.

13. (a) By selling tea which cost a certain price per lb. a merchant gains 12½ per cent. of the proceeds. He now raises his selling price to $1.00 a lb., by which he gains $36 on the sale of eighty-four dollars' worth of tea. Find the original cost price per lb. (b) Four per cent. of A multiplied by b is greater than A by 450; and 6 per cent. of A multiplied by $\frac{b}{10}$ is less than A by 315; find A.

Exercise XX.

1. How much money must be invested in the 5 per cents. at 80, brokerage 1 per cent., in order to give an income of $460 after deducting an income tax of 4½ cents in the dollar?

2. A person sells out $4600 stock in the 4 per cents. at 92, and invests in the 3½ per cents., gaining thereby $40 per annum by a change in his income. At what price did he purchase the latter stock?

3. If ·36 of a farm be worth $1600, what is the value of 7·2 of it?

4. C's daily wages are $1.20, and he receives $17 for finishing a piece of work at which A and B had worked together for 5 days; find the sum paid A, B and C for the work, given that A and B together can earn as much in 6 days as C can earn alone in 19 days.

5. How many lbs. of tea at 45 cents, 60 cents and 90 cents a lb. must be taken to form a mixture of 500 lbs., worth 75 cents a lb.?

6. Simplify $\frac{5}{8}(4\frac{1}{4}+3\frac{3}{5})$ of a £ + $\dfrac{\frac{1}{2}-\frac{1}{7} \text{ of } \frac{3}{4}}{\frac{1}{3} \text{ of } 3\cdot\dot{4}+\frac{5 9}{8 1}}$ of ·8̇3 of 15 sh. + 5·5̇71428̇d.

7. A store-room will hold 16⅔ bales of cotton and 20 casks of rum; but 13¼ bales and 2 casks will fill ½ of it. How many casks would alone fill it?

8. If the true discount on $187 for 2 years be $17, in how many years would the true discount on $429 be $169 at the same rate?

9. A crew can row from A to B, with the stream, in 2 hours, and it can row from B to A, against the stream, in 4 hours. Compare the rates of the boat and stream.

10. A bucket begins to descend into a mine at the same time that another begins to ascend from the bottom. The bucket at the top reaches the bottom 8¾ minutes, and the bucket at the bottom reaches the top 16⅔ minutes, after passing each other. What time was occupied by each in performing the distance?

11. What is the difference in cost of fencing two estates of 4000 acres each, one in the form of a square, and the other in the form of a rectangle whose sides are as 16 : 9, the fence costing 37½ cents a rod?

12. A merchant sends his agent $9009 in flour to sell on a commission of 3⅓ per cent. and instructs him furthermore to invest the balance in apples on a commission of 5 per cent. Find his total commission, and the number of barrels, at $2 per barrel, sent the merchant?

13. Forty-nine pieces of lead, each 1¾ inches thick, and in the form of an ellipse whose major and minor axis are respectively 2 ft. 11 in., and 1 ft. 9 in., are melted and re-cast into balls, each 3½ inches in diameter. Find the number of balls re-cast.

Exercise XXI.

1. A man leaves home at 4 o'clock p.m., to walk to a town where he arrives at 6.15 p.m., by the town clock. After staying in town 1½ hours, he again starts for home at a rate *4 times faster* than he went and along a road twice as long as the former, arriving at home as the clock there indicated 9.15 p.m. Find (*a*) how much the town clock was wrong ; (*b*) the distance to town, supposing his rate in going to town was 4 miles an hour.

2. A man bought a quantity of oats at 40 cents a bushel, and three times as many pease at 60 cents a bushel, paying altogether $55, which was $5 more than he would have paid had he bought the whole quantity at 50 cents a bushel. How many bushels of pease did he get?

3. A gives B 9 yds. the start in a race of 108 yards. B gives C 12 yds. the start in the same distance. How many yds. could A give C in a race of 216 yards?

FIFTH CLASS.   141

4. A pump, which stood still 3 minutes in 15 min., occupied 12 hours in draining a cellar 40 ft. by 30 ft. If the water rose 9 inches per hour in the cellar and the pump emptied 1500 cubic ft. per hour while working, how deep was the water in the cellar when the pump was *first* set in motion?

5. How long will it take a train $\frac{1}{16}$ of a mile long, going at the rate of 10 miles an hour, to cross a bridge 2 miles 80 rods long?

6. Three-two-hundred-and-fiftieths of one-fifth of a number is $\frac{2}{5}$ of 100. What is the number?

7. Reduce $\frac{23}{24}$ to a decimal, by the *contracted* method.

8. A does $\frac{1}{2}$ of a piece of work; B, $\frac{2}{3}$ of the remainder; C, $\frac{3}{4}$ of what was then left; and D the rest. How should $306.60, which was given for the work, be fairly divided among them?

9. By lending a sum of money at 5 per cent. and another sum at 4 per cent. the total interest is $60. But, if the sums are interchanged, the interest is $61.50. Find the two sums lent.

10. A and B agree to have a piece of work finished in 15 days; but A being delayed 5 days after B started to work at it, the work was prolonged $1\frac{2}{3}$ days. How should $56.70 which was paid for the work be fairly divided between them?

11. If $\frac{2}{3}$ of $(x + \frac{2}{3}$ of $x) = \frac{1}{4}$ of $(y - \frac{1}{5}$ of $y)$, find x in terms of y.

12. Simplify: $\left\{ \frac{3}{4} + \dfrac{\frac{1}{2}}{\dfrac{3\frac{1}{4}}{4} \cdot 06\frac{2}{3}} + .247\frac{17}{15} \right\}$ of $\dfrac{6 \dot{\cdot} 6}{8 \dot{\cdot} 8} \times 1\frac{1}{4}$.

13. (a) A man has two kinds of gin. The first is worth 80 cents a gallon more than the second, and 5 pints of the second are worth 4 pints of the first. Find the price of a gallon of each kind. (b) The rate of a man's rowing is 3 times the rate of the stream on which he rows, and he can row 10 miles down stream and up again in 3 hours. Find his rate of rowing, and the rate of the stream.

Exercise XXII.

1. Twelve turkeys and 12 geese cost together, $24.60, and the turkeys cost 45 cents each more than the geese. Find the value of a score of turkeys.

2. The radius of the inner circle of a race-course is 122 yards, and the course covers an area of 14 acres, 154 sq. yards. Find the width of the track. *25 yds.*

3. The height of a room is half the width and its compass is 120 feet. Find the number of yards of paper, 21 inches wide, required to cover its walls, given that 5 per cent. of the area is allowed for windows and doors, and that the length of the room is to the width as 3 : 2.

4. A cylinder, 24 inches long, fitted with a piston at one end, and with a valve at the other end, which opens with a pressure of 60 lbs. to the square inch, has, on its inner surface, 20 lbs. pressure to the square inch on starting the piston ; how far must the piston be forced into the cylinder to open the valve if the pressure of compressed air varies inversely as the space it occupies?

5. A farmer buys 7 shares in a cheese factory at $60 a share ; at the end of the second year stock rises to $70 a share, and he sells out *one* share ; the stock now falls $5 a share each succeeding year, and he sells out a share each year till all his stock is thus disposed of, when he finds he has neither gained nor lost. What per cent. interest on investment did the factory pay?

6. A cylindrical vat 9 feet in diameter and 4 feet, 8 inches deep, contains 1856·25 gallons. How many cubic inches are equivalent to a gallon?

7. What fraction of an angle of a regular hexagon is an angle of an equilateral triangle?

8. A person wishes to cover a piece of ground 60 feet square by a pyramidal tent 40 feet in perpendicular height. What will the canvas required cost him at 21 cents a square yard?

9. A pyramid of lead, altitude 3 feet, and having a regular hexagon for its base, each side being $4\sqrt{3}$ inches, is melted and re-cast into balls, each $\frac{3}{4}$ of an inch in diameter. Find (a) the number of balls cast and (b) the weight, in ozs., of the portion of lead left after casting the last ball, if the specific gravity of the lead is 13·6. ($\pi = 3\frac{1}{7}$).

10. A merchant in Minneapolis sends his agent in Halifax a consignment of flour which he sells at $6 a barrel on a commission of $1\frac{1}{2}$ per cent. and invests the proceeds in National Bank Stock at $114\frac{1}{4}$ on a commission of $\frac{3}{4}$ per cent. If the National Bank Stock pay $11\frac{1}{2}$ per cent. yearly dividends, and his first dividend be $1684.35, find the number of barrels of flour shipped from Minneapolis.

11. A boy swims two miles *down* a stream and *up* again in 2 hours, 40 minutes. His rate of swimming in still water is twice as great as that of the stream. Find his rate of swimming in still water.

12. How many balls, each 7 inches in diameter, can be made from a piece of lead 14 inches long, 11 inches wide, and 7 inches thick?

13. A offers $34364 for a farm, half of the purchase money to be paid in three years, and the balance in three years afterwards; B offers $25680, half cash, and the balance in one year. Which offer should be accepted, money being worth 7 per cent. per annum?

Exercise XXIII.

1. On a vessel from San Francisco to Melbourne, the cabin passengers were one-third the number of steerage passengers, but 20 more cabin passengers were taken on board at Aukland, when it was found that the cabin passengers were to the steerage passengers as 5:14. Find the number on board when the vessel reached Melbourne.

2. A cylindrical tank, 7 feet in diameter and 25 feet long, is filled with coal-oil; how many gallons, quarts and pints does it contain?

3. A merchant sends his agent pork to sell on a commission of 2 per cent. with instructions to invest the net proceeds in tea at $14 a box, after deducting his commission of $3\frac{3}{4}$ per cent. for buying. How many boxes of tea does the merchant receive, both commissions being $357?

4. A and B enter into partnership, their capitals being in the ratio of 7:9. After three months A withdraws a part of his capital so that the ratio is as 2:3. At the end of the year A's share of the profit is $1500. Find the whole profit and B's share thereof.

5. A customer bought, as he supposed, the value of $24.80 in tea from his grocer who used a weight $15\frac{1}{2}$ ozs. for a lb. (a) What did the grocer gain on the sale? (b) What did the customer lose on his purchase?

6. A tank, $3\frac{1}{2}$ feet in diameter and 4 feet deep, had 45 inches of water in it. It became frozen to the depth of 9 inches; the water was then drawn off by a tap in the bottom of the tank, and the ice allowed to melt. Given that water expands 10 per cent. in freezing into ice, find the number of gallons of water in the melted ice, half a gill being lost, by evaporation, during the process of melting.

7. How many cubic yards of clay will be required to make 630 sections of six-inch sewerage tile each 14 inches in diameter (external measurement) and 10 feet long? ($\pi = 3\frac{1}{7}$).

8. Find the cost of making an enclosed box, 12 ft. 6 in. long, 4 ft. 2 in. wide, and 2 ft. 6 inches deep, with inch lumber at $24 a thousand.

9. Simplify $\dfrac{6\frac{1}{5} - 3\frac{2}{3}}{6\frac{1}{5} + 3\frac{1}{3}} + \dfrac{1\frac{7}{8}}{11\frac{1}{4}}$ of $2 + \frac{1}{3}$ of $\dfrac{\frac{1}{2}}{6\frac{1}{2}}$.

10. A tank 3½ feet in diameter and 4 feet deep, has 45 inches of water standing in it. Suppose it to freeze over with ice to the depth of 9 inches, what will be the weight of the ice in the tank if ice is $\frac{19}{20}$ as heavy as water?

11. A commission merchant sells 500 bbls. salt at $1.40 a barrel on a commission of 1¾ per cent.; what does he remit?

12. A's cattle are ⅞ less in number than B's, but are 12½ per cent. better in grade. If B's herd numbers 357 head worth $72 each, what is the value of A's herd?

13. Find the volume of the frustum of a cone whose vertical height is 12 inches; the diameter of the larger base of frustum being 28 inches and the diameter of the smaller base being 21 inches.

Exercise XXIV.

1. Prove the correctness of the following statements:

PRINCIPAL.	RATE.	TIME.	SIMPLE INTEREST.	TRUE DISCOUNT.
$72	6¼%	2 yrs.	$9.	$8.
$560	7⅐%	2 yrs.	$80.	$70.
$1200	3⅓%	1 yr.	$40.	$30.
$900	16⅔%	⅔ yr.	$100.	$90.
$2200	5%	5 yrs.	$550.	$440.
$720	25%	1 yr.	$180.	$144.

2. Find the SIMPLE INTEREST on the *true discount* in each of the foregoing examples for the given time at the given rate per cent., and in each case show that the interest is equal to the *difference* between the *simple interest* and the *true discount*, as given in the foregoing table.

3. From the last example in question No. 1 show that:

(a) The Simple Interest = ¼ of the Principal.

(b) The True Discount = $\dfrac{1}{1+4}$ of the Principal.

(c) The *difference* between Sim. Int. and T. Dis = $\dfrac{1}{4 \times 5}$ of the Principal.

(d) The Interest on the T. Discount = $\dfrac{1}{4 \times 5}$ of the Principal.

(e) The Simple Interest is greater than True Discount by Simple Interest on the True Discount.

FIFTH CLASS.

4. Reduce the Simple Interest, in each case in question No. 1, to the fraction of the Principal, and from this fraction form the fraction which the True Discount is of the Principal in each case.

5. (a) Prove the correctness of the following:

SIMPLE INTEREST.				TRUE DISCOUNT.			
PRINCIPAL.	RATE.	TIME.	INTEREST.	PRINCIPAL.	RATE.	TIME.	DISCOUNT.
$288	5%	4 yrs.	$57.60	$288	5%	4 yrs.	$48
$144	5%	4 yrs.	$28.80	$144	5%	4 yrs.	$24
$144	5%	7 yrs.	$50.40	$144	5%	4 yrs.	$24
$144	10%	7 yrs.	$100.80	$144	10%	4 yrs.	41\frac{1}{7}$
$144	5%	14 yrs.	$100.80	$144	5%	4 yrs.	$24
$144	5%	2 yrs.	$14.40	$144	5%	2 yrs.	13\frac{1}{11}$

(b) Show that Simple Interest *is proportional* to PRINCIPAL, RATE or TIME.

(c) Show that True Discount *is proportional* to PRINCIPAL when RATE and TIME *remain unaltered.*

(d) Show that True Discount *is not proportional* to RATE or TIME.

6. (a) If the simple interest on a certain sum be $\frac{3}{20}$ of the principal, what fraction of the principal would represent the true discount.

(b) Given that $405 is the true discount on $3105 for 1½ yrs. at 10 per cent. per annum, find the interest without working out as a question in interest.

7. The simple interest on $420 is $21. Find (a) the true discount; (b) the difference between the simple interest and true discount; and (c) the interest on the true discount.

8. If the simple interest on $7272 for a certain time at a certain rate, be $909, what is the true discount on same sum for the same time at the same rate?

9. In what time will $650 gain $241.80 if, at the same rate, the gain on $750 for one year and 146 days is $63? What is the rate per cent. per annum charged? (365 days=a year).

10. If the true discount on $460 for a certain time at 13 per cent. is $260, what is the true discount on same sum for one fifth of that time at same rate per cent.?

11. If the true discount on $743.40 for $2\frac{1}{4}$ years is $113.40, in how many years will the discount on $570 be $70, at half the rate?

12. If the true discount on $1089 at 3 per cent. be $189, at what rate per cent. would the true discount on $1150 be $150 for $\frac{2}{3}$ of the time?

13. If the true discount on $210 for 4 years at 4 per cent. be $40, on what sum would $80 be the true discount for same time at same rate?

Exercise XXV.

1. Simplify : $\left\{ 3.875 \text{ of } 3\cdot\dot{5} \times 5\cdot\dot{0}\dot{3} \div \dfrac{3\cdot0\dot{3}}{3\cdot0\dot{5}} \times \dfrac{549}{62} \right\}$ of $\dfrac{\dot{6}\cdot\dot{3}}{2\cdot\frac{1}{4}}$ of $1\frac{1}{11}$.

2. If 13 hours are required for travelling a given distance at a given rate, what will be required when the distance is diminished by $\frac{3}{8}$ and the rate increased by 225 per cent.?

3. In what proportion must a grocer mix sugars which cost respectively, 6, 8, 16 and 19 cents a lb., in order that he may realize a profit of 30 per cent. by selling the mixture at 13 cents a lb.?

4 Bought 2 horses for $200. Sold them again gaining 5 per cent. on the second, and losing 5 per cent. on the first. If I gained on the whole transaction one per cent., find the cost price of each horse.

5. What will it cost to make a gravel walk, 7 ft. 6 inches wide, along the sides of a square field containing 2 acres, 80 sq. rods, at $37\frac{1}{2}$ cents a square yard, the walk being part of the field? *404.20*

6. Divide $870 among A, B and C, so that $\cdot75$ of C's share $= \cdot 5$ of A's share, $= \cdot\dot{6}$ of B's share.

7. I intended to gain 20 per cent. on a stock of tea and fixed my price accordingly; after selling $\frac{2}{3}$ of the stock I was obliged to reduce my price 5 cents per lb., and gained $\frac{13}{15}$ as much as I had intended. What was the original cost price of the tea per lb.?

8. A speculator sells out $5000 stock of the 3 per cents. at 96, and invests the proceeds in bank stock at 75, which pays an annual dividend of $2\frac{1}{2}$ per cent. What is his increase in income?

9. A train has 380 miles to run. After running 200 miles, its rate is reduced one-seventh, and it arrives $51\frac{3}{7}$ minutes behind time. Find its first rate of running.

FIFTH CLASS. 147

10. Owing a man $538.05, I gave him a sixty-day note; what must be the face of the note to pay him the exact debt when discounted at the bank at ten per cent. per annum? (Days of grace allowed, and 365 days — a year.)

11. Eighty lbs. of sea water contain 8 lbs. of salt. Find how much fresh water must be added so that 100 lbs. of the mixture shall contain 4 lbs. of salt.

12. The sum of two numbers added to the sum of their squares is 922, and their product is 400. Find the numbers.

13. Find the number of yards of ribbon, one inch wide, it will take to wind the surface of a cone 14 inches in diameter, and slant height 12 feet.

Exercise XXVI.

1. A grain buyer made a profit of $4\frac{44}{5}$ per cent. on a shipment of 500 bushels of wheat at $1.15, and 1275 bushels of barley at 75 cents a bushel, which he shipped his agent to sell on a commission of $2\frac{1}{2}$ per cent. The agent sold the wheat at $1.30 a bushel, and the barley at 80 cents a bushel, and paid $28.25 for expenses, remitting the balance. Find his remittance.

2. What is the rate per cent. discount on the face of a note, which a broker buys, bearing interest at 10 per cent. per annum, so as to make 25 per cent. on his investment?

3. There are two sums of money, one being 4 times the other, discounted, (true dis.), the smaller sum for two years and 6 months at 4 per cent. per annum, and the larger for 3 years and 4 months at 6 per cent. The sum of the present worths is $1400. Find the original sums.

4. Two sums of money, one being three times the other, are discounted (true discount), the smaller at 8 per cent. per annum for 9 months, and the other at 6 per cent. per annum for 4 months. The sum of the present worths is $10,500. Find the sums.

5. I shipped my agent 500 bbls. flour, with instructions to sell the flour on a commission of 2 per cent. and to invest the balance in tea after deducting his commission of $1\frac{1}{2}$ per cent. for buying. Find the price at which he sold the flour, his whole commission being $72.10.

6. The true discount on a certain sum of money for a certain time at a certain rate per cent. is $230, and the simple interest on the same sum, for the same time and at the same rate is $240. Find the sum.

7. If the simple interest on a certain sum for a certain time be $\frac{1}{10}$ of the sum, what fraction of the sum will represent the true discount? (Apply the principle involved here to the following questions in the exercise.) (See Ex. IX and 8th Ques. for another example.)

8. Sold a horse for $270, *gaining* thereby $7\frac{11}{27}$ per cent. of the proceeds. What fractional part of the cost did I gain?

9. Sold a coat for $30, *losing* thereby $33\frac{1}{3}$ per cent. of the selling price; what per cent. of the cost did I lose?

10. Sold a horse, gaining $64, which was as much per cent. as the horse cost me; what was the selling price of the horse?

11. Sold a horse for $280, gaining thereby $14\frac{2}{7}$ per cent. of the proceeds. Find my gain per cent. on cost had I sold him for $250.

12. If a kiln-dried piece of wood expands 4 per cent. in being water-soaked, what per cent. will it again contract on being kiln-dried? Prove your answer to be correct by taking a block of kiln-dried wood, measuring 650 cubic inches.

13. (a) If the bank discount on $1680, for a certain time at a certain rate, be $210, what would be the true discount on same sum for the same time at the same rate? (b) A, B and C can do a piece of work in $4\frac{4}{5}$ days working together. B does $\frac{2}{3}$ as much as A, and C does $\frac{5}{8}$ as much as B when they work together. How long will it take C alone to do it?

Exercise XXVII.

1. A shed in the shape of the letter L covers an area of 13 square rods, 28 square yards, 8 square feet, 108 square inches. It is 20 feet wide, and the shorter side measures 60 feet in length (measured from the angular point of the L); find the length of the longer side from same point.

2. A drover spent $\frac{1}{8}$ of his money in buying hogs, $\frac{3}{5}$ of the remainder in buying cattle, and the rest in buying sheep. If the hogs and cattle together cost him $375 more than the sheep, what had he invested?

3. Express in the form of a vulgar fraction the average of $\frac{1}{8}$, $\frac{\frac{7}{8}}{3\frac{2}{3}}$, ·4, ·$3\frac{1}{8}$, $4\frac{5}{8}$, ·$16\frac{2}{3}$, ·$001\frac{1}{2}$.

4. Find the L.C.M. of $17\frac{1}{2}$, $13\frac{3}{4}$, and $15\frac{5}{8}$.

5. On property worth $5000 a premium of $40 is paid on the policy. Find the rate per cent. of insurance. How many cents is it on the $100?

6. Ten men, 15 women and 20 boys earn $360 in a week, working in a certain factory. The boys earn each 75 cents a day, and a woman gets ⅓ as much as a man. Find the weekly wages of the men. $180

7. The perimeter of a semi-circle is 234 yards; find its diameter. 91

8. (a) Reduce ⅖ of an hour to the decimal of a week; (b) Reduce one day to the decimal of a week; (c) What determines the *kind* of a decimal? (d) How many kinds of decimals are there?

9. A person invests a certain sum (gold) in U. S. 6's, 10–30 which are at 10 per cent. discount, and six times as much in U. S. 9's, 5–40 which are at a premium of 21½ per cent., the interest on both being payable in gold, when gold is at a premium of 21½ per cent. What did the sureties cost him, the income from both being $2070?

10. The perimeter of a field is ·9 of a mile, and it is five times as long as it is wide; find the cost of seeding it with wheat worth 88 cents a bushel, when 2 bushels, 10 lbs. are sown per acre. 34.32

11. A publisher printed an edition of 1000 copies of a quarto book of 1554 pages. How much paper did he use, allowing 1½ quires to every ream for waste?

12. A man has $50; but, after two successive discounts at the same rate, he has $46.08. Find the rate of discount.

13. Find the square root of each of the following; (a) 1¼ of 891; (b) 14/9 of 891; (c) 17749369; (d) 7879249; (e) 25040016; (f) 57912100.

Exercise XXVIII.

1. A certain room is ¾ as wide as it is long, and requires $120 to carpet it with carpeting worth $2.50 a square yard; it also requires $4.20 to paint its four walls at 5 cents a square yard; find its dimensions.

2. A merchant bought a bankrupt stock at 70 cents on the dollar of the invoice price, which was $5000. He sold ⅔ of it at 20 per cent. advance on the invoice price, ⅓ of the remainder at 30 per cent. below the invoice price, and the balance at 80 per cent. of the invoice price. His total expenses were 5 per cent. of his investment for buying and 4 per cent. of his sales for selling the stock. Find his loss or gain, (a) in money, (b) in rate per cent. on cost of investment, (c) in rate per cent. on total cost.

3. A merchant bought goods on January 2nd, 1893, amounting as per invoice to $750. He got successive discounts of 15 per cent. and 6 per cent., and was allowed 30 days to pay the cash, after which interest at the rate of 5 per cent. per annum would be charged. On February the 1st he paid $399.25. How much did he pay on April 15th, 1893, to settle his account?

4. A circular cistern is 21 ft. deep, and holds 99 barrels, 1 gal., 1 gill of water. Find the diameter of the excavation which will allow for a water-proof lining 9 inches thick. (A cubic foot = $6\frac{1}{4}$ gallons, and a barrel $31\frac{1}{2}$ gallons.)

5. Divide the L.C.M. of $\frac{5}{8}$, $2\frac{1}{4}$ and $\frac{7}{12}$ by the H.C.F. of $9\frac{1}{3}$ and 24.

6. On a sum borrowed at 6 per cent. per annum, and loaned immediately at 8 per cent., I gained $31.20 in three months, 18 days. What do I owe the lender at the end of that period? (A month = 30 days.)

7. Jones has $80, Smith has £20, 14 sh., Sterling, and Cameron has £4, 16 sh., $3\frac{3}{4}$ d., Halifax currency. They put their money together and invested in flour at 75 cents a sack. Find the number of whole sacks bought and A's share of the money remaining.

8. A contractor bought the following :—70 pieces of cherry scantling, each 16 ft. long, 9 inches wide and 4 inches thick ; 120 pieces of pine joisting, each 24 ft. long, 8 inches wide and 3 inches thick ; 400 planed and matched inch-boards (pine), each 15 inches wide and 20 ft. long ; and 1000 pieces of maple flooring, each 24 ft. long, 6 inches wide and $2\frac{1}{2}$ inches thick. Find the cost of the whole, when cherry is worth $40, pine $15 and maple $12 a thousand feet.

9. A round stick of timber measures 16 inches in diameter at the larger end, 12 inches at the smaller end, and its *central* length is 18 feet. How many cubic feet and inches are there in the stick?

10. I have a store worth $8775. For what amount must my insurance policy be drawn at $2\frac{1}{4}$ per cent. in order that I may recover, in case of fire, both my premium and the value of my store?

11. On $6000, my income is $370, derived from part of my capital being out at 7 per cent. and the rest at 5 per cent. How much had I lent out at each rate?

12. What time after 7 o'clock will (*a*) the minute hand of a clock be midway between the figure VII and the hour hand? (*b*) the hour hand be midway between the figure VII and the minute hand?

13. Divide $235 among A, B, C, D, and E, giving A $15 less than B ; B, $5 less than C and D, together ; C, $30 more than E, and D $40 less than C and E together.

FIFTH CLASS. 151

Exercise XXIX.

1. A sum of money is $36; but after three successive advances are made upon it at a certain rate per cent., it is found to be $41.6745. Find the rate per cent. of advance.

2. What amount of stock in a company at $12\frac{1}{2}$ per cent. below par could be bought for $1225 ?

3. For what amount should a note be drawn for 9 months, which, when discounted at true discount, would produce $2000, the rate of interest being 4 per cent.?

4. British Columbia Mining Stock at 130 pays 10 per cent. per annum, and C.P.R. Stock at 115 pays 8 per cent. per annum. What would be the difference per annum in income by investing $2990 in each kind of stock?

5. A man sold out $16800 in Railway Stock, paying 5 per cent. annual dividends, at 104, brokerage $\frac{3}{8}$ per cent., and purchased Government Bonds at 165, paying 9 per cent. annual dividends, brokerage $\frac{1}{8}$ per cent. Did he gain or lose in income, and how much per annum?

6. Had $3000 in B. C. Cattle Company's Stock, paying 10 per cent. yearly. Sold out at 60, and bought in Nanaimo Coal-Mining Stock at 120, paying 25% yearly dividends. Find my change in income.

7. An agent is in receipt of $4300 with which to buy wheat for his employer at $62\frac{1}{2}$ cents a bushel, after deducting his commission of $7\frac{1}{2}$ per cent. How many bushels of wheat does he remit?

8. The net price of a piano, sold at 20 per cent. and 5 per cent. off the list price is $456. Find the list price.

9. The difference in time between two places on the globe, due east and west of each other, is 5 hrs., 58 min., and 40 sec. Find the difference in longitude.

10. Find the face value of a note drawn to fall due 2 months hence, without interest, so that if discounted immediately at a bank at 8 per cent. per annum, the proceeds may be $592.

11. A certain pipe is 7 inches in diameter, and water passes through it from a lake at the rate of 45 miles, 59 rods, 2 yards, 2 feet, $3\frac{9}{11}$ inches per hour. How many barrels of water will be discharged from the lake, through the pipe, every 4 mins., 16 secs.?

12. A has $600; but, after three successive discounts have been made on it, at the same rate per cent., he has left 514.42\frac{1}{2}$. What was the rate per cent. of discount?

13. A man has $75; but after two successive advances upon it, at the same rate per cent. of increase, he has $84.27. Find the rate per cent. of increase.

Exercise XXX.

1. (a) Reduce $26.46¼ to £.s.d. Sterling; (b) By dealing in the practical way in Canadian currency, what would a man lose in paying in English shillings, a debt of £15.

2. Reduce 1 acre, 127 sq. rods, 21 sq. yards, 2 sq. feet, 36 sq. inches to sq. yards.

3. A fruiter has 90 apples and pears in a basket, and ⅓ the number of apples in the basket is equal to ⅕ of the number of pears. If pears are selling at 20 cents a dozen, and apples at 5 cents a dozen, find the value of the basket of fruit.

4. From 20 sq. rods take 19 sq. rods, 30 sq. yards, 99 sq. inches, using compound subtraction in working it.

5. A fruit-monger bought 70 baskets of fruit at $1.20 a basket. He lost 20 per cent. of the fruit by decay, and sold the remainder at 15 per cent. advance on cost. Find the total gain or loss per cent.

6. From ⅝ of an acre subtract 74 sq. rods, 29 sq. yds., 16 sq. ft., 145 sq. in., (a) by compound subtraction, and (b) by using reduction.

7. From $\frac{5}{18}$ of an acre take 38 sq. rods, 30 sq. yds., 72 sq. ft., 36 sq. in.

8. From ⅘ of an acre, a man sold 124 sq. rods, 30 sq. yds., 100 sq. ft., 100 sq. in. What had he left?

9. A merchant sold 560 pounds of tea, using a false weight of 14 ounces to the pound. If the tea cost him 87½ cents a pound, find his gain by selling the tea at 20 per cent. advance on cost.

10. A cellar, the floor of which is 7 metres wide, is paved with 7500 paving-stones, each 20 centimetres long by 7 centimetres wide; how long is the floor in metres?

11. Find the cost of digging a trench 5 kilometres long, 3 metres wide at the surface, 1 metre, 80 centimetres wide at the bottom, and 5 metres deep, at 15 cents per stere.

12. Bought 4380 kilogrammes of prunes in Havre at 2 francs per kilogramme and sold the whole quantity in Montreal at £105 Sterling per tonneau; find my gain, in Canadian currency, exchange in Havre being 56 shillings for 73 francs.

FIFTH CLASS. 153

13. (a) From ¼ of an acre a gardener sells 13 square rods, 28 square yards, 10 square feet, 150 square inches ; what has he remaining ? (*No reduction before subtracting*). (b) Multiply nineteen hundred million, fourteen thousand and fifty thousand, thirty-six hundred and seven by two hundred and fifty thousand and ninety thousand, seven hundred and eight ; and then divide the product by eighty-nine hundred and thirty-one thousand, eight hundred and eleven.

Exercise XXXI.

1. If $\frac{5}{8}$ of 18 lbs. sugar cost as much as 2 lbs., 8 ozs. of coffee, and 7 lbs. of coffee cost as much as 4 lbs. of tea, and 5 lbs. of tea cost $2.10, how many lbs. of sugar should be given for a dollar ?

2. A coal bin is 35 feet long, 18 feet wide, and 11 feet deep. (1) How many more tons (*by measure*) of *hard coal* than of *soft coal* will it hold ? (2) How many more bushels (*by weight*) of hard coal than of *soft coal* will it hold ?

3. Add 6 cwt., 10 lbs., 5 ozs. ; 17 cwt., 21 lbs., 9 ozs. ; 575 cwt., 23 lbs., 15 ozs. Subtract 475 cwt., 75 lbs., 8 ozs. from the *sum*. Multiply the *difference* by 7 ; and divide the *product* by 5.

4. A tank is 9 feet long, 7 feet wide and 3 feet deep ; another tank is 21 feet long, 3 feet, 6 inches wide and 3 feet deep. How many more barrels of water will the *latter* hold than the *former* ?

5. If $\frac{2}{5}$ of a farm sells for $3150 less than $\frac{3}{5}$ of it, how many acres does a man get who buys $\frac{4}{5}$ of the farm at $40 an acre ?

6. Divide the L.C.M. of 8, 12, 24, 36, 40, 90, 180, 190, 570 by

$$\frac{5\frac{2}{5} \times 7\frac{2}{5}}{8\frac{7}{24} - 3\frac{5}{12}}.$$

7. A vessel is said to have gone 1760 "*knots*" in going a distance of 2028·9 miles. How many feet are there in a "*knot*" ?

8. A cistern is 9 feet square at the top, and is sunk 13·481 feet into the ground. How many barrels of water does it hold ?

9. A mow of well settled hay is 40 feet × 20 feet, and is filled to the depth of 10 feet ; what is the hay worth at $7 a ton ?

10. A man owning $\frac{4}{5}$ of a lot, sold ·3 of his share for $2800 ; find the value of the lot.

11. A cow is sold at a gain of 20 per cent., and the sum of the cost price, gain, and selling price is $192. Find the cost price.

12. How much water must be added to 81 gallons of pure wine worth $3.33⅓ a gallon, so that by selling the mixture at $3 a gallon, I may realize a profit of $15 ?   *14 gals*

13. (a) A grocer sold 18 dozen and eight eggs for $3.50, thereby gaining 25 per cent. on the sale. How much did the eggs cost the grocer per doz. ? (b) A man walking alongside a railroad, at 4½ miles an hour, observes that a train, going 45 miles an hour in the same direction in which he is walking, passes him in 40 seconds ; find the length of the train.   *15 cts   792 yds*

Exercise XXXII.

1. A, B, C and D, four adjoining farmers, have their farms drained by 960 rods of ditch, 3 feet, 6 inches deep, 5 feet wide at the surface, and 2 feet wide at the bottom. A, who benefits the most, pays half the cost of digging the ditch, and of the remainder of the cost C pays half as much as B, and D half as much as C. How much does D pay, the cost of digging the ditch being 7½ cents a cubic yard ?   *$38.50*

2. Divide the product of $\frac{37}{56}$, $\frac{51}{111}$, $\frac{142}{187}$ and $\frac{153}{171}$ by the difference between $\frac{501}{9185}$ and $\frac{3}{11}$; to the result add 12·16.   *13*

3. A bucket holds 10 pints of water when it is ⅘ full; how many bucketfuls of water will fill a barrel ?   *18*

4. A has $18150 in English standard silver ; how many lbs., etc., of pure silver are there in that amount of money, if pure silver is $40 an ounce ?

5. If coffee loses 5⅔ per cent. of its weight in roasting, how many lbs. of green coffee will produce 1530 lbs. of roasted coffee ?   */*

6. A stone-cutter dressed 8 stones per day for 8 days. Of these 62½ per cent. were circular in form, each 14 inches in diameter and 5 inches thick, and the remainder were rectangular in form, each 18″ × 15″ × 5″. How much did he earn, if he received 9 cents a square foot of surface for dressing the stones ?   *$26.25*

7. At what price must 6 per cent. bonds, maturing in 5 years from date of investment, be purchased to pay 20 per cent. on the investment ?

8. Out of a cask of brandy ⅛ is drawn, then ⅓ more than ⅔ of the remainder ; the cask is then found to contain 27 gallons of liquor. How much was in the cask at first ?   *72*

9. In what time will $610 amount to $1015.05 at 7 per cent. per annum ?

FIFTH CLASS.

10. A mow, 40 ft. long and 20 ft. wide, is filled to the depth of 10 feet with hay well settled. Find the value of the hay at $7 a ton.

11. If a ship worth $48,000 be insured for $83\tfrac{1}{3}$ per cent. of its real value, what will a man lose (in case of fire) who has a three-fifths' interest in it?

12. The premium paid is $17.50 on a house insured for $3500; how many cents is that on the $100? What rate per cent. is it?

13. By using any short method you know, reduce $\tfrac{1\frac{2}{3}}{8}$ to a decimal.

Exercise XXXIII.

1. The premium for insuring a house was $13.20 at 60 cents on the $100; for what sum was the house insured?

2. If the true discount on $960 for 4 years be $160, what will be the discount for 6 years in the same sum at the same rate?

3. Goods marked $8.40 are sold for $4.80. What is the rate of discount? $42\tfrac{5}{7}\%$

4. Average the following Ledger Account:

Dr.					Isaac Shelden.			Cr.	
1887					1887				
Apr.	2	To Mdse......	900	00	Apr.	5	By Cash......	50	00
"	11	" "	500	00	"	11	" "	1000	00
May	3	" "	100	00	"	25	" "	300	00
					May	15	" "	25	00

5. I receive $18630 to invest in flour after deducting my commission of $3\tfrac{1}{2}$ per cent. for investing. How many barrels, worth $4.50 each, do I remit? 4000

6. If $1608 be paid for 12 acres, 90 sq. rods of land, and it be immediately sold at 96 cents a sq. rod, what gain per cent. would be realized?

7. Find the cost of 162 yards, 3·6 inches of cloth at 5s. a yard.

8. Write the following in figures: Nine hundred millions, twenty hundred and ninety thousand, ten hundred and thirteen; subtract four hundred and ninety-eight hundred and fifty-seven from it and extract the *square root* of the remainder.

9. The dividend is $7\tfrac{7}{10}$; the divisor $2\tfrac{1}{2}$; the quotient $\tfrac{1}{4}$; what is the remainder? Make a statement of the relations among these.

156　　　　EXERCISES IN ARITHMETIC.

10. It cost $78.37½ to fence a rectangular field at 12½ cents a yard ; the field was 42 rods long ; how wide was it ?

11. I paid $45 to a commission merchant for selling goods at 2½ per cent. commission, and his other charges amounted to $12.75. Find the *net proceeds* of the sale.

12. How many dozens of eggs at 19 cents a dozen would pay for 1493½ ounces of tea at 57 cents a pound ?

13. A real-estate dealer sold a house and 7 acres of land for £411, 18sh. Sterling. If the house was valued at $629.99, what was the value per acre (in Canadian currency) of the land ?

Exercise XXXIV.

1. For how much is a house insured, if the premium paid is $9 at ¾ per cent.?

2. B and C are partners in a grocery business, B investing $4000 and C $3000. B is a sleeping partner, and C manages the business at a yearly salary of $800. Out of a yearly gain of $2900, what should each partner receive ?

3. What must be the asking price of a farm which cost $8721, in order to realize 20 per cent. on the sale of it after allowing a series of discounts (from the asking price) of 5 per cent., 10 per cent., and 15 per cent.?

4. A Canadian tourist went to Hamburg, Germany, with $250, which he changed for German money at 25 cents for a mark. He spent 241 marks in Hamburg, and then went to Lisbon where he exchanged his marks for Portuguese money at 23 marks for 4 milrees. He then spent 12 milrees in Lisbon, and next went to London, England, where he exchanged his milrees for English money at 5s., 9d. per milree. He then spent £14, 5s. in London, and this sum included the price of his ticket from Liverpool to Quebec. He now exchanged the remainder of his money for Canadian Currency at the ordinary rate of exchange (£ = $4.86⅔). How much money had he on arriving in Quebec ?

5. A speculator sold stock at a discount of 10 per cent., and made a profit of 20 per cent. At what rate discount had he purchased the stock ?

6. What sum of money put out at 5 per cent. for 4 years, and compounded annually, will produce $340.34 7/10 ?

FIFTH CLASS. 157

7. A man has $15000 in American standard silver; how many lbs., etc., of pure silver are there in that sum, if pure silver is worth $40 an ounce?

8. How many boys, each doing ¾ of a man's work, must be employed with 8 men to do as much work in 45 days as 50 men would do in 18 days?

9. On a debt of $500, I received on **January 1st, 1891**, 435 bushels of wheat, valued at $1.05 a bushel. The balance still due remained at interest, until March 14th, 1892. at 10 per cent. per annum. when it was paid in full. Find the receipts, March 14th, 1892?

10. If bread weighs 35 per cent. more than the flour from which it is made, how much bread can be obtained from 25 barrels of flour?

11. A rectangular plot of ground is 50 dekameters long by 50 meters wide. How many acres, etc., are there in it, an *"are"* being 3·954 sq. rods?

12. A man buys City of Vancouver bonds which pay 10 per cent. and which are to be redeemed at par in 5 years after purchased. Money being worth 12 per cent., find the price of the bonds.

13. At what price per barrel shall an agent buy flour at 5 per cent. commission so that, after paying 10 cents a barrel for transportation, it will net a profit of $12\frac{1}{2}$ per cent. when sold at $7.20 a barrel?

Exercise XXXV.

1. Stock bought at 10 per cent. discount pays 15 per cent. on investment; what per cent. will a broker make who buys at $12\frac{1}{2}$ per cent. discount, and after drawing a dividend sells out at par?

2. On March 1st, 1893, W. N. Shanley bought of J. O. Doyle & Co., merchandise as per invoice, $720, on 2 months' credit. On March 7th, W. N. Shanley paid $120, March 27th, $100, and April 11th, $200. What is the equated time for paying the balance?

3. A gentleman invested in stock at $90\frac{1}{4}$ in a government road paying 7 per cent. annual dividends, and received yearly $455. What sum did he invest in the stock, brokerage being $\frac{1}{4}$ per cent.

4. A dealer had 620 lbs. cheese, and sold a part of it at $12\frac{1}{2}$ cents a lb., realizing therefor $53.75. Find his entire receipts for cheese, the remainder being disposed of at $15 a cwt.

5. The *gross cost* of a purchase is $2342, which includes a commission of $17.25 and other charges of $24.75. What is the rate per cent. of commission?

6. A man exchanged 16 barrels of flour at $5.37½ a barrel for 20 cords of wood. What was wood worth per cord-foot?

7. From a barrel of water $\frac{2}{15}$ leaked. Find the weight, in lbs. and ozs., of the water remaining in the barrel.

8. The cost of a peach orchard is $980. One-fifth of the value of the trees is equal to one-ninth of the value of the land. Find the value of the trees.

9. A and B together bought a barrel of flour; A paid $7.35 and B paid $2.45. How many lbs. of flour did B get?

10. Multiply $\left\{ \dfrac{3\frac{9}{10} \times 1\frac{13}{25} \times 1\frac{9}{10} \times 2\frac{17}{35} \times 2\frac{1}{3}}{1\frac{1}{2} \times 1\frac{1}{4} \times 2\frac{1}{2} \times 3\frac{1}{3}} \right\}$ by $\left\{ \dfrac{18}{\frac{2}{3} \text{ of } \dfrac{4\frac{2}{3}}{12\frac{1}{3}} \text{ of } \dfrac{3\frac{4}{11}}{11\frac{1}{2}}} \right\}$.

11. How many miles does a man travel in ploughing, crosswise, a field 80 rods long by 50 rods wide, his plough turning an eleven-inch furrow?

12. Sold goods to a certain amount on 10 per cent. commission, and, having remitted the net proceeds to the owner, received $36.90 or ½ per cent. for prompt payment. What was the amount of the commission, and the value of the goods sold?

13. I sold two horses, receiving for the second ⅔ as much as for the first. On the first I gained 10 per cent., and on the second I lost 8⅓ per cent.; but gained on both $10. Find the cost price of each horse.

Exercise XXXVI.

1. A speculator bought a lot, May 1st, 1892, for $500, and gave in payment his note with interest at 7 per cent. per annum until paid. On Feb. 17th, 1893, he sold the lot for $700 cash, and redeemed his note. What did he gain?

2. What sum would be saved per annum, if the interest on a public loan of $4,000,000 were reduced from 3½ per cent. to 3 per cent.? If, in consequence, the price of the stock fell from 101 to 95⅞, how much would the property of the fundholders be diminished?

3. How much must I invest in 4 per cent. stock at 82 brokerage ¼ per cent. so that in the event of the stock falling to 78, I may lose (by selling my stock) simply the income on three hundred dollars' worth of stock? (Brokerage in each transaction.)

FIFTH CLASS.

4. Find the equated time when the balance of the following Ledger Account becomes due :—

Dr. JOHN SLOAN. Cr.

1892				1892			
Dec.	1	To Bal. from old ac't.	72 00	Dec.	8	By order on him	20 00
"	2	" Amos Ross' Order	15 00	"	9	" " " T.D.	5 00
"	3	" A. Sinclair's "	10 00	"	13	" Cash on ac't..	15 75

5. A shipment of goods is invoiced $1590. At what sum should it be insured at ⅝ per cent. so that in case of loss the shipper would recover both the invoice price and the premium?

6. What is the par value of stock if the discount is $1350, and the rate of discount 13½ per cent.?

7. A speculator bought canal stock at 85½, and sold it again at 102⅝, receiving $6150 as the net cash proceeds of the sale. What was his net gain, allowing ⅛ per cent. brokerage each way?

8. Divide 86 into two parts, such that one shall be $(2\frac{1}{2} \times \frac{3}{8} \times 5\frac{1}{3}) \times \frac{3}{4} \times \frac{2}{3} \times \frac{3}{7} \times 3\frac{1}{2})$ more than the other.

9. A grocer sold 240 lbs. of tea at 80 cents a lb., using a 15-ounce weight for a pound. If the tea cost him 50 cents a lb. by *correct* weight, what was his gain on the sale of the tea?

10. A grocer receives $11.52 for butter weighed on scales that registered 14¾ ounces to the lb. How many cents' worth did he cheat his customer?

11. A speculator sold stock at a discount of 20¼ per cent. and made a profit of 10 per cent. Find the price at which he had invested in the stock.

12. On Jan. 1st, 1893, a note for $500 is drawn up, bearing interest at 6 per cent. per annum until paid, and to be compounded whenever payments are made thereon. On March 15th the sum of $216 is paid; on August 8th, $96.96, and on October 20th, $122.40. What sum will redeem the note on Jan. 1st, 1894?

13. One-fifth of A's sheep is equal to ¼ of B's; but A buys 60 sheep, and B increases his flock 17 per cent. by buying 15 per cent. less sheep than A. Find the value of their united flocks (after these purchases) at $5 a head all round.

Exercise XXXVII.

1. Find the face value of the note, drawn May 1st, 1893, to mature in 90 days, which discounted May 18th, at 10%, will produce the *net cash* proceeds of $500?

2. I have 210 sovereigns; what weight of pure gold have I, if pure gold is worth $440 an ounce?

3. Find the cash balance due on the following account, on Sept. 7th, 1893, interest (Year=360 days.) the rate of 6 per cent. per annum:

Dr.   PETER R. EMPTY.   *Cr.*

1893				$	c.	1893				$	c.
Mar.	1	To Mdse at 30 days		500	00	Apr. 10	By Cash		....	500	00
"	31	" " " 60 "		200	00	" 19	" "		....	100	00
May	20	" " " 90 "		400	00	Sept 2	" "		....	600	00
Aug.	1	" " " 30 "		200	00						

4. A can drive round a circular track 5 times in 42 minutes, and B can drive round it 8 times in 70 minutes. If they start from the same point together, at the same time and drive in the same direction, how many times will A drive round the track before he overtakes B? What time will it occupy?

5. Find the cost to line the bottom and sides of a rectangular cistern, 4 ft., 3 in. square at the top, and 8 ft., 6 in. deep, *inside measurement*, the lead costing 32 cents a square foot.

6. A train runs at the rate of 64 Km. per hour for 35 consecutive hours. Find the approximate number of English miles the train traverses.

7. Express in decimals: $\dfrac{1}{50} + \dfrac{1}{3 \times 50^3} + \dfrac{1}{5 \times 50^5} + \ldots$

8. Find the value of a cubical block of marble whose side measures 5 dm., at $24 a cubic metre.

9. A court-yard is 1 Dm., 2 M. long by 8 M. wide; find the cost to pave it with bricks, each of which is 8 cm. square, if the bricks cost $7.20 a thousand.

10. If oak is $\tfrac{9}{10}$ as heavy as water, what length must be cut off an oak plank 4 dm. wide and 30 mm. thick, in order that the portion cut off shall weigh 21 Kg., 6 Hg.?

11. A room is 12 M., 8 dm. long by 8 M., 4 dm. wide. How much carpet 70 cm. wide, laid down lengthwise of the room, would cover the floor? Find the cost of the carpet at 75 cents a M.

12. Find correctly as a mixed circulating decimal, the value of the series: $\dfrac{4}{5} + \dfrac{4}{3 \times 5^3} + \dfrac{4}{5 \times 5^5} + \dfrac{4}{7 \times 5^7} + \ldots$

13. An accountant pays $9.10 income tax on a portion of his salary. What is his salary if $\tfrac{2}{5}$ of it is exempt from taxation, and $\tfrac{3}{4}$ per cent. is levied on the remainder?

FIFTH CLASS. 161

Exercise XXXVIII.

1. A miller bought 13500 bushels wheat, and had it insured for $\frac{2}{3}$ of its cost at $1\frac{1}{4}$ per cent. At what price per bushel must he sell it to gain 25 per cent., the premium paid for insurance being $112.50?

2. Express accurately, in decimals, the value of the series:
$$\frac{1}{4} - \frac{1}{3 \cdot 4^3} + \frac{1}{5 \cdot 4^5} - \frac{1}{7 \times 4^7} + \ldots$$

3. A square plot of land, containing 1 Da., 6 A., is covered with wood to the depth of 2 M. Find the value of the wood at 30 cents a "stere."

4. Divide $360 amongst A, B and C, so that $\frac{1}{2}$ A's = $\frac{1}{3}$ B's = $\frac{1}{4}$ C's.

5. Find the capacity of a cistern 3 M., 3 dm. long, 8 dm. wide and 5 dm., 5 cm. deep; and also the weight of water it will contain.

6. Out of a pile of wood, 8 Dm. long, 6 Dm., 5 M. wide and 8 M. high, a man reserved 35,000,000 cu. dm. and sold the rest at $37\frac{1}{2}$ cents a stere. What did he receive?

7. If gold is 19·307 times as heavy as water, what is the weight of a bar of gold 4 cm. long, 1 cm., 5 mm. wide and 5 mm. thick?

8. If mercury is 13·6 as heavy as water, what is the weight of 5 Litres of the metal?

9. What RULES in Arithmetic would the adoption of the *Metric System* simplify?

Examine the connection or relation between the UNITS of *measure* (*capacity* or *volume*) and of *weight* in the *Metric System*.

10. Find the L.C.M. of $5\frac{1}{8}$, $41\frac{9}{11}$, $4\frac{3}{5}$ and $11\frac{1}{2}$.

11. Find the compound interest and amount of $250 for 3 years at 6 per cent., interest, to be compounded annually.

12. Find the *greatest* number which will divide 941 and 1001, and leave respectively 21 and 12 as remainders.

13. How much stock at $97\frac{1}{2}$ can be purchased by investing the cash proceeds of $1950 of another kind of stock sold at 78?

METRIC SYSTEM.

The Metric System of Measurement is a *decimal* system which has for its basis a UNIT, called the "*metre*" (mē'ter).

The metre (=39·37079 in.) is the ten-millionth part of the distance from either pole to the equator, as measured along a meridian.

For the better understanding of the Metric System let us compare it (as far as the measure is concerned) with the Decimal System of Notation.

DECIMAL SYSTEM OF NOTATION.

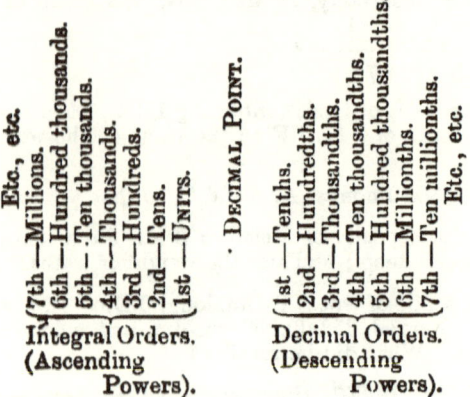

Integral Orders.	Decimal Orders.
(Ascending Powers).	(Descending Powers).

7th — Millions.
6th — Hundred thousands.
5th — Ten thousands.
4th — Thousands.
3rd — Hundreds.
2nd — Tens.
1st — UNITS.

· DECIMAL POINT.

1st — Tenths.
2nd — Hundredths.
3rd — Thousandths.
4th — Ten thousandths.
5th — Hundred thousandths.
6th — Millionths.
7th — Ten millionths.
Etc., etc.

METRIC SYSTEM OF MEASUREMENT.
(As to Length).

— Megametre 1000000 Units.
5th — Myriametre = 10000 Units.
4th — Kilometre = 1000 Units.
3rd — Hectometre = 100 Units.
2nd — Dekametre = 10 Units.
1st — Metre = Unit.

· Decimal Point.

1st — Decimetre — $\frac{1}{10}$ of a Unit.
2nd — Centimetre — $\frac{1}{100}$ of a Unit.
3rd — Millimetre = $\frac{1}{1000}$ of a Unit.
— Micrometre = $\frac{1}{1000000}$ of a Unit.

Ascending Powers of ten.   Descending Powers of ten.

Integral Multiples, **TENS.**   Decimal Parts, **TENTHS.**

FIFTH CLASS.

Table.

1000000 metres=100000 Dekametres=10000 Hectometres=1000 Kilometres=100 Myriametres=1 Megametre.
10000 metres=1000 Dekametres=100 Hectometres=10 Kilometres=1 Myriametre.
1000 metres=100 Dekametres=10 Hectometres=1 Kilometre.
100 metres=10 Dekametres=1 Hectometre.
10 metres=1 Dekametre.
1 Metre.
·1 metre=1 decimetre.
·01 metre=·1 decimetre=1 centimetre.
·001 metre=·01 decimetre=.1 centimetre=1 millimetre.
.000001 metre=·00001 decimetre=·0001 centimetre=·001 millimetre=1 micrometre.

In the Decimal Notation, commencing with the *decimal point* (which separates the *integers* from the *decimals* or the *whole numbers* from the *fractional parts*) we see that the *integral* orders are enumerated to the left, and the *decimal* orders to the right of the *point*; that the first *integral* order to the left of the UNITS' place is *tens*, and that the *first decimal* order to the right of the UNITS' place is *tenths*, etc.

Now, as far as the measurement of length is concerned, the same is true of the Metric System.

It will be observed that, for the ASCENDING POWERS OF MULTIPLES Greek prefixes are used, and they are written with *capitals*:

Deka— = 10 times the *Unit*.
Hecto— =100   "   "   "
Kilo— =1000   "   "   "
Myria— =10000 "   "   "
Mega— =1000000 "   "   "

It will be observed also, that for the DESCENDING POWERS OF DECIMAL PARTS, Latin prefixes are used, and these are written with *small* letters :

deci— = $\frac{1}{10}$ of the *Unit*.
centi— = $\frac{1}{100}$ "   "
milli— = $\frac{1}{1000}$ "   "
micro— = $\frac{1}{1000000}$ "   "

The Primary Units of Measurement.

MEASUREMENT.	PRIME UNIT.	WHERE USED.
Length.	" Metre."	Distances, lengths, dry-goods, etc.

TABLE.
(Linear.)

100 micrometers (mm.) = 1 millimetre (mm.)
10 millimetres = 1 centimetre (cm.)
10 centimetres = 1 decimetre (dm.)
10 decimetres = 1 Metre (M.)
10 Metres = 1 Dekametre (Dm.)
10 Dekametres = 1 Hectometre (Hm.)
10 Hectometres = 1 Kilometre (Km.)
10 Kilometres = 1 Myriametre (Mm.)
100 Myriametres = 1 Megametre (Mgm.)

For Measuring { Very short lengths.—decimetres, centimetres, millimetres, etc.
Short distances.—metre, etc.
Long distances.—Kilometre, etc.

MEASUREMENT.	PRIME UNIT.	WHERE USED.
AREA.	Square Metre.	Floors, ceilings, walls, carpets, etc.

TABLE.
(Ordinary Surfaces.)

100 sq. centimetres (sq. cm.) = 1 sq. decimetre (sq. dm.)
100 sq. decimetres (sq. dm.) = 1 *sq. metre* (sq. m.)

For Measuring { Ordinary areas.—sq. metres, sq. decimetres, sq. centimetres, etc.

MEASUREMENT.	PRIME UNIT.	WHERE USED.
AREA.	"Are" (=Sq. Dekametre).	Farms, townships, etc.

TABLE.
(Land.)

10 milliares (ma.) = 1 centiare (ca.)
10 centiares = 1 deciare (da.)
10 deciare = 1 "Are" (A.)
10 Ares = 1 Dekare (Da.)
10 Dekares = 1 Hectare (Ha.)

For Measuring { Land—Dekares, Hectares, etc.

MEASUREMENT.	PRIME UNIT.	WHERE USED.
VOLUME.	Cubic Metre.	Bricks, blocks of wood, stone, etc.

TABLE.
(Ordinary Solids).

1000 cu. millimetres (cu. mm.) = 1 cu. centimetre.
1000 cu. centimetres = 1 cu. decimetre (cu. dm.)
1000 cu. decimetres = 1 Cu. Metre (Cu. M.)

For Measuring { Ordinary solids.—Cub. Metres, cub. decimetres, cub. centimetres, etc.

MEASUREMENT.	PRIME UNIT.	WHERE USED.
VOLUME.	"Stere" (Cubic Metre).	Wood, excavations, gravel, etc.

TABLE.
(Greater Solids).

10 centisteres (cs.) = 1 decistere (ds.)
10 decisteres = 1 Stere (S.)
10 Steres = 1 Dekastere (Ds.)
10 Dekasteres = 1 Hectostere (Hs.)
10 Hectosteres = 1 Kilostere (Ks.)

For Measuring { Greater Solids, as wood, etc.—Decasteres, Hectosteres, etc.

MEASUREMENT.	PRIME UNIT.	WHERE USED.
CAPACITY.	"Litre" (cubic decimetre).	Dry substances, as grain, fruit, vegetables, etc; Liquids, as water, wine, etc.

TABLE.

10 centilitres (cl.) = 1 decilitre (dl.)
10 decilitres = 1 Litre (L.)
10 Litres = 1 Dekalitre (Dl.)
10 Dekalitres = 1 Hectolitre (Hl.)
10 Hectolitres = 1 Kilolitre (Kl.)
= 1 stere.

For Measuring { Large quantities.—Dekalitres, Hectolitres, etc. Moderate quantities.—Litre. Small quantities.—decilitres, centilitres, etc.

MEASUREMENT.	PRIME UNIT.	WHERE USED.
WEIGHT (or Mass).	"Gramme," (cub. centimetre of distilled water at 4° Centigrade).	Tea, Sugar, Hay, etc.

TABLE.

10 milligrammes (Mg.) = 1 centigramme (cg.)
10 centigrammes = 1 decigramme (dg.)
10 decigrammes = 1 GRAMME (G.)
10 Grammes = 1 Dekagramme (Dg.)
10 Dekagrammes = 1 Hectogramme (Hg.)
10 Hectogrammes = 1 Kilogramme (Kg.)
10 Kilogrammes = 1 Myriagramme (Mg.)

For Weighing. {
Large Quantities.—Tonneau (Ton.) or Millier (Mil.)=1000 Kg.
  Quintal (Q) =100 Kg.
Moderate Quantities.—Kilogrammes, Hectogrammes.
Small Quantities.—grammes, decigrammes, centigrammes, etc.
}

Since the Mectric System is a *decimal system*, moving the DECIMAL POINT to the *right* MULTIPLES by *ten*, and moving it to the *left*, DIVIDES by *ten*; hence to do reduction *descending* or *ascending*, we simply move the decimal point to the *right* or to the *left*, as required.

EQUIVALENTS.

(Approximate).

1 Metre = 39·37079 inches.
1 centimetre = ·3937+inches = $\frac{2}{5}$ of an inch, nearly.
1 Kilometre = 1093·633+yards = $\frac{5}{8}$ of a mile, nearly.
1 Hectare = 11960·3326+sq. yards = $2\frac{1}{2}$ acres, nearly.
1 litre = 1·7607+pints = 1 quart, nearly.
1 stere = 35·316+cubic feet = $\frac{1}{4}$ of a cord, nearly.
1 Kilogramme = 2·2046+lbs. = $2\frac{1}{4}$ lbs., nearly.
1 tonneau = 2204·6+lbs. = 2200 lbs., nearly.

COINAGE, ETC.

English Standard gold is $\frac{11}{12}$ pure.
English Standard silver is $\frac{37}{40}$ pure.
Canadian Standard silver is $\frac{37}{40}$ pure.
American Standard gold or silver is $\frac{9}{10}$ pure.

FORMULÆ IN MENSURATION.

Area of a Circle = $\frac{1}{2}$c. × $\frac{1}{2}$d. = πr^2.

Circumference of a Circle = π d.

FIFTH CLASS.

Area of a Triangle $=\frac{1}{2}$ base $\times$ the altitude or perpendicular height, or $\sqrt{s(s-x)(s-y)(s-z)}$.

Area of an Ellipse $= \pi \left[\dfrac{a}{2} \times \dfrac{b}{2}\right]$.

Convex Surface of a Sphere $= \pi d^2 =$ c. $\times$ d.—4 times the area of a circle of the same diameter.

Volume of a Sphere $= d^3 \times \frac{1}{6}\pi =$ Convex Surface multiplied by $\frac{1}{6}$ d.

Convex Surface of a Cone $=\frac{1}{2}$ circumference of base $\times$ slant height.

Surface of a Cone = Convex Surface + Area of Base.

Volume of a Cone = Area of Base $\times \frac{1}{3}$ Altitude, or Perpendicular Height.

Volume of a Pyramid of *any number of sides* = Area of Base $\times \frac{1}{3}$ Altitude (same as that of a Cone).

Volume of Frustum of Cone — *difference* between Volume of Complete Cone, and Volume of the Part Required *to complete it*.

N.B. ☞ c.—circumference ; d.=diameter ; $\pi = 3\frac{1}{7}$; r.—radius ; s.— $\frac{1}{2}$ perimeter ; x. y. and z.=respective sides of *any* triangle ; a.= major axis ; b.—minor axis.

Exercise XXXIX.

1. A man increased his farm 20% in size, and found that he had then 780 acres. How many acres did he add to it?

2. If the fraction $\frac{5}{8}$ have 3 subtracted from each of its terms, by how much per cent. is the fraction increased or diminished?

3. If 12.3946\frac{7}{8}$ is the interest on $84.75 for $3\frac{1}{4}$ years, at what rate per cent. per annum is it loaned?

4. How much is 5 times $\dfrac{\frac{1}{7} \text{ of } (\frac{1}{4} - \frac{1}{5})}{\frac{1}{10} \text{ of } \frac{5}{8}}$?

5. A clerk, who received $325 a year, had his salary raised 40%. What did he receive then?

6. A and B enter into partnership and invest capital in the ratio of $2\frac{1}{4}$ to 3. After 7 months A withdraws $\frac{2}{3}$ of his capital and B withdraws $\frac{3}{4}$ of his. At the end of the year they find they have gained $8850. Find each man's gain.

7. A man in 5 days dug 100 bushels of potatoes for 15 per cent. of them, and sold his share at 40 cents a bushel. Find his daily wages.

8. How many shares of $100 each can be purchased with $4210 cash, in the Northern Gas Company's stock at 105, brokerage being $\frac{1}{4}$%?

9. Reduce 221.55\frac{1}{2}$ to £. s. d., Sterling.

10. A merchant marks an article $1.92, but throws off $12\frac{1}{2}$% for cash. If his profit is still 40%, find the cost price of the article.

11. A dry article was exposed to damp air and having absorbed 10 ounces of water it then weighed 10 lbs. What per cent. of its weight of water did it absorb?

12. If I buy a 6 per cent. City Bond at 80, what is my rate of income?

13. By commercial discount of 8% a person would receive $60.48 less than the nominal value of a note drawn payable one year hence. If true discount only were deducted from the face value of the note, what should the person receive for it?

Exercise XL.

1. A and B together have $2700; but A spends $\frac{3}{4}$ of his money, and B spends $\frac{4}{5}$ of his, after which they find that they, together, have saved $600. How much money had each at first?

2. I received a purse of £177, 3 shillings, Sterling, how much did I receive in Canadian Currency?

3. I received a 5% dividend on Railway Stock, and immediately invested the money in the same stock at 75, after which I found that I held $32000 in the said stock. What was the amount of my dividend?

4. An agent bought a set of furniture, the catalogue price of which was $80, subject to three successive discounts of 25%, 10%, and 5% off the catalogue price. He then sold the set for $92.34 cash. Find his gain per cent.

5. Change (a) ·625 ; (b) ·875 ; and (c) ·192 into equivalent vulgar fractions in their *lowest* terms.

6. A bin, in a mill, is 20 ft. long, 16 ft. wide and 8 ft. deep, and it is filled with wheat at 56 cents a bushel. What is the value of the wheat?

7. A man paid A $\frac{1}{3}$ of his money, B $\frac{1}{5}$ of it, and C $\frac{1}{8}$ of it, and had left $2.05. How much money had he at first?

8. A and B, two boys, have ropes fastened to the same stake. A's rope is 14 ft. long and B's is 35 ft. long. They both make a circuit around the stake, keeping their ropes tight. How many yards does B go farther than A?

9. (a) What time after IX o'clock will the hands be opposite?
(b) When will the minute hand be 222 degrees ahead of the hour hand?

10. What time after VII o'clock will the minute hand be 9 minute-spaces ahead of the hour hand?

11. Reduce (a) ·625 of a bushel to gallons, pecks, etc.; (b) ·575 of a week to days, hours, etc.

12. At what rate would $650 produce $273 interest in 6 years?

13. A merchant sells an overcoat for $18 at 20% advance on the cost; but the cost price is $\frac{3}{4}$ of the marked price. At this rate, what would be the value of a case of three dozen overcoats at the marked price?

Exercise XLI.

1. Divide 52 lbs. of tea into three parcels, which shall be to one another as the numbers $\frac{1}{2}$, $\frac{1}{3}$ and $1\frac{1}{3}$.

2. The L.C.M. of two numbers is 1430 and their H.C.F. is 65 ; find all the pairs of numbers which will fulfil the conditions of the question.

3. Simplify: $2\frac{3}{4} - 5\frac{1}{2}$ of $\left(\frac{\frac{1}{3}+\frac{1}{4}}{\frac{2}{3}-\frac{1}{4}} - \frac{2\frac{1}{4}}{3\frac{1}{4}}\right) + 58\frac{87}{100}$.

4. The *sum* of the weights of two sacks of grain is 410 lbs. and the *difference* is 90 lbs. Find the weight of each sack.

5. (*a*) Name the two kinds of fractions and the sub-divisions of each.

   (*b*) Simplify: (I) $\frac{7}{8} + \frac{13}{18}$; (II) $\frac{21}{28} - \frac{117}{112}$; (III) $\frac{3}{4}$ of $\frac{7\frac{1}{2}}{16}$;

   (IV) $\frac{1\frac{13}{16}}{7\frac{1}{4}}$; (v) ·025 + ·13̇8̇ + ·2̇6̇.

   (*c*) Classify fully as stated in (*a*) the various fractional expressions together with the five fractional results obtained.

6. When lumber is $12.50 a thousand square feet, and posts are worth 13 cents each, find the total cost of building a closely-boarded guard 7 feet high for 24 rods along an embankment, inch lumber being used, the posts being set 4 feet apart from centre to centre, and labor and other expenses being $7.35.

7. What is the capacity, in barrels, of the *smallest* tank that can be filled in an exact number of minutes by *each* or *both* of two pipes, each of which respectively empties 56 and 63 gallons of water per minute? Both being opened, in what time would the tank be filled?

8. Bought 75 sheep at $2.68 per head, and 45 others at $2.20 per head. Sold the whole lot at $3.25 per head; find my gain per cent.

9. If a bag of silver containing $142 is made up of 25-cent and 10-cent pieces, there being 440 more 10-cent pieces than 25-cent pieces, how many are there of each kind in the bag?

10. If the sum of 5 times the larger and 7 times the smaller of two numbers is 1442, and the difference between the numbers is 70, what are the numbers?

11. Find the cash value of 50 shares of $100 each of mining stock at $160\frac{1}{4}$, brokerage being $\frac{1}{8}$%.

12. Divide $240 among A, B and C, so that A may have $140 more than B, and twice as much as C.

13. Ice is 90% as heavy as water, and 108 tons were packed into an ice-house 12 feet wide and 8 feet high. How many feet long was it?

Exercise XLII.

1. The sum of two numbers is 35875, and their difference is equal to $\frac{3}{5}$ of the greater number. What are the numbers?

2. The interest on $1460 for one day was 25 cents; find the rate per cent. per annum at which it was loaned. (Year = 365 days.)

3. A carriage drive, 4 rods wide and having an area of 3696 square rods, runs round a circular grass plot. Find the diameter of the plot.

4. Show that $\frac{3}{4} \div \frac{3}{5} = \frac{3}{4} \times \frac{5}{3} = 1\frac{1}{4}$.

5. Three workmen, A, B and C, earning the same daily wages, spend respectively $\frac{5}{7}$, $\frac{3}{5}$ and $\frac{8}{15}$ of their daily earnings. If the daily wages of a workman be $3.15, what sum of money will they all three save in a year's time (52 weeks), no time being lost?

6. Find the number which is as much per cent. *above* 30 as it is per cent. *below* 50. What per cent. is it?

7. An agent received $300 for selling land at $18.75 an acre on a commission of $2\frac{1}{2}$%. Find the number of acres sold.

8. Find the simple interest on $1285.44 for 5 years at 5% per annum.

9. A public garden in the form of a circle, contains 2·036 acres. It has ornamental trees planted 11 feet apart around its circumference. How many trees are there?

10. A bought B's note (drawing no interest), B allowing him 20% off the face value. What per cent. did A realize on his investment?

11. If lemons cost $1 for 30, how many dozen must I handle for $30 to gain 25%?

12. Simplify: $\frac{3\frac{1}{2}}{7\frac{1}{3}} \times \frac{5}{8} \div 1\frac{1}{8}$ of $\frac{13}{15} + \frac{1}{315}$.

13. A boy took 9000 steps in going a distance of $3\frac{21}{44}$ miles. Find the average length of his step, in feet and inches.

Exercise XLIII.

1. A's capital is to B's as 2:5, and both loan their money for one year at 8%. If the difference in the amount of interest received is $24, find each man's capital.

2. A box, without a lid, is 6' 5" long, 4' 2" wide, and 3' 3" deep (external measurement). (*a*) How many square feet of inch lumber does it contain? (*b*) How many cubic feet and inches of material are there in it?

3. A man invests $4275 in the 4 per cents at 95, and at the end of the year he sells out at 90, and invests half the proceeds in the $3\frac{1}{2}$ per cents at 81 and the other half in the 6 per cents at 108. Find the change in his yearly income.

4. A tank 11 feet long and 7 feet wide contains 13824 pints of water when filled to the top. Given that a pint holds 28·875 cubic inches of water, how deep is the tank?

5. Bought butter and sold $\frac{1}{4}$ of it at a loss of $20°/_\circ$. How much per cent. must I now advance my selling price to gain $25°/_\circ$ on the whole transaction?

6. A can do a piece of work in $7\frac{5}{7}$ days when B helps him $4\frac{1}{2}$ days, and B can do the work in $7\frac{5}{16}$ days when A helps him $4\frac{1}{2}$ days. How long would it take A and B working together to do the work?

7. If a block of toilet soap 3 inches long, 2 inches wide and $1\frac{7}{8}$ inches thick weighs 9 ounces and is worth $1.35, what is the value of a pyramidal cake whose altitude is 24 inches and whose base is a circle the diameter of which is 14 inches?

8. A has cloth marked at $1.65 a yard, which is $16\frac{2}{3}°/_\circ$ above the cost price. Find the cost price of 70 yards of that cloth.

9. Simplify: $117 \left\{ 4\frac{2}{7} \div (5\frac{1}{3} - 4\cdot 25) \times \dfrac{1}{5\frac{1}{4}} \right\} + 9.$

10. Divide the *square* of ·025 by the *cube* of ·002.

11. From 12·5 take 6·2̇2̇7̇, and to the difference add ·6̇7̇1̇.

12. A square plot, 40 yards to a side, has 8 flower beds, each 18 ft. by 10 ft., and one circular portion 21 yards in diameter for a fountain, the rest being gravelled. Find the portion of the plot gravelled, in sq. yds., sq. ft. and sq. inches.

13. Express, explicitly, 4121 (*a*) in the *denary* scale, and (*b*) in the *octenary* scale.

Exercise XLIV.

1. How many miles per hour does a train run, when it traverses 821 yards 1 foot per minute?

2. Divide 150 into two such parts that 4 times one part shall be equal to 71 times the other.

3. If 8 per cent. of A's money equals $5\frac{1}{2}°/_\circ$ of B's, and both together have $5400, how much money has B more than A?

4. Find the value of $\dfrac{(13\cdot 5)^2}{(\cdot 08)^3}.$

FIFTH CLASS. 173

5. Find the total cost of 245 lbs. of barley at 60 cents a bushel, 855 lbs. of pease at 70 cents a bushel, and 137 lbs. 6 ozs. of rye at 80 cents a bushel.

6. A discount of 20% off the list price of a $40-mandolin, and 5% off that again, is equivalent to what single rate of discount?

7. A slate cistern (without a lid) is 4 feet 3 inches long, 4 feet wide, and 5 feet 1½ inches deep (outside measurement). It is filled with water. Find the weight of the cistern and the contained water, given that the slate is 1½ inches thick, and that slate weighs 169 lbs. to the cubic foot.

8. A can do a job of work in $\frac{3}{4}$ of a day, and B in $\frac{1}{3}$ of a day. If they both work together to complete the job, what is each man's share of $5.20 paid for it?

9. Simplify:

(a) $4\frac{1}{4} + \dfrac{3\frac{1}{3} - \frac{1}{5}}{3\frac{1}{3} + \frac{1}{5}} - \frac{1}{5}$ of $6\frac{2}{3} - 5\frac{11}{36}$;

(b) $4 \div \cdot 00825$, giving the result as a repeating decimal.

10. The base of an isosceles triangle is 20 feet, and each of the equal sides is 26 feet. What is the altitude of the triangle?

11. What is the value of a house, if the insurance premium of $\frac{3}{8}$% on $\frac{2}{3}$ of its value, including $1 for the policy, amounts to $35?

12. If 28 lbs. of tea at 2/6 be mixed with 52 lbs. at 3/4 Sterling, how many dollars and cents, Canadian money, would 72 lbs. of the mixture be worth?

13. How many planks 16½ feet long by 15 inches wide will be required to floor a building 50 feet × 33 feet?

Exercise XLV.

1. Simplify:

$9 \left\{ \dfrac{1\frac{1}{4}}{\frac{16}{21}} \text{ of } 6\frac{2}{3} + 10\frac{1}{8} \right\} \div \left(7 \dfrac{\frac{1}{3} + \frac{1}{4}}{\frac{7}{10} + \frac{1}{11}} \right) \text{ of } \left\{ 5 \left(\dfrac{\frac{3}{4} + \frac{1}{5}}{\frac{4}{15}} \right) \right\}$.

2. At 25 cents a bushel, a bin of oats, 68 feet long, 8 feet wide, and 5 feet deep, costs $510.00. How many lbs. of oats were reckoned to the cubic foot?

3. A plank sidewalk 18 feet wide and 2 inches thick is to be built round a block of land 6 chains square, the walk to be no part of the block. What is the cost to build it, when lumber is $20 a thousand square feet?

4. The sum of two numbers is 253½ and their difference is 240⅔. Find the quotient arising from the division of the larger by 3 times the smaller.

174   EXERCISES IN ARITHMETIC.

5. A broker charges $\frac{7}{8}\%$ for investing money, and receives $70 for a certain transaction. Find the sum invested.

6. Which is the more profitable investment—5 per cent. bonds at 20% *discount*, or 8 per cent. bonds at 20% *premium?*
What would I gain on $1200 invested in the better concern?

7. How much must a merchant mark cloth which cost him 80 cents a yard, so that he may throw off 20 per cent. and still be selling at cost?

8. Bought a house and lot in a city for $7500; kept my property for 5 years at an annual expense of $225; sold out at a profit of 20% on my entire outlay. What was my selling price?

9. Two upright posts, set 32 feet apart, stand respectively 33 ft. and 9 ft. above the surface of the ground. What length of rope, stretched tightly, would be required to reach from the top of one post to the top of the other?

10. A commission merchant sold the following on $2\frac{1}{2}\%$ commission:—
   2800 lbs. wheat at 90 cents a bushel,
   500 boxes cheese of 70 lbs. each at 8 cents a lb.,
   605 lbs. butter at 20 cents a lb.,
   90 bags of potatoes at 55 cents a bag,
   35 bushels timothy seed at $2.50 a bushel.
Find the amount of his commission.

11. A man spends $33\frac{1}{3}\%$ of his weekly wages, and saves $780 per annum. What does he earn per week?

12. Simplify : $\left\{ \dfrac{\frac{2\frac{1}{4}}{7\frac{1}{3}} \text{ of } \frac{21}{32} \div 1\frac{9}{11}}{.35 \times .27} \times 1\frac{7}{9} \right\} + 2\frac{1}{2}.$

13. A fruiter remitted to his agent $467.62 with which to buy fruit at $2.27 a box, after deducting his commission of 3 per cent. How many boxes did the agent remit?

Exercise XLVI.

1. A and B together have $7000, and twice A's money is to three times B's as 4:9. How much money has each?

2. Find the cost of flagging, with marble slabs, a plot of ground 20 yards long by 20 feet wide, the slabs being each 18 inches long by 8 inches wide, and costing $30 a hundred.

3. A drover sold 200 cattle at $28 a head, gaining 40% on $\frac{2}{3}$ of them, and losing the same per cent. on the others. Find his net gain or loss on the entire drove.

FIFTH CLASS.

4. What is the area, in square inches, of a circle whose diameter is $3\frac{1}{2}$ yards? *12474 sq in* ✓

5. Bought 80 books for $300, and sold them at $4.20 each; find my gain per cent.

6. A can walk $4\frac{1}{6}$ miles in 50 minutes, and B can walk $3\frac{1}{5}$ miles in 42 minutes 40 seconds. How many minutes' start should A give B in 20 miles to beat him by 616 yards?

7. A man received $878.75 for a debt on which a collector levied 5% for his services. Find the amount of the debt. *$925*

8. The cost of enclosing a rectangular farm with a fence at 75 cents a rod was $375. The farm had 80 rods frontage and sold for $3060. Find the selling price per acre. *$36*

9. An agent sold a consignment of 7800 lbs. of butter at 25 cents a lb. on a commission of 4 per cent. He paid $192 for freight and storage, and invested the balance of the proceeds in silk on a commission of 5 per cent. Find the value of the silk remitted. *16c*

10. If 100 bushels of grain occupy 128 cubic feet of space, and a rectangular bin of grain $15' \times 8' \times 6'$ weigh $13\frac{1}{2}$ tons, what is the weight of a bushel of that grain? *48*

11. If $120 be gained on $584 in 125 days, what will be the gain on the same sum in 360 days at the same rate? *$345.60*

12. By selling goods at $16\frac{2}{3}$% profit a merchant clears $749; find the amount of his sales. *$5242*

13. I have an orchard 100 by 200 yards. The trees are set 20 feet apart and 20 feet from the fence which borders it. How many trees are there in my orchard? *406*

Exercise XLVII.

1. A note the face value of which is $520 is payable in 3 months with interest at 6 per cent. per annum. It is discounted at the date thereof at 10%. What rate per cent. *per annum* does the discounter realize on his money? What *per cent.* does he realize?

2. What is the value of
$$\left\{\overline{45 \div 9} \times 5\right\} \text{ times } \left\{\frac{3\frac{1}{2} \div \frac{5}{17}}{2\frac{1}{3} - \cdot 16} + \frac{9\frac{3}{8}}{39}\right\} \text{ times } 35 ?$$
6125

3. A and B together can mow a field in $3\frac{3}{7}$ days, and A can mow $\frac{3}{4}$ of it in 6 days. In how many days can B mow $\frac{2}{3}$ of it?

4. A man having drawn $7\frac{1}{2}$% of his money from the bank has still a deposit of $10027 to his credit. What was his original deposit?

176   EXERCISES IN ARITHMETIC.

5. A sold a carriage to B and gained $7\frac{1}{2}$ per cent. B sold it to C for $141.90, and thereby lost 12%. How much did the carriage cost A?

6. (a) Make out the following account *neatly, accurately,* and in *commercial form*:—

James Ross bought from you to-day :
   $10\frac{3}{4}$ lbs. cheese @ $10\frac{1}{4}$ cts. a lb.
   $7\frac{1}{4}$ "   rice   @ $24\frac{1}{2}$ "   "
   $6\frac{1}{3}$ "   cornmeal @ 10 cts. a lb.
   $41\frac{3}{50}$ "   prunes @ $1 for 12 lbs.

(b) Ross paid you the cash and you threw off 10%.
(c) Receipt the account as per data.

7. Find the amount of a note *made* February 24th, 1891, and *legally due* March 10th, 1892, the face of which is $182.50 with interest at 6% per annum. (Year = 365 days.)

8. A man insured 7000 barrels of apples worth $2 a barrel for $\frac{4}{5}$ of their value at $2\frac{1}{2}$%. A fire occurring, 200 barrels were saved. Find his loss.

9. A miller has 560 bushels of corn, 720 bushels of pease, and 815 bushels of rye to transport to his mills. What is the *least* number of the same-sized sacks that will move the grain at one moving without mixing it?

10. A farmer sold 6 loads of oats, each weighing on the average $2062\frac{2}{3}$ lbs., at $37\frac{1}{2}$ cts. a bushel; but the warehouse-man, by mistake, weighed the grain for rye, and gave the farmer a cheque for the same at 63 cents a bushel. What did the farmer gain or lose by the mistake?

11. Resolve 51480 and 3346200 into their prime factors, and from inspection of these write, *in prime factors,*—
   (i) their L.C.M. and G.C.M.,
   (ii) the quotient when the second number is divided by the first,
   (iii) the quotient when the product of both numbers is divided by their L.C.M.

12. Simplify: $\dfrac{\cdot\dot{6} - \cdot 6}{\cdot\dot{6} + \cdot 6} \times \dfrac{\cdot 3\dot{8} + \cdot 2\dot{4}}{\cdot 1\dot{6} - \cdot 1\dot{5}}$.

13. Simplify :

$$1\tfrac{4}{5}\tfrac{3}{5} \text{ of } \left\{ \left(\tfrac{\frac{1}{2}-\frac{1}{3}}{\frac{1}{5}+\frac{1}{3}} + \tfrac{\frac{1}{4}-\frac{1}{5}}{\frac{1}{6}+\frac{1}{7}} \right) \div \left(\tfrac{\frac{2}{3}-\frac{1}{8}}{\frac{1}{7}+\frac{1}{8}} - \tfrac{\frac{1}{5}-\frac{1}{4}}{\frac{1}{8}+\frac{1}{9}} \right) \right\}.$$

Exercise XLVIII.

1. A man's expenses are as follows:—Rent $\frac{1}{15}$ of income, and expenses of living 60% of the remainder. He finds that he will then save $560 per annum; find his total income.

2. (a) If 54000 pounds of wheat cost $787.50, find the cost price per bushel.

(b) A moulder cast 84 iron discs, each 56 inches in diameter and $\frac{1}{4}$ of an inch thick. How much should he get for them at 5 cents a lb., given that 7 cubic inches of iron weigh 3 lbs. 6 ounces?

3. A, B, C and D have together 1450 acres of land, and A's land is to B's as 2:3, B's to C's as 2:3, and C's to D's as 9:10. Find the size, in acres, of each man's farm.

4. A farmer sold, on the market, a load of oats at 28 cents a bushel; but the grain-dealer weighed it for barley and gave the farmer a cheque for it at 45 cents a bushel, by which the farmer was $9.30 in pocket. How many lbs. of grain had he on his waggon?

5. A music-dealer gave a discount of 8% for cash, and a second discount to teachers of 20% on all cash purchases. At what price was a book marked for which a teacher paid $4.60?

6. A and B enter into partnership to carry on a grocery business for one year. A puts in $1000 at the beginning of the year, and at the end of 6 months $500 more. B puts in $2500 at the beginning of the year, and withdraws $1000 at the end of the first three months. At the close of the year, they find they have gained $1800. Of this, what is B's share more than A's?

7. A retired merchant invests 35% of his capital in the 5 per cent. stock at 105, 20% of the remainder in 4 per cent. stock at 78, and the balance in $3\frac{1}{2}$ per cent. stock at $97\frac{1}{2}$. His total yearly income, thus derived, is $1575. Find his cash capital invested.

8. A commission merchant sold 6000 pounds of butter at 28 cents a pound. He remitted $1620, after paying freight $20, storage $19, and deducting his commission. What rate per cent. commission did he charge?

9. Sold 140 shares railroad stock at $7\frac{1}{2}$% premium. What did I receive, brokerage being $\frac{1}{4}$%?

10. The sides of a rectangle are as 3:4, and its area is 972 square yards; find the length of the *longest* straight line which can be drawn on its surface.

11. A note is drawn up as follows :—

1500\frac{00}{100}$.   VERSCHOYLE, June 1st, 1891.

One year after date, I promise to pay Robert Endsleigh or Order, the sum of fifteen hundred dollars, with interest at the rate of four per cent. per annum.   JAMES SIMCOE.

The foregoing note was endorsed as follows :—
  June 4th, 1892, $500.00.
  December 4th, 1892, $581.20.
  June 4th, 1893, $210.00.
How much would lift the note on September 4th, 1894 ?

12. The length of a rectangular field, containing 13 acres, 80 square rods, is $2\frac{2}{5}$ times its breadth, and a bicyclist can ride the length of a diagonal of the said field in 73.125 seconds. Find the time it would take him to ride round the field at the same rate of speed.

13. At what rate per cent. will $100 for 15 years amount to as much as $250 for 3 years at 6% ?

Exercise XLIX.

1. A bill due 9 months hence is discounted at 6% per annum *true* discount and $40 is received for it. What is the face value of the bill ?

2. A rectangular portion of ground, six times as long as it is wide and of the *least* possible size which could be planked with planks 10, 12, or 14 feet in length and a foot wide, is allotted by a city for a military parade ground. (*a*) Find its size in acres, sq. rods, etc.; and (*b*) the number of 14-ft. planks necessary to plank it.

3. How much ready cash would buy stock at $87\frac{1}{2}$, paying an annual dividend of 4 per cent., in order to realize an income of $720 per annum ?

4. The weight of pure gold in a guinea is $\frac{2625}{11789}$ of an ounce, and $\frac{8}{9}$ of the weight of a guinea is pure gold and the remainder an alloy 50 times less valuable. Find the value of pure gold per oz.

5. A grocer has teas at 45 cents a lb. and at 75 cents a lb., respectively. He mixes them in equal quantities, and sells the mixture at such a price that he gains as much per cent. on one kind as he loses per cent. on the other. What is his selling price per lb.? What does he gain or lose per cent. at this selling price ?

6. A man lost 5 per cent. by selling 6500 bushels of wheat at 76 cents a bushel. Find what total sum would have lost him nothing.

FIFTH CLASS.   179

7. If a merchant should sell a piece of cloth at $2.87½ a yard, he would gain $30.45 ; but if he should sell it at $2.50 a yard, he would gain only $15.45.   How much would he receive for his cloth at the average of these prices ?

8. A and B, two teachers in adjoining sections, each engage at $400 per annum to be paid *quarterly*, with the further understanding that A is to get an increase of $25 in his salary *every three months*, while B is to get an increase of $100 every year. Find the *difference* in their earnings at the end of seven years, interest being left out of the question.

9. After paying $12 for an overcoat, a man had $30 left. What per cent. of his money did he spend ?

10. A speculator insured a cargo of 40000 bushels of corn for $\frac{7}{8}$ of its value at 1⅛%, and paid a premium of $126. What was corn valued at per bushel ?

11. A rectangular field contains 60 acres, and its length is 120 rods. It is surrounded by a path 6 ft. wide as far as the corners of the field, and at the corners there are four squares of which the inner corner of each adjoins a respective corner of the field, the path and the squares containing 4700 square yards, 4 square feet. Find the length of a side of one of the square corners.

12. Sold 50 geese and turkeys for $49, the geese at 80 cents and the turkeys at $1.10 each.   How many turkeys did I sell?

13. (a) If ·257 of a farm cost $9280, what is the value of $\frac{11}{8}$ of it ?

(b) How many yards of satin ¾ of a yard wide will be required to line 22½ yards of velvet ½ a yard wide ?

Exercise L.

1. Find the result of the series :—

$$\frac{1}{5} - \frac{1}{(5)^2} + \frac{1}{(5)^3} - \frac{1}{(5)^4} + \frac{1}{(5)^5} - \frac{1}{(5)^6} + \frac{1}{(5)^7} - \frac{1}{(5)^8} + \frac{1}{(5)^9}.$$

2. The numerators of two fractions are 5 and 11, and ½ of the sum of the fractions is equal to ¾ of ⅛. What are the fractions?

3. The product of two numbers is 5103, and their G.C.M. is 9 ; find their L.C.M.

4. A farmer took a load of barley to the market where he sold it at 60 cents a bushel ; but on delivering it the warehouse-man weighed it for oats and gave him a cheque for it at 35 cents a bushel, by which the farmer lost $6. What was the weight of his load in lbs. ?

5. I invest a certain sum in the four per cents at 80, and an equal sum in the five per cents at 90. At the end of the year I receive my dividends; and each kind of stock having risen 10% in value, I sell out for cash, realizing a gain of $220. Find my total cash investment.

6. A fruiter sold apples at 5 cents a gallon, and gained 60 per cent. At this rate, find the cost price of apples per bushel.

7. What is the greatest distance between any two points on the floor of a room 36 feet long by 27 feet wide?

8. If I buy 8 per cent. Imperial Bank Stock on which there is a quarterly dividend of $120, what does the stock cost me at $137\frac{1}{2}$?

9. I invest in the $4\frac{1}{2}$ per cents at 75; what per cent. do I realize on my investment?

10. Simplify: $\left\{\dfrac{5\frac{2}{5} \text{ of } 7\frac{2}{3}}{8\frac{7}{24} - 3\frac{5}{12}}\right\} \div \left\{\dfrac{1\frac{3}{5}}{3 + \dfrac{1}{3\frac{1}{3}}} + \dfrac{1\frac{2}{3} \text{ of } 4\frac{2}{7}}{1\frac{2}{5} \text{ of } 3\frac{9}{7}}\right\}$.

11. A can mow $\frac{1}{3}$ of a field in three days, and B can mow $\frac{1}{5}$ of the field in the same time. In what time would both working together mow ·53 of the field?

12. If $\frac{2}{3}$ of the cost price of an article is equal to the gain and 25 per cent. of the selling price, find the gain per cent. at which the article is sold.

13. The extreme point of the minute hand of a tower clock moves $5\frac{1}{2}$ inches in 5 minutes. Find the length of the hand, given that it projects $1\frac{1}{2}$ inches beyond the central pivot around which it moves.

Exercise LI.

1. A wood-dealer buys wood at $3.60 a cord. Now, at what price per cord must he sell it, in order to realize a profit of 15%, and allow 10 per cent. of his sales as worthless?

2. If 20 gallons brandy, 15 gallons rye whiskey and 5 gallons cider are mixed together, what per cent. of the mixture is each?

3. A owes B $2630.88 to be paid in three *equal* payments in one year, one and one-half years, and two years, respectively, without interest. What ready cash payment should A accept, money being worth 8 per cent. per annum?

4. What principal will amount to $455.65 in $7\frac{1}{2}$ years at 4°/₀ per annum, simple interest?

FIFTH CLASS.

5. Find the cost of digging a drain 48 rods long, 3 feet deep, 3½ feet wide at the top, and 2½ feet wide at the bottom, at 4 cents a cubic yard.

6. At 30 cents a square foot, what is the value of a triangular piece of stone whose base is 9 feet and whose perpendicular height is 7 feet?

7. A gentleman insured a terrace of 7 houses for ⅞ of their value at 1½%, paying a premium of $147. Find the value of the terrace.

8. What must be the face of a note for 73 days, which discounted at the bank at 6% will produce $988 cash?

9. A drover bought 13 fat cattle at $35.00, $37.00, $37.50, $38.00, $40.00, $40.52, $41.00, $42.00, $42.75, $43.25, $45.00, $46.00, $52.00 per head, respectively. What would 50 such cattle cost at the average price?

10. If six men can do as much work as 20 boys in a given time, how much should a boy receive a day, if a man's daily wages are $2.40?

11. The difference between ⅔ of a fraction and ¾ of the same fraction is $\frac{7}{180}$; find the fraction.

12. A furnisher sold a suit of clothes for $32 and lost thereby 20%. He then sold another suit for $42 and gained as much per cent. as he lost on the first. What did both suits cost him? What was his entire gain or loss per cent. on the sale of the suits?

13. A man drew 14% of his deposit from the bank, and spent $70, which was 10⅗% of what he drew out. How much money had he in the bank?

Exercise LII.

1. A miller paid $21.50 for grain for chopping; ⅛ of it was barley at 40 cents a bushel, ½ of it was rye at 60 cents a bushel, and the rest corn at 50 cents a bushel. How many bushels in all did he get, and how many bushels of each kind of grain?

2. Find the average of 16 lbs. 10 ozs., 14 lbs. 8 ozs., 15 lbs. 7 ozs., 11 lbs. 4 ozs., and 3 lbs. 2 ozs.

3. Two places on the globe, due east and west of each other, are 125 degrees of longitude apart. What is the difference in time of the two places?

4. A merchant gained 20% by selling cloth at 60 cents a yard; find his gain on the sale of 1000 yards of the same cloth at 75 cents a yard.

5. If 8 hours constitute a day's work, and 20 men or 35 boys can do a piece of work in 5 days, how long will it take 8 men and 6 boys working together to do it?

6. A store and its contents together are valued at $7000, and the contents are worth 1½ times as much as the store. Find the value of each.

7. Find the simple interest on $438 from Jan. 16th till April 6th, 1894, at 5 per cent. per annum (civil year).

8. A merchant bought a *certain* number of pairs of shoes at 62½ cents a pair, *twice* as many pairs of boots at 75 cents a pair, and *three* times as many pairs of slippers at 25 cents a pair, paying for the lot $101. How many pairs of each did he buy?

9. A tank is 22 ft. long at the top, 20 ft. long at the bottom, 5 ft. wide and 6 ft. deep, inside measurement. How many barrels of water will it hold?

10. It takes 70 yards of 27-inch carpeting to cover the floor of a hall 45 ft. long ; how many feet and inches wide is the hall?

11. A hole 3½ inches in diameter is bored lengthwise through 576 feet of pump-log. How many cubic feet and inches of material did the auger remove?

12. Find the marked price of a bale of 1290 yards of linen that will leave a net cash price of 34 cents a yard, after two successive discounts of 20% and 15% have been made.

13. Find the equated time for the payment of the following account :—

Dr.   GEORGE LEEDS.   Cr.

1894				1894			
March	1	To Mdse...	80 00	March	15	By Cash....	100 00
"	7	" "	37 00	"	29	" "	10 00
April	6	" "	50 00				
May	4	" "	30 00				

1. A man invests the P. Worth of $2,662.40 due 8 mos hence at 6% per annm, in bank stock at 95½ (brok ½) paying 4½% yearly dividends. Find yearly Income. $120

2. I sell out $6000 stock in the 6% @ 108, and invest the proceeds in 4½% stk @ 72. Do I change my income, and how much. Increase $45.

3. I invest $10175 in Bk of Montreal stock @ 203 brok. ½ paying 8% yearly dividends, and $4960 in bank of Toronto stk @ 197½ (brok ½) paying 7½% yearly Divds Find Income $587.50

4. A & B invest capl in the proportion of 5 to 9. At the end of 5 mos A withdraws 25% of his Capl and at the end of 6 mos B withdraws 33⅓% of his. If

ANSWERS.

their profits for the year are $3051. divide it fairly between them. A $1107. B $1944

PART II.

5. $159 due in 9 mos when money is worth 8% per ann

FOURTH AND FIFTH CLASSES.

is invested in Ont. Bk Stk @ 85 paying 4% per ann find yearly income? $7\frac{1}{17}$

6. A man derives an Income of $350 from an Investment of 3½% stk @ 88. How much stk does he own and how much is it worth. $10000 stk. value 8800$

7. (a) Find the change in Income made by transferring $5000 from the 4% @ 84, to the 3½% @ 70. ans $10 g.
(b) $12750 from the 5% @ 80 to the 5⅔% @ 85 Gain $42.50
(c) $4275 from the 4% @ 80 to the 5½ @ 99¾? ans. $19 gain
d. $2500 from the 5⅝% @ 114⅛ to the 5% @ 94⅞ brok ⅛ each way? $20 gain.
e. $3600 from the 4% @ 85 to the 5% @ 102 Ans $6 gain

8. A man has left to him $2500. He invests 1/4 of it in the 6% @ 112 1/2; 1/3 of it in 4 1/2% @ 80, and the rest in 3% @ 75. Find his income $121.87 1/2

9. I invest $27225 in the 3% @ 90 5/8 and when they have risen to 91 1/8 I sell out & invest in the 3 1/2% @ 97 3/8. What is the change in my income book 1/8
   Ans. $80 Increase

10. I invest $25500 in the 4% @ 85 and when they have risen to 90 sell out and invest the proceeds in the 4 1/2% @ 108. Find the change in my income?
    $75 loss.

FOURTH CLASS.

Exercise I.

1. $90 ; B $600 ; C $300.
2. 15 minutes.
3. $6\frac{7}{9}$ days.
4. $53\frac{1}{3}$ per cent.
5. 31 lbs.
6. $140.
7. $155.52.
8. $185,600.00.
9. 70 dozen.
10. $63.
11. $\frac{1}{15}$ of an ounce.
12. $\frac{19}{210}$.
13. 450 times.

Exercise II.

1. $6750.
2. Product 518 acres, 16 rods, 3 ft., 48 inches. Quotient 57 acres, 90 rods, 20 yds., 1 ft., $125\frac{1}{2}$ inches = $361095029\frac{1}{4}$ inches.
3. (a) 50 miles ; (b) 3168000 inches.
4. 207 rods, 2 yards, 1 ft. 10 inches.
5. $385.
6. 2 inches.
7. $10.05.
8. ———
9. 25 per cent.
10. $80.
11. $768.
12. $29.60.
13. (a) $13.75 ; (b) 99 times.

Exercise III.

1. 660 yds.
2. 6 years.
3. $20.
4. 38 bushels 24 lbs.
5. $666 gain.
6. (a) $18\frac{11}{12}$; (b) $9\frac{7}{28}$.
7. $6300.
8. $.72 a cwt.
9. $5\frac{2}{5}$ days.
10. $2.92.
11. 31 miles, 219 rods, 4 yds., 1 ft., 3 inches.
12. $27\frac{9}{13}$ min. past VI.
13. (a) $6480 loss ; (b) $\left\{\begin{array}{l}50 \text{ lbs., } 0 \text{ ozs.} \\ 37 \text{ lbs., } 8 \text{ ozs.}\end{array}\right\}$; (c) $189.51.

ANSWERS.

Exercise IV.

1. 1 mile.
2. 80 rods.
3. $9.60.
4. $65.60 gain.
5. 49 days.
6. 25 gallons.
7. $5.84.
8. H.C.F. 3 inches; L.C.M. 165060.
9. 25 per cent.
10. $61200.
11. $620.
12. 176 feet.
13. $7\frac{1}{2}$ per cent.

Exercise V.

1. 4 lbs.
2. 336 yds.
3. $78\frac{3}{4}$ cents.
4. 45 gallons.
5. $4\frac{1}{2}$ per cent.
6. $192.

7. (a) 2552 cub. feet, 1088 cub. inches; (b) 1120 sq. feet, 96 sq. inches.
8. 50 per cent.
9. A's $400; B's $700; C's $350.
10. 40 tons, 500 lbs.
11. 112 days.
12. 225 cords.
13. (a) $240; (b) $902.40; (c) $95.10.

Exercise VI.

1. $23\frac{1}{13}$ min. past 5 o'clock.
2. 11.24 o'clock, or 24 min. past 11 o'clock.
3. $16\frac{4}{11}$ min.
4. (a) $21\frac{9}{11}$ min. past 7 o'clock; (b) $21\frac{9}{11}$ min. to 8 o'clock; (c) $5\frac{5}{11}$ min. to 8 o'clock.
5. $9\frac{3}{13}$ min. to 12 o'clock.
6. 48 min. past 11 o'clock, or 12 min. to 12 o'clock.
7. $4.43\frac{7}{11}$ o'clock p.m.
8. $5\frac{5}{11}$ min. to 11 o'clock.
9. 24 min.
10. $43\frac{7}{11}$ min. after III.
11. $18\frac{6}{13}$ min. past 4 o'clock.
12. 4 min.
13. (a) In 6 min. 12 seconds; (b) in $16\frac{4}{11}$ min.; (c) in 24 min.; (d) in $32\frac{4}{11}$ min.; (e) $49\frac{1}{11}$ min.; (f) in 1 hour (at one o'clock); (g) in $55\frac{5}{11}$ minutes.

ANSWERS. 41

Exercise VII.

1. $10.
2. (a) $4.80 ; (b) $1.00.
3. $940.
4. $4\frac{75}{676}$.
5. $\frac{3}{35}$.
6. 8 bushels.
7. 3 acres, 106 sq. rods, 22 sq. yds., 7 sq. ft., 72 sq. inches.
8. 79.
9. 14 days.
10. $\overline{\text{CDLIV}}\text{CDXV}$.
11. 1000.
12. $40.
13. (a) $823.44 ; (b) $40.30.

Exercise VIII.

1. £2, 13 sh., 4d.
2. 12 minutes to 10 o'clock, or 48 minutes past 9 o'clock.
3. 5750 pieces.
4. (a) 22 feet, 6 inches ; (b) 112.
5. $27.
6. 385 tons.
7. 180 bushels.
8. $2.92. per day.
9. $800.
10. $2294.
11. 100 per cent. gain.
12. 4320 times.
13. (a) $85 ; (b) $1 ;
   (c) $\begin{cases} 1050 \text{ first.} \\ 1008 \text{ second.} \\ 1200 \text{ third.} \end{cases}$

Exercise IX.

1. 320 loads.
2. 45 bushels pease.
3. $500.
4. $4.00.
5. $3600.
6. A $40, B $240, C $360.
7. $25,520.
8. $73.50.
9. $1.75.
10. $100.
11. 35 per cent.
12. $\frac{1}{2}$.
13. $12\frac{1}{2}$ per cent.

Exercise X.

1. $2^2 \times 5 \times 17$; $2^4 \times 5^2 \times 7$; $2^2 \times 5 \times 3 \times 7^2$.
2. $2^2 \times 3^5 \times 5$; $2^2 \times 3 \times 7 \times 71$; $2^2 \times 3^2 \times 5^3$.
3. $2^4 \times 3 \times 5^2 \times 7$; $2^4 \times 239$; $2^2 \times 3 \times 5 \times 23$.
4. $2^4 \times 5^2 \times 11$; $2^5 \times 3^3$; $2^3 \times 3^3 \times 5^2$.
5. $2^3 \times 5 \times 7$; $2^7 \times 5$; $2 \times 3^3 \times 11 \times 13$.
6. $2^6 \times 3 \times 5$; $2^3 \times 3^2 \times 5^2$; $2^2 \times 5^4$.
7. $3^2 \times 5 \times 7 \times 11 \times 13$; $2 \times 3 \times 7 \times 11 \times 19$; $2^3 \times 5^2 \times 7 \times 11$.
8. $2^3 \times 5$; $2^5 \times 3^3 \times 5^2$; $2^2 \times 3^4 \times 5^2$.

42 ANSWERS.

9. $2^3 \times 3 \times 5^2 \times 11$; $2^2 \times 5^3 \times 13$; $2^2 \times 3 \times 5^2 \times 13$.
10. $2^3 \times 3^3 \times 5^2$; $2^4 \times 5^2 \times 13$; $2^3 \times 3 \times 5^4$.
11. $2 \times 5^2 \times 23$; $2^3 \times 3 \times 5 \times 47$; $2^2 \times 5 \times 7 \times 13$.
12. $2^2 \times 5^2 \times 3 \times 7$; $2^2 \times 3 \times 5^2 \times 29$; $2^2 \times 5^3 \times 7$.
13. $2^2 \times 5 \times 67$; $2 \times 3^4 \times 5^2$; 7×29^2.

Exercise XI.

1. 11592.
2. 7436429.
3. 720720.
4. 672.
5. 180.
6. 504.
7. 1530.
8. 5040.
9. 6300.
10. 1673196525.
11. 10810800.
12. 3255840.
13. 565081020.

Exercise XII.

1. 510510.
2. 5040.
3. 25200.
4. 8400.
5. 2520.
6. 5019589575.
7. 277200.
8. 28728.
9. 3300.
10. 378000.
11. 864.
12. 1511640.
13. (a) 3517800; (b) 460.

Exercise XIII.

1. 477.
2. 788.
3. 192.
4. 47.
5. 1 (Prime to each other.)
6. 89.
7. 13.
8. 3.
9. 3224.
10. 39.
11. 267.
12. 43.
13. 837.

Exercise XIV.

1. 225.
2. 267.
3. 29.
4. 131.
5. 4.
6. 7.
7. 41.
8. 186.
9. 37.
10. 492.
11. 21.
12. 97.
13. 99.

ANSWERS.   43

Exercise XV.

1. 628320.
2. $32340 \div 1617 = 20$.
3. $1680 \div 168 = 10$.
4. $599760 \div 147 = 4080$.
5. $720720 \div 1001 = 720$.
6. $2227680 \div 4641 = 480$.
7. $128 \times 2304 = 294912$.
8. 232792561.
9. $60 \div \frac{5}{48} = 576$.
10. $184\frac{4}{5}$.
11. $1\frac{7}{8}$.
12. 9.
13. (a) $\frac{1}{2}$; (b) G.C.M. 3; L.C.M. 12; (c) 60 cents.

Exercise XVI.

1. $13\frac{1}{20}$.
2. $8\frac{47}{137}$.
3. $\frac{583}{1810}$.
4. $14\frac{9}{10}$.
5. $8\frac{347}{1700}$.
6. $14\frac{7}{8}$.
7. (a) $3\frac{5}{8}$; (b) $2\frac{29}{81}$; (c) $2\frac{317}{525}$.
8. $6\frac{117}{180}$ and $5\frac{87}{91}$.
9. $7\frac{61}{112}$ and $4\frac{11}{28}$.
10. (a) $5\frac{7}{24}$; (b) $4\frac{1008}{1198}$.
11. (a) $\frac{5}{18}$; (b) $2\frac{33}{37}$.
12. 3.
13. (a) $63\frac{1818}{1818}$; (b) 23 sq. yds. 5 sq. ft. 36 sq. inches.

Exercise XVII.

1. (a) $11\frac{33}{77}$; (b) 100.
2. $1\frac{4}{5}$.
3. 18.
4. $\frac{1}{8}$.
5. $16\frac{1}{4}$.
6. 85.
7. (a) $19\frac{1}{5}$; (b) $31\frac{4}{71}$.
8. (a) 16; (b) $1\frac{32}{173}$.
9. $\frac{28}{80}$ and $\frac{18}{35}$.
10. (a) $8\frac{256}{2515}$; (b) $1\frac{1087}{1180}$.
11. 5; 144; $1\frac{5}{11}$.
12. $\frac{3}{4}$.
13. (a) $3\frac{1}{2}$; (b) $\frac{7}{10}$.

Exercise XVIII.

1. 8.
2. $1\frac{1}{2}$.
3. $9\frac{7}{50}$.
4. 2.
5. 6.
6. 2.
7. 1.
8. 1.
9. $\frac{1}{2}$.
10. $6\frac{1}{4}$.
11. $\frac{1}{4}$.
12. 2.
13. $\frac{117}{100}$.

Exercise XIX.

1. $6\frac{3}{4}$.
2. 32 vests.
3. 32.
4. $93\frac{1}{2}$ yds.
5. $3135.
6. $\frac{432\_567\_525\_644}{1008}$; $\frac{53}{352}$.
7. $1\frac{1}{4}$ hours.
8. $7\frac{17}{10}$ acres.
9. $13\frac{5}{8}$ lbs., or 13 lbs., 10 ozs.
10. $\frac{7}{80}$.
11. $1\frac{17}{172}$.
12. House, $2100. Lot, $300.
13. (a) 1089.
    (b) 2 quarts, 1 pint.

Exercise XX.

1. $2\frac{3}{8}$.
2. Sum $= 1\frac{19}{36}$; Quotient 7.
3. $\frac{4}{5}, \dfrac{3+4}{4+5},$ and $\frac{3}{4}$.
4. (a) L.C.M. 382109; (b) $\frac{379}{46189}$.
5. $\dfrac{3}{5\frac{1}{2}}$.
6. $\dfrac{16}{5\frac{1}{8}}$.
7. $70\frac{793}{1280}$.
8. 3108.
9. $34\frac{43}{162}$.
10. (a) $\frac{1}{8}$; (b) $480.
11. 1.
12. $\frac{3\frac{5}{8}}{}$.
13. $\begin{cases}(a)\ \frac{1}{27};\\(b)\ \frac{29}{160};\ (c)\end{cases}$ [diagram: rectangle A E B / G H / C F D, with $\frac{2}{3}$, $\frac{1}{2}$ of $\frac{2}{3}$, $\frac{1}{3}$ labeled] $=\begin{cases}\text{A C D B}=\text{one whole rectangle.}\\ \text{A C F E}=\frac{2}{3}\text{ of the whole.}\\ \text{G C F H}=\frac{1}{2}\text{ of }\frac{2}{3}\text{ of the whole; }=\frac{2}{6}\text{ or }\frac{1}{3}\text{ of the whole rectangle, etc.}\end{cases}$

(d) $\frac{8}{15}$ ac. = 19 sq. rods, 6 sq. yds., 64.8 sq. inches; (e) 1.

Exercise XXI.

1. 28656 ounces.
2. $13\frac{1}{8}$ dozen.
3. 12 acres, 85 sq. rods.
4. $1.55.
5. $\begin{cases}\text{A 12 days.}\\ \text{B 6 days.}\end{cases}$
6. 3 feet.
7. 15 miles.
8. 5880600 sq. inches.
9. $4791.12.
10. 142992 cubic inches.
11. 25 per cent.
12. $\frac{73}{77}$.
13. 6240.

Exercise XXII.

1. $900.
2. $1540.
3. $3430.
4. $5.
5. 34.28\frac{4}{7}$.
6. $1000.
7. $8100.
8. 311.11\frac{1}{9}$.
9. $60.
10. $2.50; $3\frac{17}{36}$ cents.
11. 9000 sq. feet.
12. 1800.
13. (a) $49; (b) $1\frac{1}{5}$; $1\frac{1}{5}\times$560.00 = $672.00.

ANSWERS.

Exercise XXIII.

1. $10\frac{2}{3}$ days.
2. $5.
3. $116.34.
4. ·03̇7̇.
5. $10.
6. $1057.50.
7. The latter, by $10.
8. 607.
9. $21\frac{9}{11}$ minutes.
10. $19.78.
11. 350 bushels.
12. 1 ton, 1125 lbs.
13. (a) $80.64 ; (b) 3 days.

Exercise XXIV.

1. $\frac{3}{14}$.
2. A $120, B $105.
3. $4000, and $12\frac{1}{2}$ per cent. loss.
4. $222.
5. A 16 years, B 24 years.
6. A $60, B $80, C $90, D 205, and E $180.
7. 10 miles.
8. $6\frac{1}{4}$ gallons.
9. 54 men.
10. 76400 chains.
11. 27 cub. feet.
12. 4 lbs. green and 10 lbs. black.
13. 587 lbs., 8 ozs.

Exercise XXV.

1. $900.
2. 120 hats.
3. $87.50.
4. 40 per cent.
5. A $22.50; B $15.00; C 10.00.
6. (a) $\frac{1}{5}$; (b) $\frac{3}{10}$.
7. $12.00.
8. $99.00.
9. $200.
10. $397.50.
11. 40 per cent.
12. $8.00.
13. 96.86\frac{92}{93}$ an acre.

Exercise XXVI.

1. (a) 5 hours ; (b) 5 miles.
2. 200 yards.
3. $\frac{1}{18}$.
4. 140 lbs.
5. $60.
6. 200.
7. 105 acres, 128 sq. rods.
8. 15 gallons.
9. $42 safe, $147 contents.
10. 12 feet.
11. $150, $200 and $250 for A, B and C, respectively.
12. $750.
13. 35.

Exercise XXVII.

1. 8.36 o'clock, or 24 minutes to 9 o'clock.
2. 10 rods.
3. 1280 acres.
4. $22\frac{1}{2}$d. per lb.
5. 38 barrels, 127 lbs.; and 25 lbs. in a bag.
6. $152.90.
7. $6.
8. 1 acre, 38 sq. rods, 29 sq. yds., 5 sq. feet, 90 sq. inches.
9. $112.
10. $9.41\frac{7}{13}$ o'clock.
11. 8 days.
12. $143\frac{1}{3}$ per cent.
13. (a) 87318 bushels; (b) 351 times; (c) $126.

Exercise XXVIII.

1. $210.63.
2. $4.50.
3. $2252.25.
4. 602 carats.
5. $14000.
6. 5 dozen.
7. 1000 papers.
8. 1036 acres, 127 sq. rods, 30 sq. yds., 2 sq. feet, 36 sq. in.
9. 4 dozen.
10. $\frac{37}{850}$.
11. 12 o'clock, noon.
12. 405, 360 and 324, respectively.
13. $2,395,800, an acre.

Exercise XXIX.

1. 280 sheep.
2. $900.
3. $7.30 an acre.
4. $4 a cwt.
5. 1400 five-cent pieces; $74.
6. The first, by 763 lbs.
7. $71.28.
8. 27390 feet.
9. 109 feet.
10. (a) $\frac{1}{2}$; (b) $2\frac{3}{4}$.
11. $37800.
12. $42834.00.
13. 1 foot, 6 inches.

Exercise XXX.

1. 17136 times.
2. (a) $(2 \times 2 \times 3 \times 3 \times 5)$, $(2 \times 3 \times 3 \times 5 \times 7)$, $(2 \times 3 \times 5 \times 5 \times 7 \times 7)$.
(b) I. G. C. M. = $(2 \times 3 \times 5)$ the *greatest* selection of common factors of these numbers = 30. II. L. C. M. = $(2^2 \times 3^2 \times 5^2 \times 7^2)$ the *smallest* selection of factors, including the factors of each given number = 44100.

3. (a) $(3 \times 5 \times 7 \times 13)$ and $(2 \times 5 \times 5 \times 7 \times 13)$. (b) (I.) G. C. M. is equal to $(5 \times 7 \times 13) = 455$; (II) L. C. M. is equal to $(2 \times 5 \times 5 \times 7 \times 13 \times 3) = 13650$. (c) (I.) From (b) (I.) and (II.) we have G. C. M. × L. C. M. $= (5 \times 7 \times 13) \times (2 \times 5 \times 5 \times 7 \times 13 \times 3) = (3 \times 5 \times 7 \times 13 \times 2 \times 5 \times 5 \times 7 \times 13)$ all the factors of 1365 and 4550; (II.) from (c) (I.) we see that G. C. M. is composed of the factors of 1365 and 4550 rejected by L. C. M. and *vice versâ*; (III.) G. C. M. and L. C. M. are made up of all the factors of 1365 and 4550 [c. (I.)]; therefore G.C.M. × L. C. M. = product of the two numbers (because G.C.M. and L.C.M. = *all the factors* of the given numbers); (IV.) since G.C.M. × L. C. M. of the two numbers = product of numbers; therefore their product ÷ one of the numbers = the other number, and *vice versâ*; (V.) since product of the two numbers = G. C. M. × L. C. M.; therefore their product ÷ G. C. M. = L. C. M. and *vice versâ*.

4. 180.
5. (Theory).
6. 740.
7. The smallest number we could have for one is 240; therefore, 240 and 2880, or 720 (third multiple) and 960, etc. (N.B. all the multiples of 240 will not do, however).
8. L. C. M. 40; Quot., 525.
9. H. C. F., 5; L. C. M., 30.
10. (a) H. C. F., $\frac{1}{105}$; L. C. M., $\frac{3}{4}$; (b) 1 and 81 times, respectively.
11. 243,706,050.
12. L. C. M., 90, and H. C. F., $\frac{1}{105}$.
13. 272.

Exercise XXXI.

1. 312 bushels.
2. 4.
3. 25 of each.
4. (a) The latter kind by $\frac{1}{28}$ of a cent, per inch. (b) 40 sticks of the 7-inch kind.
5. 410 and 615.
6. 4840 times.
7. 21 lbs., $0\frac{7}{8}$ ounces, $(21\frac{7}{128}$ lbs).
8. 650 lbs. at 4, 6 and 8 cents, respectively, and 1560 lbs. at 15 cents.
9. $5\frac{10}{13}\%$.
10. $96.24.
11. $20 cost.
12. $240.
13. (a) 514 bushels. 16 lbs.; (b) 9600; (c) $18.48.

Exercise XXXII.

1. 11½ cents.
2. 3¾ ozs.
3. A $78.32. B $121.04.
4. 3 : 13.
5. $4,150,000.
6. 416 sq. ft., 96 sq. inches.
7. $240.
8. 7 cents.
9. 5 days.
10. $1613.20.
11. £16, Sterling.
12. $691.
13. (a) 56 cents. (b) L.C.M., 90; 73 times.

Exercise XXXIII.

1. A $4.50. B $2.00. C $1.80.
2. 200.
3. $5,700.
4. 20 per cent.
5. 1$\frac{25}{48}$.
6. 210.
7. 22.
8. 567, L.C.M.
9. 357, the greater; and 136, the less.
10. 160 lbs. of the dearer, and 120 of the cheaper.
11. 70 cents.
12. 2$\frac{6}{7}$ per cent.
13. (a) $7000 cost, $8000 asking price, $7500 selling price; (b) $32.60.

Exercise XXXIV.

1. $2.
2. November 19th, 1888.
3. 40 per cent.
4. $200.
5. First cost, $4; second cost, $2.
6. $131.25.
7. 200 bushels.
8. 4 per cent.
9. 66¾ per cent.
10. $6875.
11. (a) 57$\frac{11}{12}$; (b) 35¼.
12. 9 years.
13. (a) 16 feet; (b) 36 years.

Exercise XXXV.

1. 3½ years.
2. 4 per cent.
3. $1800.
4. 112 barrels, and 560 boxes.
5. 20, 80 and 160.
6. 510 cords, 60 cubic feet.
7. 5166 acres, 119 sq. rods, 6 sq. yds., 2 sq. ft., 36 sq. in.
8. $4800.
9. $54.
10. $504.
11. 4 times.
12. G:B::2:3 (or 120 lbs. green and 180 lbs. black).
13. (a) 336; (b) $2.35.

ANSWERS.   49

Exercise XXXVI.

1. $607.50 amount (principal and interest).
2. 5 per cent.
3. 12½ years.
4. The latter by $5440.
5. ¼.
6. $4.50.
7. $33.75.
8. 5585 miles, 1650 yards.
9. 16 tons, 1860 lbs.
10. 13 acres, 157 sq. rods, 139 sq. yds., 5 sq. feet.
11. $16.20.
12. $·90.
13. 3176 miles, 80 rods.

Exercise XXXVII.

1. 4 per cent.
2. 25 per cent.
3. 3600 men.
4. $57.60.
5. 2640 times.
6. 40 cents.
7. 99 days.
8. $1750.
9. 20 lbs. at 46, 50 and 75 cents, respectively, and 9 lbs. at 80 cents.
10. 38⅝ per cent.
11. $13333⅓.
12. $92.
13. 104 yds. at $1.80 = $187.20 (practically); 25%.

Exercise XXXVIII.

1. $1880.
2. $327.00.
3. 9$\frac{13}{18}$ days.
4. 3 min. per hour.
5. 90 gallons.
6. 31,536,000 seconds.
7. $180.00.
8. 4 months.
9. (a) Side measurement, 32 sq. ft. to a cord. (b) In tiers lengthwise of the pile.
10. $271.25.
11. 8 lbs. at 50 cents, 5 lbs. at 70 cents.
12. 18 gallons.
13. (a) $10 ; (b) 30 cents.

Exercise XXXIX.

1. 4 hrs., 35 min.
2. 150 per cent.
3. 20.
4. 420 sq. inches.
5. 62$\frac{8}{11}$ per cent.
6. $24.80.
7. ½.
8. 6732 ; 1679, sum.
9. $8.
10. $4.20.
11. $75.
12. $22.50.
13. (a) 70 tons ; (b) $384

Exercise XL.

1. $2.51⅞.
2. First, 70; second, 140; third, 60.
3. 17136.
4. 10 bags.
5. 1875 bushels.
6. 841.
7. 56 lbs.
8. A, $9.00; B, $4.30; C, $2.90; D, $12.60.
9. 90 fives; 80 tens.
10. $1432.32.
11. $36.50.
12. 113.
13. (a) 16 cents; (b) A, $350; B, $50; C, $250.

Exercise XLI.

1. $7000.
2. (a) $\frac{1}{8}$; (b) $\frac{40}{81}$; (c) $\frac{1}{2}$.
3. $1075.20.
4. 9 miles.
5. $175.50.
6. $\frac{1}{8}$ of an inch to the mile.
7. 90 cents.
8. $\frac{2}{25}$.
9. 4 per cent.
10. 107 cart-loads.
11. 5200.
12. 80 per cent.
13. 5 p.m.

Exercise XLII.

1. (a) 10 minutes; (b) 3 miles.
2. 432 days.
3. $333.
4. 12 days.
5. $1440.
6. 24762 tons, 1678 lbs., 2 ozs.
7. 2 games.
8. 33⅓ per cent.
9. $1950.
10. $216.
11. 16 days.
12. 1¼ per cent. gain.
13. 5 per cent.

Exercise XLIII.

1. (a) 80 cents; (b) 3⅛ per cent.
2. 2000 gallons.
3. 48 tons.
4. $156.06.
5. 5 per cent.
6. $27.50.
7. A, $40; B, $120; C, $180.
8. 2 lbs. 8 ozs.
9. 12 per cent.
10. 15 cents a doz., before; 12 cents a doz., after.
11. $244.48.
12. 20.
13. $84.

Exercise XLIV.

1. $1.46.
2. $\frac{34}{75}$.
3. 7 years.
4. A, $81 ; B, $90 ; C, $108.
5. 49 boys.
6. 420.
7. $\frac{1}{2}$.
8. $6.12.
9. $1880.
10. $53.82.
11. November 19th, 1888.
12. 8 hours.
13. $4.00 loss.

Exercise XLV.

1. $737.10.
2. $436.48.
3. 20.
4. $46.30.
5. 20 days, 12 hrs., 48 minutes.
6. 50 per cent.
7. 2254 casks, and $3\frac{2}{3}$ pints left.
8. 24 miles.
9. $41.60.
10. $517.11.
11. $2200.00.
12. 24 miles an hour.
13. 1089.00.

Exercise XLVI.

1. 435.
2. 1120.
3. 40 cents.
4. 2105.
5. $1530.
6. 150.
7. 32.
8. 112.
9. $125 and $280.
10. $\frac{2\frac{1}{4}}{}$ of a sq. inch.
11. $8688.80.
12. 7:5.
13. (a) 6 turkeys, 3 ducks, 2 geese and 2 chickens; (b) £10 14sh. 11d.

Exercise XLVII.

1. $\frac{1}{225}$.
2. Yes; because it is the measure of a quantity.
3. Due Dec. 13th, 1891, but must be paid on the 16th Dec. (3 days' grace); $654 will redeem it.
4. $1.55.
5. 5.
6. A, $560.00; B, $784.00; C, $1120.00.
7. $180.00.
8. 132.
9. 42.
10. $1287.45.
11. $420.
12. 25 per cent.
13. (a) 840 ; (b) 1 ft. 4 in.

Exercise XLVIII.

1. $146000.00.
2. A $14.00 ; B $70.00 ; C $28.00.
3. 13 sq. feet, 153 sq. inches.
4. A $\begin{cases} 20\frac{55}{144} \text{ gallons of wine.} \\ 9\frac{89}{144} \text{ gallons of water.} \end{cases}$
   B $\begin{cases} 9\frac{89}{144} \text{ gallons of wine.} \\ 10\frac{55}{144} \text{ gallons of water.} \end{cases}$
5. 750.
6. $36.00.
7. Sum $800.00 ; Shares $\begin{cases} \text{A's } \$500.00. \\ \text{B's } \$60.00. \\ \text{C's } \$240.00. \end{cases}$
8. 4.
9. $33.33\frac{1}{3}$ less.
10. $73\frac{1}{2}$ cents.
11. 18 lbs., 12 ozs.
12. $90.
13. (a) 504 rails ; (b) 515 yds.

Exercise XLIX.

1. $122.88.
2. 115 yards.
3. 12 horses ; 108 sheep.
4. 100 gallons.
5. 8 per cent.
6. 700.
7. $2\frac{3}{11}$.
8. 81.
9. 66 trees.
10. $13\frac{1}{3}$ % gain.
11. 135 ounces.
12. 660 times.
13. $\begin{cases} 20 \text{ lbs. at } 60 \text{ cents.} \\ 30 \text{ " " } 70 \text{ "} \end{cases}$

Exercise L.

1. $11,900.00.
2. 80.
3. 7,115,505.
4. $183.
5. $\begin{cases} \text{A. } \$118.80 \\ \text{B. } \$1608.00 \end{cases}$ Total, $1726.80.
6. $145.71..
7. $8\frac{1}{2}$ per cent.
8. 32 dozen.
9. $37\frac{1}{2}$ per cent.
10. 7×907 ; $2^3 \times 3^2 \times 5^3$; $2^3 \times 5^2$.
11. 35.
12. $\begin{cases} 64\frac{8}{15} \text{ min.} \\ 32\frac{7}{15} \text{ "} \end{cases}$
13. 246.31\frac{1}{4}$.

Exercise LI.

1. A, $36 ; B, $48 ; C, $40.
2. $16.
3. $1\frac{7}{8}$.
4. Clay, 60 feet ; sand, 12 feet ; rock, 18 feet.
5. 13 days.
6. 28.
7. 5040.
8. 5 days.
9. Both (a) and (b) Theory ; (c) (I.) $\frac{32}{55}$; (II.) 62 ; (d) (I.) 9091 ; (II.) 61 ac., 96 rods, 26 yds., 6 ft. 108 in.
10. $103,000.
11. $72.
12. A, $615 ; B, $1025.
13. 40 cents.

ANSWERS. 53

Exercise LII.

1. 560 acres.
2. 60 per cent.
3. 2.
4. 5 lbs.
5. −$60. (He is $60 in debt.)
6. (a) 71 ; (b) 1,244.880.
7. A, 60 days ; B, 180 days.
8. ·027045.
9. $100.
10. 2880 times.
11. Lose, $1400.
12. 25 ft. 6 in. long ; 17 ft. 0 in. wide.
13. (a) $91.26 ; (b) 28 cents.

Exercise LIII.

1. $1 25.
2. $200.
3. 649.97\frac{193}{253}$.
4. $6864.
5. 5⅓ cents.
6. $677.60.
7. $28.75.
8. $44.00.
9. $764.00.
10. $32.
11. 242.
12. $497.61.
13. 114.

Exercise LIV.

1. $80 per annum.
2. $8500.00.
3. (a) ⅓ ; (b) $\frac{41}{108}$.
4. 17 days.
5. 40 days.
6. $192.
7. A, $480 ; B, $360.
8. $3.
9. $\frac{20}{77}$.
10. $170·555264.
11. 40 barrels.
12. −$\frac{403}{13530}$.
13. (a) $189.00 ; (b) $75.60.

Exercise LV.

1. A, $242.10 ; B, $121.05.
2. The ninth = 9 × 450 = 4050.
3. 7½ per cent.
4. 28000.
5. 1048 yds.
6. $500.
7. $400, first ; $350, second.
8. 225 bushels.
9. 2 tons, 913$\frac{11}{8}$ lbs.
10. L.C.M. 40320 ; H.C.F. 133.
11. $15.48.
12. 456 bushels.
13. (a) $12.75 ; (b) 15 acres.

Exercise LVI.

1. 18 times.
2. 43 tons, 400 lbs.
3. 704 bushels.
4. $2154.27.
5. 2 tons.
6. $54.45.
7. A : B : : 45 : 32.
8. $4375.
9. $1.05.
10. 5.
11. 330.03\frac{3}{4}$.
12. 121.21\frac{7}{8}$.
13. $7.00 gain.

Exercise LVII.

1. 45 sheep.
2. $320.00.
3. 4 per cent.
4. $963.90.
5. $192.50.
6. 1$\frac{5}{27}$.
7. $81.60.
8. $8.00.
9. 23 H.C.F.; and 211 L.C.M.
10. $19.80 + $33.75 = $53.55.
11. 1$\frac{1}{8}$ of cost.
12. $9405.
13. (a) $34.56; (b) $18.

Exercise LVIII.

1. $\frac{1}{4}$.
2. $20.00.
3. (a) $\frac{43}{88}$; (b) $\frac{44}{88}$; (c) 1.
4. 28$\frac{4}{7}$%.
5. 117,612 tons.
6. 2 tons, 56 lbs.
7. $84.00.
8. $4.80 (80 cents each).
9. $31,500.00.
10. $\frac{19}{7}$.
11. 3$\frac{1}{2}$.
12. 20 miles.
13. $1000.

Exercise LIX.

1. $30.00.
2. The former; $6.00 saved.
3. 2$\frac{1}{2}$ L.C.M.
4. 35 days.
5. $21.07.
6. 10 years; 6 per cent.
7. 4 per cent.
8. $30,000.
9. $532. (Quintal = 1 cwt.)
10. $13.80.
11. $350.00.
12. 3 days.
13. 60.

ANSWERS. 55

Exercise LX.

1. $17.04.
2. {First, 176 bushels.
   Second, 176 "
   Third, 348 "}
3. $1\frac{5}{16}$.
4. $1.60.
5. $107\frac{2}{21}$.
6. A, 800 ; B, 300.
7. $\frac{4}{25}$ of a ton.
8. 6,198,089,008,491,993,412,800.
9. A, $32.00 ; B, $30.00.
10. 870 bbls.
11. 4 acres.
12. 15·83.
13. $280.

Exercise LXI.

1. $34.40.
2. $\frac{4}{85}$; $2400.00.
3. 32 days.
4. A, 450 ; B, 400.
5. $125.
6. 1 ton, 625 lbs.
7. $38.70.
8. $240.
9. $1400.
10. $\frac{3}{8}$.
11. $40.
12. 80 dozen.
13. (a) Gains 10 per cent.;
    (b) 27 times.

Exercise LXII.

1. $270,000.00.
2. A, $480 ; B, $160 ; C, $640.
3. $24.00.
4. $73.60.
5. 243.
6. $153.60.
7. $27,375.
8. 408 yards.
9. 8%.
10. B, $1.02 ; G, $2.04.
11. 45 gallons.
12. $87.50.
13. 1, 4, 3 and 2 lbs. resp., (or 1 lb. of each, for another set.)

Exercise LXIII.

1. $13\frac{1}{2}$.
2. 81 tons.
3. $1300.
4. 20 per cent.
5. $10.40 a head.
6. 60 miles.
7. $360.
8. 1 day.
9. 117,628.
10. $1364.
11. 8.
12. 5.20 p.m.
13. (a) 110 sq. inches ; (b) 1320 sq. inches ; (c) 2354 sq. inches.

Exercise LXIV.

1. 154 sq. inches.
2. 10 feet, 6 inches.
3. 56 yards.
4. 1886 sq. yards, 4 sq. feet, 72 sq. inches.
5. 8 acres, 23 rods, 8 yards, 2 feet, 36 inches.
6. $\pi(80^2 - 60^2)$ sq inches $= 3\frac{1}{7} (140 \times 20)$ sq. inches $= 6$ sq. yds., 7 sq. feet, 16 sq. inches.
7. 1078 cubic inches.
8. 505.14 ... + ... sq. inches.
9. 891 cubic inches.
10. 20 inches.
11. 42 rods.
12. 20 inches.
13. (a) 9 feet, 4 inches; (b) 44 sq. rods, 6 sq. yards, 6 sq. feet, 72 sq. inches.

Exercise LXV.

1. $60.
2. $1261.40.
3. $165.12.
4. 8 : 5 respectively.
5. $230.
6. (a) of, first; ÷, second; ×, third; (b) $3\frac{51}{175}$.
7. (a) $\frac{25}{180}$, (b) $\frac{175}{243}$, (c) $\frac{21}{25}$.
8. $50\frac{10}{13}$ days.
9. 303 dozen and 4, chairs.
10. He would neither gain nor lose.
11. $120.
12. $\frac{348}{300}, \frac{87}{300}, \frac{75}{300}$; $1\frac{5}{13}$.
13. 10 years.

Exercise LXVI.

1. (a) $9\frac{1}{2}$; (b) $9\frac{1}{2}$.
2. $6.00.
3. Either *directly* North or South.
4. $121.70.
5. 7800 miles.
6. 9 acres, 52 rods, 24 yards, 3 feet $21\frac{3}{4}$ inches.
7. 21,315 lbs.
8. $2707.20.
9. $133.20.
10. 1st, 205; 2nd, 328; 3rd, 4th, 5th, etc. ... to 11th, 123 each.
11. $160.70.
12. $390.
13. (a) $8\frac{1}{2}$; (b) 48 cents, tea; 40 cents, coffee.

ANSWERS.

Exercise LXVII.

1. 1.
2. $1.26.
3. $9\frac{1}{11}$ lbs.
4. 45 sheep.
5. 733 yds., 1 ft.
6. $4\frac{1}{5}$ hours.
7. 1 pint.
8. At A's corner; once. (But A will have reached his corner the second time).
9. Horse, $240; carriage, $400.
10. $560.
11. 630.
12. 20 per cent.
13. $9\frac{1}{2}$ inches.

Exercise LXVIII.

1. (a) Book-work; 3341520; (b) 37; 3rd, 4th, 5th, 6th, 7th, 8th, and 9th.
2. (a) Book-work; (b) 14.37\frac{1}{2}$; (c) 25 per cent.
3. (a) Book-work; (b) 150 barrels.
4. 75 cents.
5. July 13th, 1890.
6. 2 days.
7. 7.
8. Book-work; $375 \cdot 70\dot{4}4635\dot{5}$.
9. (a) $32; (b) 104 days.
10. $46.71.
11. 11 dozen.
12. 67.
13. $60, A's share; $50, B's share and $36, C's share.

Exercise LXIX.

1. 5 days.
2. 4 hrs., 22 min., 30 sec.
3. $4.50.
4. 13 miles.
5. 4 lbs.
6. $26\frac{1}{2}$ per cent.
7. $\frac{1}{8}$ of an acre.
8. 13 lbs., 8 ozs.
9. $43,200.
10. (a) 2,505,600 sec's.; (b) 7 times.
11. A, $70; B, $80.
12. 664 lbs.
13. $16,044.

Exercise LXX.

1. 80 yards.
2. 45 acres.
3. 63 cents.
4. $2400.
5. $3942.
6. $60.
7. A, $100; B, $150; C, $250.
8. $13500.
9. 1st, $600; 2nd, $1200; 3rd, $900; 4th, $2700.
10. 192.85\frac{5}{7}$.
11. 147 sq. rods, 0 sq. yds., 8 sq. ft., 90 sq. in.
12. 70 times.
13. $86.69.

Exercise LXXI.

1. 28 per cent.
2. 50 lbs. and 37½ lbs.
3. $221.
4. $902.40.
5. 300.
6. 80 per cent.
7. $40.30 gain.
8. 244 acres, 88 rods, 22 sq. yards, 7 sq. feet, 72 sq. inches.
9. A $440; B $87.50, and $262.50.
10. (a) $10; (b) £3, 3s, 3d.
11. $18.90.
12. 37.

13. (a) 28512; (b) (I.) By the '*local value*' of a digit is meant its value *according to the position it occupies* in our scale (decimal scale) of NOTATION. (II.) First its *real* or *intrinsic* value as the number 7 (7 times the unit); and second, its '*local value*' in the TENS' PLACE (7 tens, or 70 TIMES *the unit*). (III.) $\overline{\text{CXLI}}\overline{\text{CLXXXI}}\text{CMXXIV}$.

Exercise LXXII.

1. (a) Book-work; (b) 247; (c) ·14285$\dot{7}$.
2. (a) *Theory*: Finite, Pure Repetend, Mixed Repetend, respectively. (If the denominator of a fraction contains *no other factors* than 2 or 5, the decimal is *finite*; if the denominator contains *neither of the factors* 2 or 5 it is a *pure* repetend; but if it contains *either of the factors* 2 or 5 it is a *mixed* repetend.) (b) (I.) $\frac{77}{180}$; (II.) $\frac{5}{81}$; (III.) $\frac{2274}{4995}$.

3. $\frac{1}{8}$.
4. $610.
5. $10.
6. ·078125.
7. $675.
8. H.C.F., 41; L.C.M., 34,440.
9. $\overline{\text{LIX}}\text{CCXXIV}$.
10. $384.
11. $41.25.
12. 101 barrels.
13. 1036 acres, 128 sq. rods.

Exercise LXXIII.

1. 72 gals.
2. $37\frac{1}{2}\%$.
3. The *latter*, by $1 on $100.
4. $17.81.
5. 10 hrs., 48 min., a.m.
6. Length, 27 ft.; breadth, 18 ft.; height, 13 ft.
7. $4.07.
8. $240.57.
9. $\frac{2}{3}$.
10. 3 sh. St'g.
11. 2 miles.
12. 7 ft.
13. $100.

Exercise LXXIV.

1. $72.
2. Total, 14215.
3. 2 ozs., 13 dw.s., 4 grs.
4. $1313.
5. 60%.
6. (a) 3636; (b) 81.(☞Brackets)
7. A, 54; B, 36; C, 60 sheep; $5 per head.
8. A, $10; B, $8; C, $22; $2 a day.
9. 15·045.
10. 71 ac., 98 sq. rods, 29 sq. yds., 1 sq. ft., 54 sq. in.
11. $\frac{8}{10}$.
12. $22.16.
13. $5.10.

Exercise LXXV.

1. $604.80.
2. A, 123 lbs., 6 ozs.; B, 164 lbs., 8 ozs.
3. 54 yards; $2 left.
4. $23.04.
5. $2646.
6. $19.08 gain.
7. 28 hours.
8. 27 acres, 20 sq. rods, 15 sq. yards.
9. 54 minutes.
10. 15 miles.
11. 42 acres, 108 rods, 7 yards, 81 inches.
12. $\left\{\dfrac{41+(\frac{1}{2} \text{ of } \frac{9}{10})+(\frac{1}{8} \text{ of } \frac{9}{10})}{83\frac{1}{4}}\right\} = \frac{1}{2}$.
13. 236250.

Exercise LXXVI.

1. 216 yds., 2 ft.
2. 15 days.
3. 60 per cent.
4. 240 lbs.
5. 5 per cent.
6. 13 cents.
7. $43.20.
8. 24 days.
9. 9 cents.
10. 30 lbs.
11. $967.50.
12. $46\frac{2}{3}\%$.
13. 3 cents.

Exercise LXXVII.

1. 25 cents.
2. $3872.
3. 32 bbls. at $4.50 ; 113 bbls. at $5.00.
4. A, $90 ; B, $70 ; C, $640.
5. 99.
6. 3 dirks.
7. 175 hours.
8. 45 minutes.
9. A, $180 ; B, $100 ; C, $280.
10. $16\frac{2}{3}$ per cent.
11. Tom, $5.91; and Bob, $3.44.
12. $55.12 gain.
13. 41 acres, 120 rods, 19 yards.

Exercise LXXVIII.

1. $43.20.
2. $9\cdot41\frac{7}{13}$ p.m.
3. Each man $15 ; each woman $5 ; each child $1.
4. $81.
5. $95.
6. 23 lbs.
7. 33.
8. $360.
9. $50.
10. A must pay B $0.50.
11. 486 lbs. $10\frac{2}{3}$ ounces.
12. 67.
13. 492 bushels ; $\frac{14}{14}$.

Exercise LXXIX.

1. $28.
2. $48.64.
3. 20.
4. 1522 yards.
5. $6000.
6. 13 miles.
7. 30 cents.
8. 5 per cent.
9. $7.20.
10. Note (*face value*), $584.
11. $112.
12. $73.
13. (a) $9210 ;

(b) (1), H.C.F. 896 $\left\{ \dfrac{16128}{81536} = \dfrac{18}{91} \right.$; (2) $\dfrac{16128}{81536} - \dfrac{2304}{11648} = \dfrac{288}{1456} = \dfrac{18}{91}$;

(3) $\dfrac{\not{7}}{\not{18}} \times \dfrac{\not{72}}{91} \times \dfrac{\not{2}}{\not{8}} = \dfrac{18}{91}$

Exercise LXXX.

1. 2 quarts, 1 pint.
2. The *multiplier* $= 1\frac{1}{5}$; $1\frac{1}{5} \times \$560 = \$672$, the amount.
3. $\dfrac{319}{7632}$ of a lb. troy.
4. 20 per cent.
5. 40.
6. 18 tons.
7. $700.
8. 10 doz.
9. (a) The L.C.M. of *two numbers* consists of the *smallest selection of factors which contains* the factors of each given number; and the H.C.F. of *two numbers* consists of the *greatest selection of factors common* to both numbers. The H.C.F. is composed of *all the factors rejected* by the L.C.M. and *vice versâ*; therefore, the *factors* of the H.C.F. and L.C.M. comprise *all the factors of the two numbers;* and consequently, the H.C.F. multiplied by the L.C.M. is equal to the *product* of the *two numbers*, *e.g.* :—Question 9 (*b*). H.C.F. and L.C.M. of 2340 and 2520, which *resolved* into their *prime* factors =
$\begin{cases} 2340 = 2 \times 2 \times 3 \times 3 \times 5 \times 13. \\ 2520 = 2 \times 2 \times 2 \times 3 \times 3 \times 5 \times 7. \end{cases}$ Now, the *greatest selection of factors, common* to these numbers, is $2 \times 2 \times 3 \times 3 \times 5 = 180$, the H.C.F.; and the *smallest selection of factors* which CONTAINS the factors of each of the given numbers, is $(2 \times 2 \times 3 \times 3 \times 5 \times 13) \times (2 \times 7) = 32760$, the L.C.M.; but these *are all the factors* of these two numbers; therefore the H.C.F. × L.C.M. of *any two* numbers is the product of the *two* numbers; ∴ $\dfrac{\text{H.C.F.} \times \text{L.C.M. of } any\ two \text{ No's.}}{\text{One of the No's.}}$ = the other No. (c) $\dfrac{31 \times 28520}{713} = 1240.$ (d) $\dfrac{38760}{323} = 120.$
10. L.C.M. = 158230800; H.C.F. = $\frac{2}{9}$ ∴ $158230800 \times \frac{2}{9} = 35162400$.
11. (I.) $5.30; (II.) $4.80.
12. A, $90; B, $60; C, $50.
13. (a) A, $160; B, $150; C, $180. (b) A, $30; B, $20; C, $16.

Exercise LXXXI.

1. $7200.
2. 16 days; $\frac{1}{3}$ of the work.
3. 10 per cent.
4. 3 cents a pint.
5. 10 per cent.
6. 70×56 rods.

7. In $brackets = \left\{4\tfrac{1}{3} \div (\tfrac{3}{4} \text{ of } \tfrac{13}{12})\right\} + \left\{(\tfrac{5}{8} \text{ of } \tfrac{3}{4}) \div 2\tfrac{8}{15}\right\} - \left\{\tfrac{1}{3} \times (\tfrac{8}{10} \div 1\tfrac{7}{20})\right\} - \dfrac{5\tfrac{1}{3}}{7} = \dfrac{4\tfrac{1}{3}}{\tfrac{3}{4} \text{ of } \tfrac{13}{12}} + \dfrac{\tfrac{5}{8} \text{ of } \tfrac{3}{4}}{2\tfrac{8}{15}} - \tfrac{1}{3} \times \dfrac{\tfrac{8}{10}}{1\tfrac{7}{20}} - \dfrac{5\tfrac{1}{3}}{7} = 18.$

8. 20 at $3.00; 13 at $0.50.
9. 60 tons.
10. Length, 64 ft.; breadth, 48 ft.; height, 5 ft. 4 in.
11. 12 days.
12. 60 gallons.
13. $10.50.

Exercise LXXXII.

1. A, 20 days; B, 27½ days.
2. 30.
3. 25 times.
4. $80.
5. 4 per cent. loss.
6. $1.20.
7. A, $180; B, $240.
8. $3024.
9. 15 days.
10. $429.
11. $9000.
12. 373.06 net.
13. $\tfrac{5}{8}$ of an inch.

Exercise LXXXIII.

1. Of *all the factors* of the two numbers; hence L.C.M. × H.C.F. =*Product* of the two numbers; 170,690.

2. In the simple rules the *unit* is uniform; in the compound rules it varies; $\sqrt[2]{\left(\dfrac{\text{Product}}{\text{Quotient}}\right)} =$ smaller number = 6,081; and $\sqrt[2]{(\text{Product} \times \text{Quotient})} =$ large number = 1,866,867; 1 ℔, 2 ozs., 12 dwts., 10 grs.

3. Same difference as between *simple* and *compound* rules; in decimal fractions the unit is uniform (*decimal scale*), and in vulgar fractions the unit varies; 2; 13·00069615.

4. (5 strips=2 double rolls) $245.
5. $1425.
6. $22.50.
7. $5000.
8. 250 gallons.
9. A, $80; B, $90; C, $100.
10. 15 ozs.
11. 2.
12. 3 horses=2 oxen.
13. $18.

Exercise LXXXIV.

1. $\frac{1}{4}$.
2. $42.
3. $\frac{1}{2}$.
4. $\frac{81}{100}$.
5. 14 lbs. tea; 36 lbs. coffee.
6. $63.75.
7. £65.
8. 637560.
9. A, $40; B, $60; C, 90.
10. 33.
11. $1.50.
12. $504.
13. 13064.

Exercise LXXXV.

1. £24 6s. 2d.
2. Wheat, 40 bushels; barley, 60 bushels.
3. $100.
4. 30 rods.
5. 69 cents.
6. A, $60; B, $75; C, $90.
7. $122.20.
8. 6 ft.
9. $50.40.
10. $\frac{1}{135}$.
11. $45.
12. $7488.
13. $310.10.

Exercise LXXXVI.

1. 10 days.
2. $531.
3. 8 days.
4. $8.89.
5. 8 miles, 80 rods.
6. 6.
7. $79.
8. $90.
9. Each equals—64 sq. rods, 9 sq. yds., 5 sq. ft.
10. 9 hours.
11. 360.
12. $8\frac{2001}{2738}$.
13. $329.

Exercise LXXXVII.

1. 6 days.
2. 25 cents per hour.
3. A, $627; B, $2090 and C, $3443.
4. $3\frac{1}{8}$ per cent. gain.
5. 700 bbls., 7 gals., 2 lbs., 14$\frac{3}{4}$ ozs.
6. Rye, 70c. per bush.; barley, 56c. per bush.
7. 750.
8. 11.30 o'clock p.m. (every 10$\frac{1}{2}$ hrs.)
9. 31.
10. 9.
11. $140.
12. $14.40.
13. A, $81; B, $90; C, $108.

ANSWERS.

Exercise LXXXVIII.

1. 10 days.
2. 7.
3. A, $32.20 ; B, $16.10 ; C, $48.30.
4. $1.75.
5. $38.40.
6. 300 feet.
7. $\left\{\begin{array}{l}\text{Oats, } \$361.80 \\ \text{Wheat, } \$990.99 \\ \text{Barley, } \$293.30\end{array}\right\} = \$1646.09.$
8. 18 gallons, 2 quarts.
9. $17.50.
10. 24 bushels, 27 lbs.
11. 2381400.
12. $\frac{1}{3}$.
13. A, $350 ; B, $420 ; C, $560.

Exercise LXXXIX.

1. 3 years.
2. $701.10 net.
3. 37 bushels, 24 lbs.
4. 41 cwt., 16 lbs.
5. 14 acres, 15 rods, 8 yards, 2 ft., 36 inches.
6. A, $27 ; B, $36 ; C, $45.
7. $7.00.
8. $1510.00.
9. $131,384,009\frac{209}{841}$.
10. 6.
11. 3 cents.
12. 8 per cent.
13. Sum of quotients, 437.

Exercise XC.

1. 289.
2. (a) 6,414,408 ; (b) 180.
3. 80 pounds.
4. $270.00.
5. $945.00.
6. 55 cents.
7. 8 per cent.
8. $820.00.
9. 39 animals.
10. $7560.
11. First, $21.60 ; second, $18 ; third, $15 ; fourth, $12.50.
12. $17.00 and $8.20.
13. 84 inches.

Exercise XCI.

1. £95, 16 sh., 8d.
2. 36 cents.
3. $290.00.
4. 82 dozen and 6 eggs.
5. 100 acres.
6. 18.
7. A, $450.00 ; B, $400.00 ; C, $350.00.
8. 10 per cent.
9. 45 square yards, 1 square foot, 72 square inches.
10. 90 times.
11. 3.55 o'clock, p.m. (or it lacks 5 minutes of 4 o'clock, p.m.)

ANSWERS.   65

12. $\begin{cases} 7560 = 2\times2\times2\times3\times3\times3\times5\times7. \\ 8820 = 2\times2\times3\times3\times5\times7\times7. \\ 44100 = 2\times2\times3\times3\times5\times5\times7\times7. \end{cases}$

Now the *smallest* selection of factors which contains the factors of each given number is :

$[\{(\underline{2}\times\underline{2}\times\underline{2}\times\underline{3}\times\underline{3}\times\underline{3}\times\underline{5}\times\underline{7})\times\underline{7}\}\times 5] = 264,600$ L.C.M.

And the *greatest* selection of factors common to these numbers is : $2\times2\times3\times3\times5\times7 = 1260$ H.C.F.

13. (a) 21 years ; (b) $745.

Exercise XCII.

1. $\frac{4}{5}$ of a ton.
2. 100 rods.
3. 1440.
4. 1089.
5. (a) 6048 ; (b) 112320.
6. 30 miles.
7. 6 miles, 240 rods.
8. $\frac{2705172}{61} = 44352$ times.
9. $579.43.
10. 56 gallons.
11. $56.25.
12. $\frac{40320}{32} = 1260$ times.
13. 866.

Exercise XCIII.

1. 2640 dozen.
2. $\frac{1}{10}$.
3. $16,000.00.
4. 37½ cents.
5. 40 barrels.
6. 15 acres.
7. $748.80.
8. James, $145 ; Andrew, $132 ; Robert, $119.
9. $20.90.
10. $42.00. (☞ Ceiling three times ordinary height.)
11. $264.00.
12. $17.00.
13. $15.00.

Exercise XCIV.

1. $\frac{1}{8}$ S.P.=$\frac{1}{5}$ C.P. ∴ $\frac{1}{8}$ of 80 yds. at 10c.=$\frac{1}{5}$ of $9.60.
2. 7101 sum.
3. 90 days.
4. $54.40.
5. £616, 1sh.=$2998.11.
6. 240 rods.
7. H, $550 ; L, $440.
8. $1950.
9. $27.00.
10. $20.59.
11. $182.
12. 11,948,160.
13. (a) 8649 ; (b) 25%.

Exercise XCV.

1. $405.00.
2. 84.
3. (a) Reduce them to fractions having a common denominator. (b) $\frac{27}{155}$. (c) $\frac{7}{13}$, $\frac{72}{155}$, $\frac{21}{55}$.
4. 4,735,008.
5. 47 times.
6. 5 per cent.
7. 8 years.
8. $16.00.
9. 87½ cents.
10. 48 weeks, 3 days.
11. 50,424,201.
12. $18.00.
13. (a) $20.75; (b) $9,441 + · · ·

Exercise XCVI.

1. $160; 400 dozens.
2. $\frac{15}{88}$.
3. 2 miles, 263 rods, 1 yd., 2ft., 6 inches.
4. $24.00.
5. 12½ per cent.
6. 14¾ per cent.
7. $630.
8. 4.
9. $\frac{25}{27}$, $\frac{5}{6}$, $\frac{7}{5}$, $\frac{59}{88}$.
10. 14.
11. $\frac{2198\frac{3}{4}}{2613}$.
12. 115 lbs.
13. (a) 25 per cent. (b) 12 lbs.

Exercise XCVII.

1. 2 miles, 99 rods, 2 yards, 0 feet, 6 inches.
2. 87120 times.
3. $339.57.
4. A, $1014; B, 2535; C, $3549.
5. $6.65.
6. (a) 12 acres, 80 rods; (b) $3250.00.
7. $6624.00.
8. $26.46.
9. 7 per cent.
10. 128,755.
11. 4⅔ miles an hour.
12. $3.05.
13. A, $6.12; B, $5.10; C, $2.04.

ANSWERS. 67

Exercise XCVIII.

1. $34.15.
2. 3.
3. John $567; Robert $42.
4. $63.
5. 35.
6. $40,32.
7. $1300.
8. 5.
9. 411 miles, 266 rds, 3 yds, 2 ft.
10. $60.
11. $\dfrac{\text{L.C.M.}=840}{\text{H.C.F.}=15}=56.$
12. 4449.
13. $147.00.

Exercise XCIX.

1. 6.
2. $85.
3. $8.
4. L.C.M., $10\tfrac{1}{2}$; G.C.M., $\tfrac{1}{4}$.
5. 12 sq. rods.
6. 25 per cent.
7. A, $108; B, $144; C, $288.
8. 3 days.
9. 13 acres.
10. S., $420; T., 3 years.
11. $7\tfrac{1}{2}$ days.
12. $\left\{\begin{array}{l}\text{Papering, }\$1.76\\ \text{Painting, }\$22.63\end{array}\right\} = \$24.39.$
13. $91.01.

Exercise C.

1. (a) 13 (H. C. F.); (b) 7176 (L. C. M.)
2. $17.50.
3. *Product*, 69,610,086; sixty-nine millions, six hundred and ten thousand and eighty-six.
4. 350 tens; 475 twenties.
5. 625.
6. 10 gallons.
7. 23.37\tfrac{1}{2}$.
8. (a) $25,600.00; (b) $21.40.
9. 13,689.
10. 20 cents.
11. (a) $\tfrac{3}{4}$ of $\tfrac{1}{2}$ of 1; (b) A compound fraction;

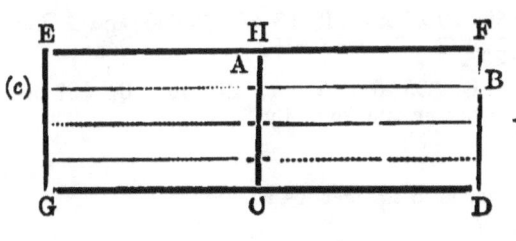

(c) Finish out, *dividing* the whole Fig. E G D F, so as to show it as composed of *eighths*; then, A C D B is *three* out of the *eighth*, eighths, or $\tfrac{3}{8}$ of whole Fig. E G D F.

12. A, $20; B, $60; C, $20.
13. $126.00.

Exercise CI.

1. $347.50.
2. 27 cows ; $35 each.
3. $15.75.
4. 9·44+ . . . .
5. A, $4.00, B, $3.00, C, $2.00.
6. 6 per cent.
7. (a) Book-work. (b) A, 4 days, B, 6 days.
8. $180.00.
9. $276.00.
10. 25 cents.
11. 90 cents.
12. A $60.00, B $72.00.
13. 150 per cent.

Exercise CII.

1. 24 cents.
2. G.C.M. = 329 ; L.C.M. = 29610.
3. 20 cows.
4. 93.
5. 31 acres, 130 rods, 27 yds., 4 ft., 72 in.
6. $3.50.
7. *Multiplication*: Ex. $42 \times 73 = 73$ taken *42 times as an addend* $= 3066$. Multiplicatian is a *short form* of Addition.
8. $22.40.
9. $43\frac{7}{11}$ minutes past 12 o'clock.
10. ·16.
11. 7 dozen $\div 3 + 2 = 30$ marbles.
12. 30 days.
13. $425.00.

Exercise CIII.

1. $380.
2. $9\frac{1}{2}$ per cent.
3. 625 leaps.
4. £1291, 10 sh.
5. $10350 = 2 \times 3^2 \times 5^2 \times 23$.
   $113022 = 2 \times 3^3 \times 7 \times 13 \times 23$.
   $169533 = 3^4 \times 7 \times 13 \times 23$.
   $\therefore$ L.C.M. $= 2 \times 3^2 \times 5^2 \times 23 \times 3 \times 7 \times 13 \times 3 = 8{,}476{,}650$; and G.C.M. (or H.C.F.) $= 3^2 \times 23 = 207$.
6. (1) A, $70.20 ; B, $35.10 ; (2) A, $67.80 ; B, $37.50 ; (3) The first mode is the better one for by $2.40.
7. 2 cwt., 24 lbs.
8. 1640 dozens.
9. 1 sq. rod, 16 sq. yards, 8 sq. feet, 54 sq. inches.
10. (a) $1\frac{1}{2}$; and (b) $\frac{43}{137}$.
11. 21 cents.
12. (a) $4.80; (b) $16\frac{2}{3}$ lbs. for a dollar.
13. (a) 17 ; (b) 49.

ANSWERS. 69

Exercise CIV.

1. 810 doz.
2. 6 tons, 1950 lbs.
3. (a) Integral, Prime, Odd, Abstract. (b) Fractional, Vulgar, Proper, Simple (representing 4 fractional units whose prime unit is one inch). Denominate.
4. 7 hours, 15 minutes.
5. $56.51 ; Receipt :

Burnside, May 13th, 1893.

56\frac{51}{100}$.

Received from John A. Bruce, the sum of fifty-six dollars and fifty-one cents (56\frac{51}{100}$) in full payment of account.

A. B. BURNS & Co.

6. 24 sq. rods, 2 sq. yards, 2 sq. feet, 24 sq. inches.
7. £15, 15s. Sterling.
8. $90.
9. $30.25.
10. $198.76.
11. $1.50 an acre ; 128 acres.
12. 40 cents.
13. $4660.50.

Exercise CV.

1. A, $10.00 ; B, $2.40 ; C, $2.00.
2. 54 tons.
3. $32.
4. $266.70.
5. $19.65.
6. 240 trees.
7. 13.
8. 11323.
9. A, 3 miles ; B, 4 miles ; C, $4\frac{1}{2}$ miles ; D, 5 miles.
10. (a) The multiplicand. (b) The multiplier. (c) When both numbers are *abstract*. (d) $\left\{\begin{array}{l}3\times4=4+4+4=12\\4\times3=3+3+3+3=12\end{array}\right\} \therefore 3\times4=4\times3.$
(e) 6×7.
11. 1980
12. 240 barrels R.I.G's. ; 420 barrels N.S's.
13. ·0138.

Exercise CVI.

1. Q. 38984, Rem. 78 ; P. 37,050,342,912.
2. Q. 273, Rem 380.
3. A, $22.50 ; B, $24.00 ; C, $46.50.
4. A, $3200 ; B, $4000 ; C, $5040.
5. 106 lbs., 4 ozs.
6. Oranges, 36 cents ; lemons, 28 cents.
7. 200 acres.
8. 16 bushels.
9. 7 chains, 7 feet.
10. 64 cents.
11. 65 dozen.
12. 3⅜.
13. $49.

FIFTH CLASS.

Exercise I.

1. 54 and 6.
2. $59.40.
3. 4.
4. 45 pairs.
5. 17187 tons, 1000 lbs.
6. 93 cents a lb.
7. $45.
8. 192 men.
9. $1000.00.
10. 24 miles an hour.
11. 60 cents.
12. L.C.M., 45 ; H.C.F., $\frac{1}{2}$.
13. 84 times.

Exercise II.

1. 54 miles.
2. 88 cubic feet.
3. $704.00.
4. A, $70 ; B, $42 ; C, $30.
5. 144 miles.
6. 70 bushels at 90 cents ; 130 bushels at 85 cents.
7. (a) $7\frac{1}{2}$ days ; (b) 15 days ; (c) $17.25.
8. 12 miles.
9. A, $40 ; B, $20 ; C, $40 ; D, $280.
10. $13\frac{3}{5}$ days.
11. 45 bushels @ 60 cents ; 75 bushels @ 80 cents.
12. 32 per cent.
13. 1987.

Exercise III.

1. $373.06 net.
2. 45 bushels.
3. $17.60.
4. $7.00.
5. 7 brooms.
6. 42 gallons.
7. 30 hours.
8. $\dfrac{345982 \text{ L.C.M.}}{1901 \text{ H.C.F.}} = 182$ times.
9. $72.00.
10. $\dfrac{107140644 \text{ L.C.M.}}{1807 \text{ H.C.F.}} = 59292$ times.
11. $64.00.
12. $\dfrac{1493382 \text{ L.C.M.}}{1331 \text{ H.C.F.}} = 1122$ and $(1122)^2 = 1258884$.
13. 6 tons.

Exercise IV.

1. 21 lbs. chicory ; 7 lbs. coffee.
2. $4052.00.
3. $988.
4. £300.
5. $90 \times 90 = 8100$ product.
6. $2^{22} \times 3^4 \times 7 \times 11^2 \times 13^2 \times 17 \times 19 \times 23$.
7. (a) $2.88 ; (b) 60 per cent.
8. $2^9 \times 3^5 \times 5 \times 7^2 \times 11 \times 13 \times 17 \times 19$.
9. 106 feet, 4 inches.
10. Green, 16 lbs ; Black, 44 lbs.
11. 9 lbs.
12. 6 per cent.
13. 2 feet, 9 inches.

Exercise V.

1. $75.00.
2. $1875.00.
3. $1639.30.
4. $1752.00.
5. 28 sheep.
6. $100.00.
7. $1120.00.
8. (a) 515 ; (b) 5 quarts.
9. (a) 225 ; (b) 330.
10. (a) 12 apples ; (b) 8 pears.
11. $409.40.
12. $42.00.
13. 61·44 lbs.

Exercise VI.

1. 1st time, $9\frac{9}{11}$ minutes past IX o'clock ; 2nd time, $22\frac{2}{11}$ minutes past IX o'clock.

2. With the Romans, the symbols used maintained their relative values, no matter in what order they were written ; thus, IX stood for 11, and was read *eleven*, just as XI ; and XL stood for 60, and was read *sixty*, just as LX, etc. Their system of notation was by *units, fives, tens, fifties, hundreds,* etc., instead of *units, tens, hundreds,* etc., as in our system, the symbols being written in that order, and each one repeated in accordance with their system of notation—I and X might be repeated *four* times, but V or D would not be required to be repeated as two V's = X, and two D's = M,

ANSWERS.   73

etc., etc. In writing them down, place like symbols under each other, *i.e.*, units under units, fives under fives, tens under tens, etc.

(a) DCC LX
    CC XXXX
    DCCC   XXVIIII
――――――――――
MM CCC XXXXV sum.

(b) MM   L XVIIII
    MDCC XXV
――――――――――
CCCXXXXIIII diff.

(c)   XXXX II
        LXXXXV
―――――――
MMC
  CCCC XX
  CCCC XX
  CCCC XX
  CCCC XX
    CC   X
――――――――――
MMMDCCCCLXXXX prod.

(d)
XXV)MDCCC XXV(LXXIII quot.
    M CCL
―――――
  D   LXXV
    CCL
―――――
  CCC XXV
  CCL
―――――
    LXXV
    XXV
―――――
  L
    XXV
―――――
    XXV
    XXV

3. $7000.00.
4. 3 miles, 60 rods.
5. $5670.00.
6. $496.10.
7. $33.75.
8. 16 hours.

9. $5011.20.
10. Lose $4.50. 4.20
11. 270 sheep.
12. 117.
13. 233½ per cent.

Exercise VII.

1. $20.
2. $40.
3. $45.
4. $60.
5. $7.
6. 8 dozen.
7. 63 gallons.

8. $77.
9. 12 per cent.
10. 31.
11. A, $48 ; B, $72.
12. $65.
13. 54 cents.

Exercise VIII.

1. $93\frac{83}{144}$ barrels.
2. 3636.
3. $31\frac{83}{132}$ quarts.
4. A, $200.00 ; B, $125,00.
5. $156\frac{1}{4}$ barrels.
6. 30 barrels, $18\frac{1}{2}$ gallons.
7. $108.
8. $1.00.
9. Principal, $350.00, time 5 yrs.
10. (a) $1.20 ; (b) $2.00.
11. $2.00.
12. Principal, $725, time, 7 yrs.
13. A, $27.00 ; B, $36.00 ; C, $45.00.

Exercise IX.

1. $825.00.
2. $500.00 ; $300.00
3. $24 : $40.
4. $9.10.
5. 1444.
6. 4141.
7. 30 cents.
8. 60 per cent.
9. 90.
10. $\frac{1}{3}$.
11. $2.00.
12. (a) 15. (b) The 7th.
13. 49 yards, 2 ft., 5 inches.

Exercise X.

1. $180.00.
2. $1.80 an hour.
3. $501.00.
4. 21.
5. L.C.M. 250208595 ; Quotients, 6643, 3285, 4095 ; Sum, 14023.
6. A, $256.50, or $8\frac{1}{7}$ cents a lb. ; B, $96.30, or $7\frac{9}{14}$ cents a lb.
7. 24 days.
8. $514.50. (See P.S. arith., p. 88).
9. A, $560.00 ; B, $370.00.
10. A, $7400.00 ; B, $8400.00.
11. 21 miles.
12. 20 days.
13. 6455753577.

Exercise XI.

1. L.C.M. = 289, 692, 179, 960, 656, 200, 943, 335, 120. (Test question.)
2. L.C.M. = 783,029,520.
3. $892.08.
4. (a) 8641 ; (b) 2801 ; (c) 98079; (d) 707; (e) 6041; (f) 2841; (g) 8056.
5. (a) 506 ; (b) 287 ; (c) 4547 ; (d) 4070.
6. $18.60.
7. $448.00.
8. $420.00.
9. 4 per cent.
10. 5 years.
11. $73.00.
12. 13 years.
13. A, $1690.00 : B, $1820.00 ; C, $1950.00.

ANSWERS. 75

Exercise XII.

1. $84.
2. (a) $777; (b) $950.
3. $364.
4. A, $81.75 ; B, $245.25 ; C, $654.00.
5. 5.
6. I. The number of equal parts (fractional parts) of the *prime unit*, 1 lb. II. The number of fractional parts (units) in the fraction. III. That the prime unit, 1 lb. is divided into *five equal parts*; the name of each part; the weight (in this instance) of each part or fractional unit. IV. 1 lb. V. $\frac{1}{5}$ of a lb., $\frac{2}{5}$ of a lb., $\frac{3}{5}$ of a lb., $\frac{4}{5}$ of a lb., ($\frac{5}{5}$ of a lb.) VI. The TERMS of the fraction. VII. Yes ; because it is the *measure of a quantity*.
7. 5·4 inches.
8. $18,360.00.
9. 15 lbs.
10. $\frac{9}{85}$.
11. 26 ; 27th.
12. 18 lbs.
13. (a) (1) Write out in succession, the MULTIPLES of these numbers :—

24 :—24, 48, 72, 96, 120, 144, 168, 192, 216, 240, 264, 288, 312, 336, 360, 384, 408, 432, 456, 480, 504, 528, 552, 576, 600, 624, 648, 672, 696, 720, 744, 768, etc.

42 :—42, 84, 126, 168, 210, 252, 294, 336, 378, 420, 462, 504, 546, 588, 630, 672, 714, etc.

Now we see, by inspection, the *common multiples* of these numbers, and of these *multiples* 168 is the least; therefore it is the L.C.M.

2. Write out *all* the *prime factors* of these numbers :—

24 = 2 × 2 × 2 × 3.
42 = 2 × 3 × 7.

Now the L. C. M consists of the smallest (*least*) selection of *factors* that contains the factors of each given number; therefore the L. C. M. is 2 × 2 × 2 × 3 × 7 = 168.

(3). 2) 24, 42
    3) 12, 21
       4, 7   L. C. M. = 2 × 3 × 4 × 7 = 168.

ANSWERS.

(b) (1) All the measures of

(Factors). (Co-factors).
96=1, 2, 3, 4, 6, 8.   12, 16, 24, 32, 48, 96.
240=1,2,3,4,5,6,8,10,12,15.   16,20,24,30,40,48,60,80,120,240.

Now the *common measures* are: 1,2,3,4,6,8,12,16,24,48, and *48*, the *greatest* of these, contains all the other measures; hence it is the G.C.M.

(2) Write out *all prime factors* of these numbers:

$$96 = 2 \times 2 \times 2 \times 2 \times 2 \times 3.$$
$$240 = 2 \times 2 \times 2 \times 2 \times 3 \times 5.$$

Now the greatest selection of measures (factors) common to these numbers is: $2 \times 2 \times 2 \times 2 \times 3 = 48$, the G.C.M.

(3) 96)240(2
    192

   48)96(2
     96

    0   ∴ 48 is the G.C.M.

Exercise XIII.

1. 960 men.
2. 32 per cent.
3. 5 dwts., 18⅜ grains.
4. 33 days, 18 hours.
5. $15000.
6. (a) 20 hours. (b) At starting point. (c) A, 4; B, 7; C, 12 times round the island.
7. Reduce to decimals of same order, then divide as in long division, striking out a figure in divisor every division, instead of adding to the dividend by bringing down additional figures:

    378·7878 . . . .)31666·666666 . . . .(83·6 Ans.
                   30303 03030 . . .

                   136363636 . . .
                   113636363 . . . .

                   22727272 . . .
                   22727272 . . .

8. 2·71828 . . .
9. 60 yds., and $1.50 per yd.
10. 2100 ft. by 1680 ft.
11. 6⅔ per cent.
12. 89⅞.
13. (a) 5 ft., 6 in.; (b) F., $1200; S., $500.

Exercise XIV.

1. $3889.69.
2. $11664.00
3. 6 inches.
4. A, $5187.50; B, $2812.50.
5. (a) $1\frac{478}{5359}$ of an oz.; (b) $1\frac{400}{5359}$ of an oz.
6. 500 birds.
7. $85.25 gain.
8. 26 feet.
9. 210 miles.
10. 4.
11. £103, 4s, 1d.
12. 28 rods.
13. 1900 square yards.

Exercise XV.

1. 6 o'clock p.m.
2. $5\frac{5}{11}$ minutes past 7 o'clock p.m.
3. 9 o'clock p.m.
4. $40\frac{520}{1427}$ seconds after 4 o'clock.
5. $12\frac{878}{1427}$ seconds after 5 o'clock.
6. $29\frac{4}{8}$ seconds after 9 o'clock.
7. $56\frac{188}{287}$ seconds after 1 o'clock.
8. $51\frac{153}{287}$ seconds after 2 o'clock.
9. First time, $32\frac{8}{11}$ minutes after 8 o'clock; second time, $54\frac{6}{11}$ minutes after 8 o'clock.
10. 5 minutes too fast.
11. 6 minutes too slow.
12. 9 miles.
13. 24 minutes.

Exercise XVI.

1. 8 lbs.
2. 25 per cent.
3. 5 miles, 110 rods.
4. $33\frac{1}{3}$ per cent.
5. 20 per cent.
6. (a) B's time is to C's time as 14:9. (b) $1120, B's gain.
7. $11\frac{11}{19}$ per cent.
8. 12 per cent.
9. 40 cents.
10. 12 rods.
11. (a) 1842 lbs., $4\frac{9}{16}$ ozs. (b) 9 sq. ft., 90 sq. in.
12. Grapes, $30.00; apples, $40.00; cherries, $50.00.
13. $40.00.

Exercise XVII.

1. $11,520.
2. $180.
3. 18 acres, 120 sq. rods.
4. 30 children purposed going and 15 went.
5. 10 lbs., 2 ozs.
6. $11\frac{1}{9}$ per cent.
7. $18\frac{2}{11}$.
8. 25 per cent. gain.
9. 10 per cent.
10. 24000 bricks; and $6\frac{2}{3}\%$.
11. 6 boys.
12. 7033 and 9197.
13. $4800.

Exercise XVIII.

1. 3696 gallons (or 117⅓ bbls.)
2. 19.
3. 170,414,521,200 L.C.M.
4. 8 average men.
5. The circuitous, by $2.
6. 7½ gallons.
7. 36⅔ cents a bush., 35\frac{11}{12} lbs. per bush.
8. Half-and-half; or 50 per cent. brandy.
9. $6240.
10. $1098.50.
11. A, $480 ; B, $240.
12. 14 inches.
13. 6 balls.

Exercise XIX.

1. 12 per cent.
2. $269.75.
3. 6⅔ per cent.
4. 3 hours, 8 min., $55\frac{85}{269}$ sec.
5. Cash, by $50.
6. $7920, B. of C. Stock.
7. A, $750 ; B, $200 ; C, $315 ; D, $400 ; E, $210.
8. 385 cords.
9. $10.
10. $1000 M.; $600 W.; $480 B.
11. 10 per cent. discount.
12. 8 per cent. on former and 10 per cent. on latter.
13. (*a*) 70 cents ; (*b*) 450.

Exercise XX.

1. $7776.
2. 66⅔.
3. $32,000.
4. $36.
5. 100 lbs. @ 45 cts.; 100 lbs. @ 60 cts.; 300 lbs. @ 90c.
6. £6, 6sh, 5d.
7. 30 casks.
8. 13 years.
9. 3 : 1.
10. 20⅘ min., 28⅘ min.
11. $50.00.
12. Total Com. $715.00; No. bbls. remitted, 4147.
13. 2160 balls.

Exercise XXI.

1. (*a*) Town clock 15 minutes slow ; and (*b*) 10 miles.
2. 75 bushels.
3. 40 yards.
4. 3 feet deep.
5. 13 minutes, 52½ seconds.
6. 25,000.

ANSWERS. 79

7. 9565217391304347826086. (5, the fourth remainder, is $\frac{1}{3}$ of 15 the second remainder; therefore $\frac{1}{3}$ of 6, the third number in quotient, is 2 which is the next figure to set down in the quotient, etc.)
8. A, $102.20, B, $58.40, C, $54.75, and D, $91.25.
9. $600 and $750, respectively.
10. A, $14.70 ; B, $42.00.
11. $x = \frac{2}{15} y$.
12. 1.
13. (a) $4 and $3.20 respectively. (b) Man's rate 7$\frac{1}{2}$ miles an hour. Stream's rate 2$\frac{1}{2}$ miles an hour.

Exercise XXII.

1. $25.
2. 25 yards.
3. 260$\frac{4}{9}$ yards.
4. 16 inches.
5. 1$\frac{2}{3}$ per cent. (or $1 a share).
6. 276.48 cubic inches.
7. $\frac{1}{2}$.
8. $140.
9. (a) 31278 balls ; (b) $\frac{425}{8584}$ of an oz.
10. 2850.
11. 2 miles an hour.
12. 6 balls.
13. A's, by $1460.00.

Exercise XXIII.

1. 1140.
2. 6015 gallons, 2 quarts, 1 pint.
3. 441 boxes.
4. $3660 whole profit and $2160 B's share.
5. (a) 80 cents ; (b) 77$\frac{1}{2}$ cents.
6. 41 gallons.
7. 203 cubic yards, 19 cubic feet.
8. 4.34\frac{1}{4}$.
9. $\frac{2}{3}$.
10. 4 cwt., 10 lbs., 2$\frac{1}{2}$ ozs.
11. $691.
12. $20655.00.
13. 3 cubic feet, 514 cubic inches.

Exercise XXIV.

6. (a) $\frac{3}{23}$. (N.B.—The *sum* of the numerator and denominator of the fraction, representing the simple interest, forms the denominator of the fraction representing the true discount.) (b) $465.75 simple interest.
7. (a) $20 ; (b) $1 ; (c) $1.
8. $803.
9. 6 yrs., 73 days, and 6 per cent.
10. 94.92\frac{4}{8}$.
11. 3$\frac{1}{2}$ years.
12. 5 per cent.
13. $420.

Exercise XXV.

1. 2240.
2. 2 hours, 30 minutes.
3. 6 lbs. at 6 cents, 6 lbs. at 8 cents, 3 lbs. at 16 cents, and 2 lbs. at 19 cents (other sets of answers may be got).
4. $80 first, and $120 second.
5. $404.20.
6. A, $360 ; B, $270 ; C, $240.
7. 50 cents a lb.
8. $10.
9. 35 miles an hour.
10. $547.50.
11. 120 lbs.
12. 16 and 25.
13. 88 yards.

Exercise XXVI.

1. $1600.
2. 12 per cent.
3. $330 and $1320.
4. $2703 and $8109.
5. $2090.90 (or 4.18\frac{9}{50}$ per bbl.)
6. $5520.
7. $\frac{1}{11}$.
8. $\frac{2}{25}$ of cost ($=\frac{2}{27}$ S. P.).
9. 25 per cent. (or $\frac{1}{4}$ of cost).
10. $144.
11. $4\frac{1}{6}$ per cent.
12. $3\frac{11}{13}$ per cent.
13. (a) 186.66\frac{2}{3}$; (b) 24 days.

Exercise XXVII.

1. 150 feet.
2. $1125.
3. $\frac{593}{800}$.
4. $3657\frac{1}{2}$.
5. $\frac{4}{5}$ per cent.; 80 cents on $100.
6. $180.
7. 91 yards.

8. (a) ·0̇04761̇9 ; (b) ·1̇4285̇7 ; (c) The *nature of the denominator* of the vulgar fraction to which it corresponds. If the denominator is made up of *no other factors* than 2's and 5's, the decimal will be finite ; if either 2 or 5 with other factors, it will be a mixed repetend ; if neither 2 nor 5, it will be a pure repetend. (d) *Finite* decimals ; and *pure* and *mixed repetends*.

9. $28,350.00.
10. $34.32.
11. 437 reams, 10 quires.
12. 4 per cent.
13. (a) 24.75 ; (b) 36 ; (c) 4213 ; (d) 2807 ; (e) 5004 ; (f) 7610.

ANSWERS. 81

Exercise XXVIII.

1. L, 24 ft.; B, 18 ft.; H, 9 ft.
2. (a) $837.00; (b) $22\frac{18}{49}$ per cent.; (c) $21\frac{2877}{4941}$ per cent.
3. $202.00.
4. 7 feet.
5. $8\frac{3}{4}$.
6. $5293.60.
7. 266 sacks; 20 cents.
8. $946.80.
9. 19 cub. feet, $658\frac{2}{7}$ cub. inches.
10. $9000.
11. $2500 @ 5 per cent.; $3500 @ 7 per cent.
12. (a) $36\frac{12}{23}$ min. past 7; (b) 42 min. past 7.
13. A, 60; B, $75; C, $50; D, $30; E, $20.

Exercise XXIX.

1. 5 per cent.
2. $1400.
3. $2060.
4. $22.
5. Gained $105.
6. Gained $75.
7. 6400 bushels.
8. $600.
9. 89°40'.
10. $600.
11. 900 barrels.
12. 5 per cent.
13. 6 per cent.

Exercise XXX.

1. (a) £5, 8sh., 9d; (b) $1.00.
2. 8703 square yards.
3. $1.00.
4. 1 square foot, 81 sq. inches.
5. 8 per cent. loss.
6. 13 sq. rods, 26 sq. yards, 2 sq. feet, 35 sq. inches.
7. 5 sq. rods, 5 sq. yds., 6 sq. ft.
8. 2 sq. rods, 19 sq. yds., 2 sq. ft., 116 sq. inches.
9. $159.25.
10. 15 metres.
11. $9000.00.
12. $602.98.
13. (a) 39 sq. rods, 11 sq. yds., 138 sq. inches; (b) Product, 478,687,021,724,583,756; quotient, 53,593,500,996.

Exercise XXXI.

1. 25 lbs. for a dollar.
2. (1) 45 tons; 535$\frac{5}{7}$ bushels.
   (See P.S. Arith. p. 88).
3. 171 cwt., 92 lbs., 7 ozs.
4. 6$\frac{1}{4}$ barrels.
5. 250 acres.
6. 6840 ÷ 8 = 855.
7. 6086·7 feet.
8. 216$\frac{2}{3}$ barrels.
9. $126.
10. $18,900.
11. $80.
12. 14 gallons.
13. (a) 15 cents; (b) 792 yards.

Exercise XXXII.

1. $38.50.
2. 13.
3. 18.
4. 34 lbs., 11 ozs., 14 dwts., 9 grs.
5. 1620 lbs.
6. $26.25.
7. 65.
8. 72 gallons.
9. 9$\frac{1}{2}$ years.
10. $126.
11. $4800.
12. 50c.; $\frac{1}{2}$ per cent.
13. ·$\dot{9}2307\dot{6}$.

After the first division we have 3 as remainder, which is one-fourth of 12, the numerator of the fraction; now, complete the repetend from this point by reducing each remainder to *tenths* of the next lower order and dividing by 4, *e.g.* :—

$\frac{12}{13}$ = ·9, and **3** as *remainder;* now 3 is $\frac{1}{4}$ of 12.
  $\frac{1}{4}$ of 9 (first figure in decimal), etc.
  = 9 ÷ 4 = **2** and 1 over,—10 × 1 + 2 = 12.
  12 ÷ 4 = **3** and 0 over,—10 × 0 + 3 = 3.
  3 ÷ 4 = **0** and 3 over,—10 × 3 + 0 = 30.
  30 ÷ 4 = **7** and 2 over,—10 × 2 + 7 = 27.
  27 ÷ 4 = **6** and 3 over,—10 × 3 + 6 = 36.
  36 ÷ 4 = **9** and 0 over, etc.
    Dec. = ·92307692, etc.
        = ·$\dot{9}2307\dot{6}$.

(N.B.—The operation should be performed *mentally*.)

Exercise XXXIII.

1. $2200.
2. $1040.
3. 42⅔ per cent.
4. Focal date, April 0, 1887; Bal. due, Jan. 16th, 1887.
5. 4000 barrels.
6. 20 per cent.
7. £40, 10s., 6d.
8. 30034 square root.
9. $6\frac{11}{20}$; Rem. = Dividend − (Divisor × Quotient.)
10. 15 rods.
11. $1742.25.
12. 280 dozens.
13. $196.37 per acre.

Exercise XXXIV.

1. $1200.
2. B, $1200; C, $1700.
3. $14400.
4. $98.55.
5. 25 per cent. discount.
6. $280.
7. 28 lbs., 1 oz., 10 dwts.
8. 16 boys.
9. $48.44.
10. 66 cwt., 15 lbs.
11. 6 acres, 28 sq. rods, 15 sq. yds., 1 sq. foot, 18 sq. inches.
12. 93¾.
13. $6.00.

Exercise XXXV.

1. 29⅗ per cent.
2. June 17th, 1893.
3. $5915.
4. $81.25.
5. ¾ per cent.
6. 53¾ cents.
7. 303 lbs., 12 ozs.
8. $350.
9. 49 lbs.
10. 1188.
11. 225 miles.
12. $820; $8200.
13. $300 first; $240 second.

Exercise XXXVI.

1. $108.64.
2. $20,000; $225,000.
3. $990.
4. Bal. due Nov. 25th, 1892. (Focal date, Dec. 0, 1892.)
5. $1600.
6. $10,000.
7. $1012.50.
8. 46 and 40.
9. $79.50.
10. 90 cents.
11. 72.
12. $80.96.
13. $3930.

Exercise XXXVII.

1. $490.
2. 2 ozs., 2 dwt., 14 grs.
3. $103.55.
4. 25 times: 3 hours, 30 min.
5. $52.02.
6. 1400 miles.
7. ·0200026673068495806̇98412̇.
8. $3.
9. $108.
10. 2 Metres.
11. 153 M., 6 dm.; **$115.20.**
12. 1·081075031̇841269̇.
13. $900.

Exercise XXXVIII.

1. $1.00.
2. ·244978683713832688492063̇.
3. $960.
4. A, $80; B, $120; C, $160.
5. 1 Kl., 4 Hl., 5 Dl., 2 L., 145 Mg., 2 Kg.
6. $2475.
7. 5 Dg., 7 G., 9 dg., 2 cg., 1 mg.
8. 68 Kg.
9. Compound Rules; **1 cubic metre (volume or capacity) = 1 gramme (weight)**, or capacity : weight :: 1 cu. cm. : 1g.
10. 460.
11. $47·754 interest; $297·754 amount.
12. 23.
13. $1560.

Exercise XXXIX.

1. 130 acres.
2. Diminished by 36%.
3. 4½%.
4. 3.
5. $455.
6. A, $3900; B, $4950.
7. $1.20.
8. 40 shares.
9. £45, 10sh., 6d.
10. $1.20.
11. 6⅔%.
12. 7½%.
13. $700.

Exercise XL.

1. A, $1200; B, $1500.
2. $862.13.
3. $1500.
4. 80% gain.
5. (a) ⅔, (b) ⅞, (c) 24/125.
6. $1146.88 (or using 25 qts. to the cub. ft., which is practically wrong for grain, the answer would be $1120).
7. $6.00.
8. 44 yards.
9. (a) 16 4/11 min. past IX
   (b) 24 "   "   "   "
10. 48 min. past VII.
11. (a) 2 pks. 1 gal.
    (b) 4 days 36 min.
12. 7%.
13. $810.

ANSWERS. 85

Exercise XLI.

1. 12 lbs., 8 lbs., 32 lbs., respectively.
2. 65 and 1430, 130 and 715.
3. 13.
4. 160 lbs., 250 lbs.
5. (a)
   1. Vulgar
      1. Simple $\begin{cases}(a)\text{ Proper.}\\(b)\text{ Improper.}\end{cases}$
      2. Mixed.
      3. Compound.
      4. Complex.
   2. Decimal
      1. Finite decimals.
      2. Pure Repetends.
      3. Mixed Repetends.

   (b) (I.), $1\frac{3}{25}$; (II.), $\frac{1}{10}$; (III.), $\frac{45}{125}$; (IV.), $\frac{1}{4}$; (V.), $\cdot 4265\dot{1}$.

   (c)
   1. Vulgar
      1. Simple: $\frac{7}{8}, \frac{13}{58}, \frac{31}{28}, \frac{117}{112}, \frac{1}{16}, \frac{1}{4}, \frac{45}{125}$.
      2. Mixed: $1\frac{3}{25}$.
      3. Compound: $\frac{3}{4}$ of $\frac{7\frac{1}{2}}{16}$.
      4. Complex: $\frac{11\frac{3}{5}}{7\frac{1}{4}}$.
   2. Decimal
      1. Finite decimal: $\cdot 025$.
      2. Mixed Repetend: $\cdot 13\dot{8}$ and $\cdot 4265\dot{1}$.
      3. Pure Repetend: $\cdot \dot{2}\dot{6}$.

6. Lumber \$34.65, Posts \$13.00, Labor \$7.35 ; Total \$55.00.
7. 272 barrels ; and 72 minutes.
8. 30%.
9. 280 twenty-fives, 720 tens.
10. 91 and 161.
11. \$8018.75.
12. A, \$152 ; B, \$12 ; C, \$76.
13. 40 feet.

Exercise XLII.

1. 25625 and 10250.
2. $6\frac{1}{4}$%.
3. 290 rods.
4. $\frac{3}{4}=\frac{15}{20}$ and $\frac{3}{5}=\frac{12}{20}$ ∴ $\frac{3}{4}\div\frac{3}{5}=\frac{15}{20}\div\frac{12}{20}=\frac{15}{12}=\frac{3\times 5}{4\times 3}=\frac{3}{4}\div\frac{3}{5}=\frac{5}{4}=1\frac{1}{4}$.
5. A, \$280.80 ; B, \$546.00 ;
   C, \$458.64; total, \$1285.44.
6. $37\frac{1}{2}$; 25%.
7. 640 acres.
8. \$321.36.
9. 96.
10. 25%.
11. 60 dozen.
12. $\frac{1}{2}$.
13. 2 feet 2 inches.

86   ANSWERS.

Exercise XLIII.

1. A's, 200 ; B's, $500.
2. (a) 92 sq. ft. 102 sq. inches.
   (b) 7 cu. ft. 1254 cu. inches.
3. $20 of an increase.
4. 3 feet.
5. 75%.
6. 6 days.
7. $147.84.
8. $99.
9. 99.
10. 78125.
11. 7.
12. 1093 sq. yards. 4 sq. ft. 72 sq. inches.
13. (a) $4121 = 412(10)+1.$
    $= \{\,41(10)+2\,\}(10)+1.$
    $= 41(10)^2 + 2(10) + 1.$
    $= 4\{\,(10)+1\,\}(10)^2 + 2(10) + 1.$
    $= 4(10)^3 + 1(10)^2 + 2(10) + 1.$
    $= 4121.$
    (b) $4121 = 515(8)+1.$
    $= \{\,64(8)+3\,\}(8)+1.$
    $= 64(8)^2 + 3(8) + 1.$
    $= \{\,8(8)+0\,\}(8)^2 + 3(8) + 1.$
    $= 8(8)^3 + 0(8)^2 + 3(8) + 1.$
    $= 8031.$

Exercise XLIV.

1. 28 miles.
2. One part 142, the other 8.
3. $1000.
4. 355957·03125.
5. $\begin{Bmatrix} \text{B, } \$3.06\tfrac{1}{4} \\ \text{P, } \$9.97\tfrac{1}{2} \\ \text{R, } \$1.96\tfrac{1}{4} \end{Bmatrix} = \$15.00$ total.
6. 24%.
7. $\begin{Bmatrix} 4687\tfrac{1}{2} \text{ lbs. water,} \\ 2049\tfrac{1}{8} \text{ lbs. slate,} \end{Bmatrix} = 6736\tfrac{5}{8}$ lbs. in all ; or 3 tons 736 lbs. 10 ozs.
8. A, $1.60 ; B, $3.60.
9. (a) 3 ; and (b) 484·84.
10. 24 ft.
11. $8500.
12. $53.29.
13. 80 planks.

Exercise XLV.

1. 6.
2. 25½ lbs. to the cub. ft.
3. $1192.32.
4. 13.
5. $8070.00.
6. The latter ; $5 gain.
7. $1.00.
8. $10350.00.
9. 40 feet.
10. $77.50.
11. $22.50.
12. 7.
13. 200.

ANSWERS. 87

Exercise XLVI.

1. A, $2800; B, $4200.
2. $360.
3. $960.
4. 12474 sq. inches.
5. 12%.
6. 22 minutes.
7. $925.
8. $36.
9. $1600.
10. 48 lbs.
11. $345.60.
12. $5243.
13. 406.

Exercise XLVII.

1. $51\frac{1}{9}$%; $12\frac{7}{8}$%.
2. 6125.
3. 4 days.
4. $10840.
5. $150.
6. $\begin{cases}(a)\ \$7.00\ \text{bill.} \\ (b)\ .70\ \text{discount off.} \\ (c)\ \$6.30\ \text{cash.}\end{cases}$ ☞ For *form*, etc., see P.S.A. pages 56 and 57.
7. $193.90.
8. $3000.
9. 419.
10. Gained $2.73.
11. $51480 = 2 \times 2 \times 2 \times 3 \times 3 \times 5 \times 11 \times 13.$
    $3346200 = 2 \times 2 \times 2 \times 3 \times 3 \times 5 \times 5 \times 11 \times 13 \times 13.$
    (i) L.C.M. $= 2 \times 2 \times 2 \times 3 \times 3 \times 5 \times 11 \times \overline{13} \times 5 \times 13.$
        G.C.M. $= 2 \times 2 \times 2 \times 3 \times 3 \times 5 \times 11 \times 13.$
    (ii) Quotient $= 5 \times 13.$
    (iii) Quotient $= 2 \times 2 \times 2 \times 3 \times 3 \times 5 \times 11 \times 13.$
12. 3.
13. 12.

Exercise XLVIII.

1. $1500.
2. (a) $87\frac{1}{2}$ cents; (b) $712.80.
3. A, 200 acres; B, 300 acres; C, 450 acres; D, 500 acres.
4. 8160 lbs.
5. $6.25.
6. $300.
7. $37500.
8. $1\frac{1}{4}$%.
9. $15015.
10. 45 yards.
11. $315.
12. 3 minutes $11\frac{1}{4}$ seconds.
13. 13%.

Exercise XLIX.

1. $41.80.
2. (a) 24 acres, 47 sq. rods, 18 sq. yds., 2 sq. ft., 36 sq. in.
   (b) 75600 planks.
3. $15750.
4. £3, 18 shillings.
5. 56¼ cents ; and 6¼ % loss.
6. $5200.
7. $107.50.
8. $262.50.
9. 28 4/7 %.
10. 32 cents.
11. 26 feet.
12. 30.
13. (a) $22000 ; (b) 15 yards.

Exercise L.

1. ·166666752.
2. 5/32 and 11/12.
3. 567.
4. 2720 lbs.
5. $1440.
6. 25 cents.
7. 45 feet.
8. $8250.
9. 6 %.
10. 4.
11. 3 days.
12. 33 1/3 %.
13. 12 inches.

Exercise LI.

1. $4.60.
2. 50% ; 37½ % ; and 12½ %.
3. $2351.00.
4. $350.50.
5. $10.56.
6. $9.45.
7. $11200.00.
8. $1000.00.
9. $2077.00.
10. 72 cents.
11. 2 1/10.
12. $75.00 ; loss 1⅓%.
13. $5000.00.

Exercise LII.

1. 40 bushels in all : barley 5 bushels, rye 20 bushels, corn 15 bushels.
2. 12 lbs. 3 ozs.
3. 8 hours 20 minutes.
4. $250.00.
5. 8 days 6 hours.
6. S., $2800 ; C., $4200.
7. $4.80.
8. 56 pairs shoes, 112 pairs boots, 168 pairs slippers.
9. 125 barrels.
10. 10 ft. 6 inches.
11. 38 cub. ft. 864 cub. inches.
12. $645.00.
13. March 27th, 1894.

www.ingramcontent.com/pod-product-compliance
Lightning Source LLC
Chambersburg PA
CBHW021811230426
43669CB00008B/716